Mercedes AMG
Gold Portfolio
1983-1999

Compiled by R M Clarke

ISBN 185520 7451

BROOKLANDS BOOKS LTD.
P.O. BOX 146, COBHAM,
SURREY, KT11 1LG. UK
sales@brooklands-books.com

www.brooklands-books.com

Printed in China

ACKNOWLEDGEMENTS

Brooklands Books primary aim is to inform and help second and subsequent owners of interesting cars by making available once again the best contemporary articles that were written about their vehicles. Readers will find within this book the views of expert motoring writers drawn from the leading automobile journals of three continents. I am sure that AMG and Mercedes-Benz enthusiasts will wish to join with me in thanking the publishers of *Autocar, Automobile, Car, Car and Driver, Fast Lane, Motor, Modern Motor, Motor Australia, Motor Trend, Performance Car, Road & Track, Road & Track Specials, Top Gear* and *Wheels* for their ongoing support.

R M Clarke

AMG are the initials of a once small company that modified Mercedes-Benz cars for wealthy enthusiasts. Excellent though Mercedes-Benz cars might be - conservatively styled, well made and superbly engineered-they were never known for their élan. They were thoroughly executed luxury saloons and sports cars for the discerning motorists who appreciated them for their German-ness, if you like.

Centred in the village of Affalterbach, AMG began in 1967 when two enthusiasts, Werner Aufrecht and Erhard Melcher, went into business with the aim of improving the performance of Mercedes-Benz cars, to make them more exciting to drive. Incidentally, the initials AMG came from Aufrecht + Melcher + G for Grossaspach, Aufrecht's birthplace. The company gained international recognition when it entered a Mercedes-Benz 300SEL 6.3 AMG with a modified engine and chassis in the gruelling 1971 Spa Francorchamps 24-Hour race. Co-driven by Daimler-Benz experimental engineer Erich Waxenberger, the big, heavy saloon finished first in its class, second overall! AMG had arrived with a bang.

In 1983 AMG introduced its first "customer" car, the Mercedes-Benz 190E 3.2 AMG. The 190E was a very good car but it lacked sparkle, it lacked personality. The AMG revisions transformed it; the chassis was far more responsive and the 3.2-litre six-cylinder engine's power was raised to 234bhp, acceleration from O-100km/h (62mph) was reduced to just 6.8 seconds and its maximum speed was raised to 244kmlh (152mph). Interestingly, it was a quicker car than the original 300SEL 6.3 AMG!

As the company grew it explored new ideas, always concentrating on Mercedes-Benz cars. One of its more outrageous versions was known as "The Hammer." Based on the W124 series coupes, AMG fitted a monster 5.6-litre V8 under the hood; its 402bhp propelling it from rest to 100kmlh in 5.6 seconds and on to a top speed of more than 300kmlh.

The first formal joint collaboration with Daimler-Benz came with the 1993 release of the C36 AMG. Based on the 190E saloon body, it was powered by a 3.6-litre engine developing 280bhp permitting a 0-100km/h time of 6.9 seconds and a maximum speed electronically limited to 250kmlh. This was the first tentative steps towards direct competition with BMW's successful M cars and the BMW Alpinas.

To demonstrate the depth of its engineering capabilities, AMG designed and built 25 CLK-GTR gull wing coupes powered by a high performance 6.9-litre V12 engine; it was a road-going supercar built at a time when such machines were very much in vogue.

For the 1988 racing season AMG teamed up with Daimler-Benz to compete in the German Touring Car Championship; this ultimately led to a merger in 1999. Today Mercedes-Benz clients can select from an AMG version of almost any model in the vast lineup. Excitement had arrived in Stuttgart!

Gavin Farmer

CONTENTS

PHOTOGRAPHY AARON KILEY

AMG Mercedes-Benz 500SEL

The running mother of all rocketships.

• We refer to this mighty machine as the Atomic Blueberry. This seems entirely appropriate for a car of its capacity and coloring that will easily attain 139 mph. Its color is officially referred to by Mercedes-Benz as Lapis Blue, a deep, metallic shade that alters with the light, varying mystically from an almost bright blue to navy blue to royal purple. The bumpers and the lower body are painted to match, and the trim is all black, laced around the gleaming body like the dark markings of a perfectly ripened blueberry.

This Atomic Blueberry, however, is in no danger of being gobbled up. It is ungodly fast, more than a match for all but one or two of the most accomplished sports cars volume-sold in this country, and it maintains this superiority with all due composure. It is a Mercedes, so it has had a thorough upbringing in the social graces. It is, however, an AMG-modified Mercedes, and capable of exceptionally highhanded behavior. AMG is Germany's preeminent Mercedes tuning firm, owned and operated by Hans-Werner Aufrecht in the town of Affalterbach, near Stuttgart, whence the almighty 5.0-liter motorcars emanate.

As they come from Mercedes, the 500SELs, SECs, and SLs are already among the fastest big cars in the world, scions of dedication to the ideals of solidity, utility, and, particularly as embodied in the 5.0-liter flagships, performance. Unfortunately, their performance has remained the province of other markets, never reaching the States because of our tight emissions requirements and Mercedes' aversion to adding a gas-guzzler surcharge. Thus a mild 3.8-liter powerplant is the only factory-offered V-8 here. Several U.S. emissions-and-safety-certification firms rectify this by bringing in 500-series cars and affixing the necessary hardware, thus enabling America's well-heeled to run neck and neck with their European counterparts.

This does not make Mercedes-Benz particularly happy, since it is ever vigilant of its good name and thus predictably concerned with the modifications to its cars (though the company has enough pride in its products to provide a limited service-and-parts channel here for its big-engined models). Mercedes, along with Ferrari and BMW, philosophically supports pending congressional legislation endorsed by Volkswagen that would effectively put an end to pipsqueak competitors by requiring them to meet exactly the same 50,000-mile certification standards set for major importers.

One of the pipsqueak competitors is Classic Motors (233 West Ogden Avenue, Westmont, Illinois 60559; 312-971-2002), a specialty import center run by Richard Buxbaum, who has recently entered into an agreement with O'Gara Coach Company (9501 Wilshire Boulevard, Beverly Hills, California 90212; 213-278-6713) that calls for O'Gara to handle business west of the Rockies. In addition to handling trick, Euro-version BMWs, Ferraris, Porsches, and the like, Classic and O'Gara are AMG's exclusive U.S. distributors. They can provide fully certified but otherwise stock Mercedes, or they can boost performance from stirring to sensational. In support of the attendant expense, we offer up the Atomic Blueberry's performance statistics: 0 to 60 mph in 7.4 seconds, the quarter-mile in 15.5 seconds at 93 mph, 0 to 100 mph in 18.3 seconds, and 70-to-0-mph braking in 185 feet. (The stellar braking performance is due to the vice-free ABS anti-lock four-wheel discs, not available here from the factory.) And above it all looms that monumental 139-mph top end, effortlessly provided by the exceptional aerodynamic detailing, despite the big Merc's hefty frontal area, massive passenger compartment, and 3772-pound burden.

Alas, a confession: this Atomic Blueberry is not yet a certified car, and its performance might slip a little with the requisite hardware aboard. However, in its defense, it has already served 50,000 miles of duty as an AMG engineering mule (including several hundred laps at Hockenheim during the process of gaining Germany's TUV type-approval for the new five-spoke, eight-by-sixteen-inch AMG wheels) and as a press car, its only real concession to ill-treatment being a touch of looseness in the steering. AMG has a selection of smaller steering wheels for customers at odds with Mercedes' colossal wheel, but some of us prefer the big one for the ballistic, high-speed accuracy it lends (this being one of those inherently stable cars that feel even better as you go more quickly), and for the unimpeded view it provides of M-B's excellent instruments.

The fuel gauge indicates that, even at our brutally applied 13 mpg, the 25.4-gallon tank has an impressive 300-plus-mile range (an add-on AMG trunk tank increases capacity to 40 gallons). Once and only once we have endured the unendurable, a sustained 55-mph doze-off, which produced over 20 mpg, no small accomplishment for a 139-mph limousine capable of carrying five notably comfortable and relaxed occupants in quiet luxury amid velour upholstery, the restrained banding of wood veneer, and legroom adequate even for stilt walkers in full parade regalia. Moreover, the crudest gas we could dump down the filler was fine, though unleaded will be necessary once the catalysts go on.

None of this tells you how sensationally exciting this car is to drive. It is uncommonly deceptive. Only when you toe into the throttle do you have an inkling of what lies hidden within the single-overhead-cam V-8 and its AMG heads, valves, cams, and assorted detailing. No rocky idle gnashes back through the superb four-speed automatic drivetrain. Instead, the monstrous output is entirely in concert with a most accomplished chassis, thanks to AMG's special Bilstein shocks and shorter, somewhat stiffer springs, which detract little from ride quality, even on the wide-set 225/50VR-16 Pirelli P7s. The monster is deceptively poised and agile, suggesting that a twist of the wrist is all that's necessary for the accomplishment of any task. You will find that the mirrored world recedes with zoom-lens speed. Two unfortunates in Z28 and 924 thought they were racing across Ohio until the Atomic Blueberry rocketed si-

lently past with a 30-mph cushion and disappeared.

Stout stuff, this stuff of the real thing. We can only hope that pending legislation to eliminate the importation of such machinery fails. Its passage would be doubly sad, because not only would it eliminate a source of real automotive excitement, it would also eliminate

pressure on the large importers to better their current offerings. Only free competition leads to the quickest possible progress. For that reason alone, never mind the adrenalin adjunct that goes hand in hand, we all owe thanks to companies like Classic Motors and to the Atomic Blueberries of our world.
—*Larry Griffin*

Vehicle type: front-engine, rear-wheel-drive, 5-passenger, 4-door sedan

Price as tested: $75,000

Options on test car: AMG high-output engine, $8088; 16-inch AMG wheels and Pirelli P7 tires, $2614; blacked-out chrome, $1964; AMG suspension, $1128; front and rear spoilers, $691.

Sound system: Blaupunkt AM/FM-stereo radio/cassette, 4 speakers

ENGINE

Type	V-8, aluminum block and heads
Bore x stroke	3.80 x 3.35 in, 96.5 x 85.0mm
Displacement	303 cu in, 4973cc
Compression ratio	9.4:1
Fuel system	Bosch K-Jetronic fuel injection
Emissions controls	none
Valve gear	chain-driven single overhead cam
Power (SAE net)	265 bhp @ 5500 rpm
Torque (SAE net)	293 lbs-ft @ 4000 rpm
Redline	6000 rpm

DRIVETRAIN

Transmission	4-speed automatic
Final-drive ratio	2.72:1, limited slip

Gear	Ratio	Mph/1000 rpm	Max. test speed
I	3.68	7.2	32 mph (4500 rpm)
II	2.41	11.0	66 mph (6000 rpm)
III	1.44	26.6	111 mph (6000 rpm)
IV	1.00	26.6	139 mph (5250 rpm)

DIMENSIONS AND CAPACITIES

Wheelbase	120.9 in

Track, F/R	59.8/59.1 in
Length	202.0 in
Width	73.6 in
Height	56.7 in
Curb weight	3772 lbs
Weight distribution, F/R	55.2/44.8%
Fuel capacity	25.4 gal
Oil capacity	8.5 qt
Water capacity	15.8 qt

CHASSIS/BODY

Type	unit construction with one rubber-isolated crossmember
Body material	aluminum and steel stampings

SUSPENSION

F	ind, unequal-length control arms, coil springs, anti-sway bar
R	ind, semi-trailing arm, coil springs, anti-sway bar

STEERING

Type	recirculating ball, power-assisted
Turns lock-to-lock	2.9
Turning circle curb-to-curb	40.4 ft

BRAKES

F	10.9 x 0.9-in vented disc
R	11.0 x 0.4-in disc
Power assist	vacuum with Bosch anti-lock system

WHEELS AND TIRES

Wheel size	8.0 x 16 in
Wheel type	cast aluminum
Tire make and size	Pirelli P7, 225/50VR-16
Test inflation pressures, F/R	35/35 psi

CAR AND DRIVER TEST RESULTS

ACCELERATION

	Seconds
Zero to 30 mph	2.8
40 mph	4.2
50 mph	5.7
60 mph	7.4
70 mph	9.4
80 mph	12.1
90 mph	15.0
100 mph	18.3
110 mph	23.6
120 mph	30.6
130 mph	44.9
Top-gear passing time, 30–50 mph	3.2
50–70 mph	5.1
Standing ¼-mile	15.5 sec @ 93 mph
Top speed	139 mph

BRAKING

70–0 mph @ impending lockup	185 ft

Fade	**none** moderate heavy

HANDLING

Roadholding, 282-ft-dia skidpad	0.74 g
Understeer	**minimal** moderate excessive

COAST-DOWN MEASUREMENTS

Road horsepower @ 50 mph	18.0 hp
Friction and tire losses @ 50 mph	8.5 hp
Aerodynamic drag @ 50 mph	9.5 hp

FUEL ECONOMY

C/D observed fuel economy	13 mpg

INTERIOR SOUND LEVEL

Idle	55 dBA
Full-throttle acceleration	75 dBA
70-mph cruising	70 dBA
70-mph coasting	69 dBA

THROUGHOUT Europe a new spoiler-clad ground-hugging supercar is turning the heads of even the most blasé of enthusiasts. Park one next to a Rolls-Royce and so effectively will the new car pull the crowds that the Spirit of Ecstasy is likely to get lonely. Park one next to a Ferrari and the prancing horse is likely to jump with jealousy. Even the long time champion car of European poseurs, the Lamborghini Countach, has cause to feel threatened. Surprisingly the new head turner comes, mostly, from that doyen of styling conservatism, Mercedes-Benz. But the three-pointed star on the grille does not tell the whole story. For, like a three-piece suited businessman who has just spent the morning shopping in Chelsea, these new Mercedes-Benzes have had their standard formal clothes stripped off and replaced with a brand new outfit. The cars are lowered, fitted with front and rear spoilers, side skirts, wide alloy wheels wearing huge tyres, and have had their chrome colour-keyed. The metamorphosis can be effected on any Mercedes-Benz, but it is

MERCEDES MIT MUSCLE

AMG has been modifying Mercedes Benzes for 16 years, but it took the AMG 500SEC, with its 35kW power boost and extrovert body modifications to bring the company fame. Gavin Green tested a wilder AMG product — a red 280CE with a 206kW 5.0 litre V8

particularly striking on the S class coupes.

The company behind the transformations is AMG, the German tuning firm which has been making Benzes go faster and look bolder for the last 16 years. But in the last four years business has really boomed. Now — despite the recession — things are growing at the rate of 30 percent a year.

Export markets, in particular, are expanding at a phenomenal rate. "As cars become more and more similar in appearance, so people are more interested in getting modifications done, which make their cars look different and become more individual," says AMG's chief, former racing driver and Mercedes development engineer, Hans-Werner Aufrecht.

Happily the next export market in line for the AMG expansion is Australia. Although some local firms have been privately importing AMG bits and fitting them to Mercedes-Benzes Down Under, there has never been an officially sanctioned AMG concessionaire — until now. The new distributor is an English firm, Stratton, which is based near Manchester. Its director, Mike Hinde, is due in Australia this month to talk to dealers interested in selling the AMG goodies.

Traditionally a strong country for both Mercedes-Benz sales and for car customising, Australia should be one of the world's biggest markets for the three-pointed star transformation, predicts Hinde. But, at an English price of just under $10,000 for the suspension lowering (by three cm) and the appearance metamorphosis (including the chrome colour keying), the transformation on the S class coupe is not cheap. For an extra $5000 in the UK, you can have the engine modifications as well, which boost power for the five litre 500SEC by 35 kW and helps it rocket to more than 240 km/h. For the 380SEC, power can be boosted by 25 kW at a price of $3000. Australian prices, needless to say, are probably going to be significantly higher.

Appropriately, AMG is based near Stuttgart, not far from the Mercedes head office, in a town called Affalterbach. Even more appropriately the address is number 1, Daimlerstrasse. "The address is just a coincidence," says Herr Aufrecht, a short man who finds it hard to sit still, hates being photographed, loves drinking local Swabian wine and eating Swabian food,

and is also very friendly. He also loves Mercedes-Benzes, which he unequivocally considers to be the best make of car in the world. "We don't make Mercedes cars any better," insists Aufrecht. "We just make them less of a compromise. We make them a better sports car."

AMG modifies about 1500 cars a year, and works only on Mercedes models. The most unusual assignment, says Aufrecht, was to transform a classic 1955 Mercedes 300SL Gullwing, worth at least $50,000 in Germany in its standard form. "The owner wanted us to gut it and fit AMG modified 5.0 litre V8 parts from the 500SEC. He wanted the engine, gearbox, suspension, brakes, rear axle — the works." It took six months and cost $220,000.

When I arrived in Affalterbach on a wintry February day with the weather trying to make up its mind whether it was snowing or raining, there was the usual impressive display of Mercedes hardware parked in the AMG forecourt — all awaiting collection by their wealthy owners. The gathering of super Mercedes-Benzes included a 500SEC with $25,000 worth of interior modifications — including a video player (the screen was built into the facia centre console ahead of the gear knob; the player was built into the back seat) and full leather interior, a superb sound system more likely to be found in a disco than a car, and carpet which wouldn't look out of place in the lounge at Buckingham Palace. Naturally all the exterior and engine modifications had been carried out as well. It was the most expensive 500SEC AMG had modified. Completed, it cost double the price of a standard 500SEC. It was about to be air freighted to its owner in the Middle East.

There was also a collection of Mercedes W201s — the new small Merc — which had undergone the metamorphosis. AMG is starting to fit 121 kW 2.3 litre fuel injected engines to the sweet handling machines. "Shortly we'll start

bar

PHOTOGRAPHY: MERVYN FRANKLYN

6

fitting 5.0 litre V8s as well. When we do that it will be the quickest thing we make.'' Aufrecht is so impressed with the potential of the W201 series Mercedes that he thinks it will be the most popular car for the transformation. He's expecting to modify between 1000 and 2000 W201s in some way in a year — be it by simply adding spoilers or fitting the 5.0 litre motor.

But until these beasts hit the road, the best machine for the sporty driver that the tuning doyen makes is, according to Aufrecht, the W123 coupe body (the 230CE and 280CE) fitted with the big 5.0 litre motor. And that was what I went to Germany to collect.

The object was to bring one from Affalterbach to England where British concessionaire Stratton could use it for display and promotional purposes. But it wasn't just any old 5.0 litre W123 coupe that I picked up.

"This car," said Aufrecht before I hopped into the leather encased cockpit, "is the best production based road car for the enthusiast we've built.'' Read the specification of this special one-off machine and it's not hard to work out why. Take a 280CE, strip out the mechanicals and then fit one of the AMG modified 206 kW 5.0 litre V8 motors, 500SEC series automatic four speed transmissions and rear axle assembly, ABS brakes and rear end self levellers. Then add Bilstein gas shock absorbers, specially uprated and shortened coil springs (which help reduce the ride height by five cm over standard), eight inch wide alloy five spoke AMG alloy wheels and vast Pirelli P7 225/50VR16 tyres. "It's faster accelerating than the AMG modified 500SEC because it's lighter," says Aufrecht. "It handles better because of the shorter wheelbase." Final weight is 1520 kg, 70 kg more than the 280CE but 90 kg less than the standard 500SEC.

But the transformation wasn't restricted to the mechanicals. In looks AMG has taken the wolf in sheep's clothing 280CE and turned it into a ferocious tiger-gone punk. For a start there is the usual AMG fitment of chin

9

AMG 280CE is gaudy in red, but interior is more tasteful after $9000 worth of modifications, including British Connolly leather upholstery

spoiler (although this is a brand new one piece moulding which incorporates the front bumper), and side skirting. The wheel arches have been cut back at the front to accommodate the monstrous rubber and lowered body. But then, as was specially requested by the Arab customer who ordered the car, the beast got the sort of paint job of which even Aufrecht does not approve. A bright candy apple red. It is so loud and garish that it makes you wonder whether Henry Ford's colour choice policy did have some merits after all. Even the hallowed three pointed star has been tainted. In its bright red colour it looks more like a dissected toffee apple than the ultimate symbol of motoring excellence.

Inside, things are less gaudy — although with $9000 worth of modifications, the cost is totally in keeping with the rest of the car. The cream coloured Connolly leather upholstery, with its tasteful dark brown piping, would look entirely appropriate inside any upmarket British luxury car. It is the first time AMG has used Connolly hides. Now, says Herr Aufrecht, 80-90 per cent of all interior modifications will use the British treated skins. An excellent Pioneer KP909G stereo cassette player, together with speakers worth $2000, helps look after the tapes whether it be Mozart or Men At Work. Also inside, the usual Mercedes seats have been discarded and replaced with Recaros which, with their myriad of adjustment, can accommodate anyone from the emaciated to the corpulent. Total cost of the car in

THE MB 190 is clearly going to be a hit, even beyond those bulging Daimler Benz order books. The smaller Mercedes was hardly announced when AMG, produced its own version, which has every evidence of being a success.

AMG will tell you that it isn't easy to improve on a new Mercedes. Granted, this Swabian tuner is easily the most-established shop specialising in faster or fancier "star" products, but even AMG was a little daunted at the idea of bettering the 190, a whole new concept which has kept DB engineers occupied for most of the past decade.

AMG knew of course that the baby Mercedes was coming, but it didn't actually get one to work over until early last December. Labouring virtually night and day right through Christmas and New Year, AMG produced the 190 E/2.3 for a late February introduction.

If it isn't wildly different — well, AMG customers aren't given to boasting. They do

...and mini-muscle

Burning the midnight oil allowed AMG to come out with a version of the new 190 Mercedes straight after the car's official release. The 'baby' of the AMG range uses a 120kW 2.3 litre four, which Jerry Sloniger reports, will be another AMG success

Germany is $80,000. Herr Aufrecht refers to the beast as an AMG 500CE.

When you step behind the wheel you look over a normal Mercedes facia with only one alteration: a speedo calibrated to 300 km/h. The large Mercedes steering wheel has also been discarded in the transformation: instead there's a smaller AMG sports steering wheel, which feels much nicer even if it does block the view to the top of the instruments.

Fire up the motor and listen to the throaty, uneven idle of the AMG 5.0 litre unit and you soon get the idea that this V8 has a good deal more grunt than its tamer Unterturkheim forefather. (It gets its 35 kW boost over the standard motor from different valves, modified combustion chambers and camshafts which give more valve overlap. The bottom end of the motor is untouched.) Adjust the firm but comfortable Recaro, and the typically excellent Mercedes wing and rear view mirrors, select Drive, and you're away. Fast.

Bluntly, the AMG 500CE accelerates like no automatic car I have driven. Held in Drive, but with the right pedal mushing the thick carpet, you'll see 100 km/h from rest in only 6.5 sec — faster, for instance, than an Aston Martin V8 or that other doyen of slushmatic acceleration, the Jaguar XJS. To 100, the AMG 500CE is a mighty 1.5 sec quicker than the standard Mercedes 500SEC and about 0.5 sec quicker than the modified AMG S-class coupe.

Swing the car out onto the autobahn, squeeze the accelerator and, in perfect symphony with the rising growls of the big V8, you'll see the speedometer needle swing quickly around the clock. Held in Drive and with the accelerator hard down, you'll hear the four speed auto select top at 185 km/h. Progress does not start to falter until an indicated 240. Given a straight enough piece of road you'll be able to beat that by an indicated 10 km/h. However, allowing for the speedo error, the AMG 500CE is nonetheless a real 240 km/h road car — or 150 mph in the old language. And it must be said that at 240 km/h motoring is neither dangerous nor dramatic. Unfortunately however the German autobahn held one nasty shock in store. In a temporary 80 km/h speed zone (due to roadworks in the slow lane), the punctilious Teutonic policeman did not smile kindly when the 500CE thundered through at 160. A $300 on the spot seemed to cheer him up but didn't do me much good. When I told him, in my best schoolboy German, that I didn't own the car and wasn't rich it made not a jot of difference. Either you pay the fine or stay in jail until you can get the money, he said. Thus relieved of my cash for fuel and the ferry ticket to England, I kept more of an eye on the economy gauge than the speedo. And fortunately the ferry people accepted cheques.

Nonetheless, well before the officious policeman flagged me down, I had discovered that there is more wind noise with this special W123 coupe at speed than there would have been on an S class coupe, with or without the AMG mods. The old unaerodynamic body accounts for that. The car is also affected more by cross winds, and tends to wander in its lane. Floor the throttle at 100, and drop the automatic back into third, and you'll see 160 in only 8.7 sec — half a second faster than an Aston Martin V8, and a stunning 5.0 sec faster than a normal Mercedes 500SEC.

Happily the super W123 coupe is also excellent in tight going. Like the 500SEC with AMG suspension mods, the car displays considerably less body roll than the excellent handling standard Mercedes. The firmer springs, more precise Bilstein dampers and huge low profile Pirelli tyres make the machine more taut and responsive. The steering too (even though the box is standard W123 fitment) is just a touch sharper. The end result is that you can hustle down tight country lanes with more precision, more speed and more security. The ride is less supple than on a standard Merc but it is never uncomfortable. You will feel the nastier bumps and hear them, but you are unlikely to curse them.

AMG claims to improve the fuel consumption of the 5.0 litre V8 with its mods, but my figures disagreed. The best I got for the 500CE was 6.8 km/l (19 mpg on a fairly leisurely trip from London down to Thomas Hardy country in Dorset), while the worst was 5.4 km/l (15 mpg) at high speed on the autobahn. A standard 5.0 litre V8 would surely have done better.

When AMG is officially represented in Australia this year, you too could have one of the special 500CEs built. For, as Herr Aufrecht says. "We can do whatever modifications anyone wants to their car". All you'll need is a lot of money.

However rest assured that if you do get your 280CE so transformed, or if you get your 380SEC kitted out with the AMG goodies, you will undoubtedly have the best pose machine in either Double Bay or Toorak. The only danger may come from a Lamborghini Countach. But then if you order the candy apple red paint, the chances are, even the bull from Sant'Agata will be upstaged. □

want to go faster than Stuttgart suggests, or even be individuals in a restrained manner and in those terms this latest AMG expands the 190 range nicely. Also, it isn't the final word on the subject.

For one thing, initial AMG deliveries will use the standard manual or automatic gearbox. Special ratios must wait until Mercedes produces its expected five-speed. In similar manner, there will be a new type of limited slip differential which will appear later.

AMG's order book is full too, thanks to BMW-type buyers rather than previous AMG owners trading down from a tuned version of some larger Mercedes. AMG naturally expect some 190/2.3 cars will go to current owners of the 230/280 line, at least until it is also replaced in another year or so. But so far, most AMG customers for this compact have either come from other brands or selected one as a good second car to go with their 500 SEC by AMG. This 190 range will be a larger project for the tuner so they can spread development costs over more units.

One thing they don't see is a track version, at least not in the near future. DB would have to homologate the right basic parts first. Even then AMG, like most German tuners today, finds a racer sideline too expensive. The company started that way of course but its business now lies in visuals, spoilers and highway power.

Here AMG took an obvious path in providing more displacement. AMG fits a 2.3 litre, injected Mercedes four from the next-larger range, altering cylinder head, camshaft and intake manifold to achieve 120 kW (18 more than the 230E) with peak revolutions lifted to 6000 rpm. Normal torque is rated as satisfactory. AMG customers want extra power and speed, not softer driving.

Those who take the full kit, also have wider, 225/50 tyres on 8 x 16 alloy wheels which require subtly recontoured fenders. Altering springs and shock absorbers and lowering the car by 2.5 cm, gives it a more bullish look and flatter ride, at the expense of eliminating Mercedes' negative scrub.

AMG does work in a wind tunnel normally but here that ran out of time. A deeper front skirt and small spoiler, both designed by AMG itself, are there to retain the fine MB drag coefficient despite a somewhat greater frontal area, while simultaneously increasing downforce for better high-speed handling. AMG claims both goals were achieved, based on highway comparison tests which returned a top speed of 210 km/h with a 0-100 acceleration time of 8.2 seconds.

Inside, the first 190 E/2.3 has fully-automatic Recaro seats and an AMG steering wheel but no other alterations have been made.

The whole AMG idea results in Mercedes quality and performance — only more so. It works well and is bound to be a surefire success.

Painting the brightwork is just the beginning

PHOTOGRAPHY BY RICH COX

When the phone call came in, most of the staff was understandably expectant. The voice belonged to Joe Molina, P.R. representative for O'Gara Coachworks of Beverly Hills, purveyors of AMG Mercedes conversions. Joe was telling us that the brothers O'Gara would like to make one of AMG's latest projects available to us. What could we say besides "when?" and "what color?" As you can see, there isn't much doubt about the color. It's all red. With the emphasis on the all.

Hans-Werner Aufrecht, a former Mercedes development engineer and founder of AMG, once explained that painting a Merc, grille and all, is a moderately easy way to lend an ultra-conservative car a decidedly individualistic look. One look at the car displayed here vindicates at least the individualistic part of this premise. Aufrecht has devoted himself exclusively to modifying M-Bs since 1967. At the time of its inception, most of AMG's business was preparing the bigger Benzes for European Group 1 and Group 3 racing. Modifying (Aufrecht's own word) production cars for street use started as an offshoot of

the competition work, but now is pretty much all AMG does. Aufrecht has said time and time again that his company doesn't improve M-Bs, since by his own admission "Daimler-Benz has the finest engineering of any car company in the world." Rather, AMG is in the business of making Mercs "better sports cars."

The idea of matching Mercedes-Benz sports cars, even big 4-door ones, to the exotic West Coast car market yields a marriage unequaled since Bollinger champagne and Beluga caviar first met at Tour d'Ar-

gent in 1921. Never ones to turn their corporate backs on such an opportunity, the O'Gara brothers cut a deal with Herr Aufrecht and are now the exclusive importers of AMG cars and components for the western United States. O'Gara imports AMG Mercs of any variety with a heavy emphasis on SEL, SEC, and SL models of the 5.0-liter variety. The AMG modifications available include front air dam with side skirts, uprated suspension, BBS mesh or AMG 5-spoke aluminum wheels, Recaro seats, additional leather interior trim, the aforementioned body-colored chrome trim, higher-output engine, and a 5-speed manual gearbox.

For our test O'Gara provided us with a well-equipped AMG 500SL roadster, indistinguishable from the 380SL save for an additional 1.2 liters of displacement. The 500 produces 231 hp and weighs in at 3381 lb. Starting with this far from humble clay, AMG fits a pair of ported and polished heads with reshaped combustion chambers, larger intake and exhaust valves, and new camshafts with more lift and overlap. As a result, engine output is upped to 276

Rhapsody in Red

hp at 5750 rpm while torque drops 2 lb-ft and is produced at 1000-rpm-higher engine speed—297 lb-ft at 4000 rpm.

The SL we drove was fitted with M-B's excellent 4-speed automatic transmission. Normally mated to a 2.24:1 axle ratio, our roadster was fitted with a 3.08:1 ring and pinion with optional limited slip. While the shorter final drive helps launch the car well without going so far as to compromise its long-legged feel at freeway speeds, the speedometer of our sample hadn't been re-calibrated for the numerically higher axle showing a bit over 175 kph at an actual 100 kph (62 mph). Terminally optimistic speed aside, the powertrain mods work very well, with 0-60 times just a fraction over 7 sec. The 500 would run the quarter mile in 15.5 sec, with a trap speed of almost 89 mph—this with the excellent auto gearbox being left to shift on its own. We believe the AMG 500 could run faster, but the 6200-rpm rev limiter was cutting in as low as 4500 rpm when the pedal was mashed down all the way. As noted, a 5-speed manual is available at an extra $4000.

To match this considerable infusion of power, AMG has uprated the suspension with the addition of Bilstein gas-filled shocks, firmer springs front and rear, plus a larger front anti-roll bar. The basic SL geometry is unchanged, with production upper and lower control arms up front and the usual semi-trailing arm arrangement in the rear. The various AMG suspension pieces lower the car by 1.5 in. and substantially increase roll stiffness both front and rear—maybe even too much in front. A pronounced but stable understeerer, the car was able to generate only 0.79 g on the skidpad. This is a good figure, but with 225/50VR16 Pirelli P7s on humongous 16

x 8-in. alloy wheels we expected a little more. O'Gara will be offering a larger rear anti-roll bar later this year, which should help balance the roll stiffness problem and be good for a bit more lateral g in the bargain. The combination of the previously mentioned superbig supertires, 4-wheel ventilated disc brakes, and ABS anti-skid brake system means the AMG SL has the ability to stop as well as it can go. The system can bring the 1.75-ton car to a halt from 60 mph in 156 ft with superb control.

Aside from a color-coordinated instrument panel top and 4-spoke AMG steering wheel, the interior of our 500 was essentially the same as 380SLs on this side of the Atlantic. The standard Mercedes seats are superb in almost every way, needing only a bit more lateral support to make them ideal. The thick-rimmed steering wheel allows a good view of the informative albeit styleless instrument cluster. A good deal of harshness is transmitted through the wheel as well. Chalk it up to the less compliant suspension in league with the substantial contact patches of the 225 Pirellis. At any rate, this is one of the compromises you make when you try to do away with the compromises built in by the factory.

One of the most noticeable compromises made by Mercedes itself is in the style department. M-B's clientele is made up of some of the most conservative people in the world. This is very apparent in every modern Benz. The design philosophy of Daimler-Benz seems to be one of evolutionary innovation. The people at AMG have taken this attitude and swathed it in a blanket of high-tech taste (although some call it paint). The very idea of completely color keying every part of a car to paintwork is radical, if nothing else. Some people say it

looks too "military," others complain the car has the appearance of having received a quick paint job without masking. All we know is we like it. A lot. And judging from the glances from other drivers in this part of the world where standard SLs clutter the thoroughfares like Checker Cabs in Manhattan, the Eurotech look, as Bruce Zeigler at O'Gara calls it, is meeting with far more cheers than jeers.

So what kind of money is this Teutonic exoticar going to set you back? For the full AMG treatment on a new 500SL, it would be wise to have $60,000-75,000 extra sitting in your checking account. To some, that seems like a lot to pay just to have your chrome painted over, but *those* people won't be buying an AMG anything. And curiously, while O'Gara has set up a large facility northwest of Los Angeles in the Simi Valley for uprating customer's cars to AMG cosmetic spec, Zeigler reports most people wanting the AMG look on a Mercedes also want the whole package—engine, bodywork, suspension, and paint.

To us, the SL roadster seems to be the likeliest candidate for the AMG treatment in California, but the SEL 4-door sedan has been the most popular, followed closely by the SEC coupe. With the Mercedes 190E going on sale late in October, Zeigler is looking for the *kinder-benz* to be the new favorite for Herr Aufrecht's AMG magic.

The AMG 500SL shows Aufrecht's ability to wring some more appeal out of an aging car (the first version of the current SL went on sale in April, 1971), making the 12-year-old convertible think it's an Italian exotic. And now, thanks to the brothers O'Gara, you too can participate in the fun. Just be sure the Dow is up the day you write your check. _{MT}

AMG

Making the best of a very good thing

BY PETER EGAN
PHOTOS BY JEFFREY R. ZWART

I F YOU WERE to offer the average car enthusiast (if there is such a person) the use of a Mercedes-Benz 500SEC for a weekend of travel and then ask upon his return what should be done to improve the car, you'd probably be answered with a long, blank stare. As with the 380SE or the 190E, driving a 500SEC causes very few flaws to leap quickly to mind. Mercedes-Benz has a worldwide reputation for building solid, well engineered cars with better handling and acceleration than anyone could expect from sedans of such satisfying heft and luxury. Right out of the box—or the shipping container—M-Bs probably give their owners less reason to grumble of shortcomings than any cars on earth.

No car is perfect, of course, and most performance-minded drivers will tell you that any car can be made to go faster and handle better. This opinion is especially prevalent in that rarified automotive air, the fast lane of the German *Autobahn*. To a wealthy German businessman with a flair for high speed driving, no car is ever quite fast enough as long as there is another car in his mirrors, blinking its lights impatiently. It's no fun moving over to let those Porsches howl by.

And that is where a company called AMG comes in.

What, you ask, do those three letters stand for? A is for Hans-Werner Aufrecht, M is for Erhard Melcher, his former partner, and G is for Grossaspach, the town where Hans-Werner Aufrecht was born. Aufrecht is a former development engineer in the racing department at Daimler-Benz. He left the mother company and in 1967 set up his own business, a small workshop dedicated to the high-performance tuning and modification

of Mercedes-Benz automobiles.

AMG's work on the 300SEL and 450SLC produced a respectable series of wins and high finishing positions in European sedan and endurance racing at such circuits as Spa-Francorchamps, Monza and the Nürburgring during the Seventies, planting the company name firmly in the minds of Mercedes enthusiasts. Since its inception the business has grown considerably and AMG is now Europe's largest supplier of Mercedes-Benz performance parts and accessories. The small company that began life in an old mill in Burgstall has since moved into a large, modern workshop and test facility in the city of Affalterbach, not far from Stuttgart. AMG's business interests are now worldwide, with U.S. distribution being handled by AMG of North America (233 West Ogden Ave, PO Box 346, Westmont, Ill. 60559; 312 971-2002), a branch of Classic Motors, a specialty import shop owned by a gentleman named Richard Buxbaum.

What does AMG do to improve the already redoubtable Mercedes lineup? Modifications are made to engines, suspensions, aerodynamics and cosmetics. Most AMG engine work goes into the cylinder heads, which are ported and polished for better flow and given valves with smaller stems for reduced intake restriction. Intake and exhaust manifolds are also ported, and on some of the upper stage engines tuned exhaust headers are fitted. AMG makes its own plenum chamber castings to get more air to the ports. Lighter-weight cam followers are used and, depending upon what stage of tune the customer needs, an appropriate cam is selected. Unlike some cammy exotics that run like hell on

the upper end but shake and burble at idle, AMG's engines are tuned for tractability and even-tempered running around town as well as all-out acceleration and 140-mph cruising on the *Autobahn*.

Taking a German market Mercedes, which is more powerful than its U.S. counterparts to begin with, and then breathing on it can produce some pretty spectacular results. The claimed power output on AMG's 5.0-liter engine, as found in the 500SEC or 500SL for instance, is 286 bhp DIN at 4000 rpm, and the company lists its developed 190E engine at 145 bhp at 5750 rpm. Considering that the current U.S. versions of those same engines are rated at 184 and 113 bhp SAE net, respectively, AMG owners should find the accelerator pedal an entirely new source of entertainment and driving pleasure. Different stages of tuning are possible, of course, and AMG offers a number of kits as well as complete in-house engine rebuilds for the full line of Mercedes engines. Five-speed manual transmissions are also available throughout the range.

There's more to performance than sheer horsepower, of course, and the complete AMG treatment includes chassis modifications to lower the car and tighten up the handling.

The suspension kit includes lowered coil springs with higher than stock spring rates coupled with Bilstein shock absorbers especially built to AMG's specifications. Color-coordinated AMG alloy wheels, built for the company by ATS, are used for lighter weight and the best possible combination of offset and rim width.

While the car's mechanical improvements might go unnoticed (until you tried passing one of these cars), AMG cannot be accused of building nondescript sleepers. Those alloy wheels, along with a complete set of front and rear spoilers, side skirts and rear apron, all matched to the car's color, give the AMG creations a low, monolithic and slightly menacing look that alerts other drivers to the nonstandard nature of your Mercedes. Matte-black or color-matched chrome trim adds to the effect. The inside of the car is also changed, with a smaller leather-covered steering wheel and Recaro sport seats.

Buyers who don't want completely reworked cars from AMG can purchase any of the tuning kits, suspension parts, air dams or cosmetic and interior parts independently and install them on their own cars, or have them installed at AMG outlets (though the company, of course, would rather

"...AMG owners should find the accelerator pedal an entirely new source of entertainment..."

see its banner carried by complete high-performance versions than by profilers with a few parts bolted on). In addition to the accessories already mentioned, AMG is now also marketing such things as sound systems and "boutique" clothing items to go with the cars.

All this performance modification might be a little depressing to the U.S. enthusiast if the car were not available in this country, but for once it is. AMG of North America is bringing in not only the performance kits and accessories, but also complete AMG cars and having them certified to meet U.S. specifications. This treatment includes DOT certification, requiring such changes as stronger bumper brackets, seatbelt buzzers, internal door bracing, proper running lights, etc. EPA certification entails the addition of a catalytic converter, a different black box for the fuel injection and ignition control, an exhaust-gas recirculation system and a sealed fuel system to prevent the escape of vapors. On the customer's behalf, AMG of North America can order a new German market version of a car directly from the Mercedes factory, have AMG in Affalterbach perform its modifications, then bring the car into the U.S. and do all necessary certification at a federal

testing station in the Chicago area. Prices vary according to what is done, but importer Richard Buxbaum notes that the complete process is "not cheap."

While Buxbaum hopes to bring in around 150 complete cars this year, he says his main business is still in parts and accessories from AMG, sold to people who already own M-Bs and want to improve the performance or appearance. Relative standardization of Mercedes engines all the way back through the Seventies, he says, makes the AMG parts catalog useful to current owners.

With the recent announcement that Mercedes-Benz is introducing a 2.3-liter, 16-valve dohc version of the 190 for the European market, it might appear that Mercedes is playing AMG's own game in catering to buyers who want more sparkling performance. After all, the new 190 comes right from the factory with sport suspension, wider wheels and Pirelli P7 tires to complement that Cosworth-designed cylinder head. Word has it, however, that AMG doesn't mind a bit and is already working on the new version. No good tuner, after all, has ever found a stock factory engine that made quite enough horsepower. A little something extra is what AMG is all about. ⊛

AMG Mercedes-Benz 500 SEC Supertest

Start with one rather bland but immaculately executed high-performance coupé and breathe some fire into it, and the result is, among other things, probably the fastest accelerating car with an automatic gearbox that is currently available in Britain. It could cost you up to £60,000 though . . .

Photographs by Rowan Isaac

". . . IT ENABLES you to give the impression that you have grown up and put away foolish things, even though this may be far from the truth . . . (it) subtly suggests high class motoring without a hint of extravagance".

In case you are in any doubt, those remarks do *not* refer to the AMG Mercedes-Benz 500 SEC 'Wide Body' which is the subject of this test. They come instead from the introduction to our Supertest of the standard 500 SEC in last December's issue.

The AMG version does not mess about with concepts like subtlety. It makes no attempt to hide the extravagance of its owner. It suggests muscle-car performance and a whopping price tag, and in these respects it gives no misleading impressions.

This is not only probably the quickest Mercedes road car that anyone has ever tested, it's also probably the quickest road-registered automatic that anyone has tested.

AMG have been converting Mercedes-Benzes for 18 years now, initially mainly for competition. Their UK concessionaire, Stratton's of Wilmslow (just south of Manchester) is much more than simply an importer. AMG cars sold in Britain are put together by Strattons to AMG

specifications.

The car tested here is just one of a wide range of conversions that may be specified by the customer, based on most models in the Mercedes range. There are two other engine conversions, based on this big V8, for example; one takes the capacity out to 5.2-litres, the other to 5.4-litres. Both are high-torque conversions, though neither produces as much power as this 32-valve motor based on the 5.0-litre.

A Mercedes-Benz 500 SEC cannot be described as underpriced: with all taxes paid, the cheque adds up to £34,965. This AMG version, as tested, bumps that up to a stinging £63,695, which is £11,000 more than an Aston Martin Vantage.

The costs break down as follows (all prices include VAT): heated front seats £269, 'Memory' front seats £586, radio/cassette player £600, wide body kit (including wheels and tyres) £9,367, lowered suspension £674, four-valve engine £13,196, sports exhaust £754, interior woodset £1,093, wooden gearknob £209 (yes, really!), AMG boot badge £32, recalibrated speedometer and instruments in white £314, uprated rear axle £1,450, and AMG steering wheel £186.

Naturally, many of these individual items may be deleted

from the specification if the customer does not feel the need for them.

AMG claim a maximum speed of between 163 and 165 for the 500 SEC in this highly altered state, and a 0-60mph time of under six seconds.

We were able to verify the latter, the Wide Body squealing and roaring to that speed in a mere 5.8sec, and on to 100mph in 14.8sec, respectively two and 7.5sec better than the standard car.

As far as the top speed is concerned, we could not equal the claim around Millbrook's banked bowl, recording a lap at 152.8mph and a fastest quarter-mile at 156.3.

The effect on maximum speeds of tyre scrub around a banked circuit like Millbrook is a moot point. Jaguar engineers reckon that the 3.6-litre XJ-SC will lap the faster Nardo track in southern Italy at 145mph, but its speed at Millbrook is about 138mph. On this basis, AMG's claim looks as if it may be no exaggeration.

In any case, this AMG 500 is a great deal faster than the standard SEC with which we recorded 141.8mph (also at Millbrook).

To achieve such a dramatic improvement, AMG start off with the basic 4,973cc all-alloy V8, with its total of 16 valves driven by a single camshaft per bank. On a 9.2:1 compression ratio, this engine produces 231bhp at 4,750rpm and 299lb ft of torque at 3,000rpm.

When AMG have finished with it, power is up to 340bhp at 5,750rpm and torque to 337lb ft at 4,500rpm (with more than 275lb ft from 1,500rpm onwards).

These increases are achieved without altering the 96.5mm bore and 85mm stroke. The main change is the switch to four valves per cylinder, with inlet valves 20 per cent larger than the exhaust valves, and the compression ratio is raised to 9.8:1.

Other modifications consist of a revised exhaust system and adjustments to the timing and ignition, and a different sump. The pistons are machined in order to give adequate valve clearance.

In the standard 500, even if you don't quite get the near-silent running of the Jaguar XJ-S, you do get a remarkably refined and quiet car. If you want AMG-type performance, you'll probably be prepared to sacrifice some of that peace just for the sheer excitement of being able to blow off most Ferraris.

We are sure that Mercedes-Benz would not unleash such a noisy beast on to the public as an official member of the three-pointed star club, but AMG's customers will no doubt enjoy the racing car sounds as much as we did. Whether they will at times find the mid-range boom, as well as all the extra road noise, as hard to tolerate as we did remains to be seen.

After correcting the odometer's rampant optimism (no less than 17 per cent fast!) we were impressed with our overall consumption – for nearly 900 hard-driven miles – of 15.9mpg. It is quite likely that as much as 18mpg could be attainable while still maintaining rapid progress. This would allow a practical range of about 330 miles.

Incidentally, the speedometer was equally wild in its assessments of the car's relationship with the world passing by in a blur: it is rather unnerving, when you're cornering hard on a banked circuit, to see that 185mph is being suggested, even when you *know* you are being told a sizeable fib . . .

Part of the credit for the Wide Body's speed capabilities seems to be due to the bodywork modifications. These consist of the front air dam, side sills, rear spoiler and rear lower apron, and widened front and rear arches, in grp. It would appear that whatever advantage is lost in enlarged frontal area is more than cancelled by better air penetration.

The frontal area is also substantially increased by the enormously squat Goodyear Eagle tyres, 245/45 VR16 on front 9J and 255/50 VR16 on rear 10J rims. The wheels are alloy, a five-spoke AMG design.

These tyres (new to the market) provide astonishing levels of grip on a dry surface, and remain acceptable in the wet, where blame for the difficulties of driving this car are due more to the transmission than anything else.

Steering feel is improved, and so also is straight line stability at high speed. One of the prices of those big tyres is a significant increase in the diameter of the turning circle.

The widened arches take the width out from 72 to 75.6in (in our test of the standard SEC, we inadvertently quoted the width as measured from the outside tips of the door mirrors; this remains at 78.8in), while the track has increased by 2.5in at the front and 3.5in at the rear, so that it is almost identical now at each end. The height has been reduced by 1.5in.

It would be surprising if using such fat tyres – a vast change from the standard 205/70 VR14 rubber and 6½J

Top: Interior is virtually standard except for red-on-white dials, gearchange knob and steering wheel.

Above: MB's five-litre V8 is given four ratios per cylinder to boost output.

Left: No self-respecting sheik could survive without one – a cellular telephone.

rims – resulted in enhanced ride comfort. Particularly when they are combined with suspension modifications aimed at the virtual elimination of body roll (in which AMG have been very successful) and generally tauter handling, the result is predictable.

Even in standard form, the big Mercedes' ride quality is firm by any standards, smoothing out high-speed undulations but becoming nervous and jiggly over our dismally-maintained suburban surfaces.

With the stiffened and shortened springs and with increased damping rates, the 500 becomes fairly uncomfortable around town, lots of noisy bump-thump resulting from every raised manhole cover and pothole. Even so, overall comfort is not unreasonable, but for the price one might expect the superb damping control of a Ferrari or Porsche 928S.

We are not *totally* convinced by the handling, either. As mentioned, grip is tenacious, certainly in the dry, and traction – as might be expected with those tyres and a limited slip differential – is excellent. Exiting a tight bend, the LSD and the tyres combine to cause noticeable squirm, but not to an alarming extent.

(2.72 is also available), but with the standard internal gearbox ratios. With the different tyres, this gives 28.2mph/1,000rpm in top. The change-up point in the four-speed 'box is 5,950rpm except from 1st to 2nd where it is restricted to 4,200rpm. This gives speeds in the gears of 35, 70, and 117mph, and there's not much that can be argued with there.

Changes however, are often lumpy, and the harshness of the kickdown is coupled with a delay of a second or so between buried pedal and neck-snapping surge. It seems to us that the 47 per cent increase in power illuminates deficiencies in the transmission which are kept in virtual darkness in the standard car.

The brakes are unchanged from standard, and we didn't feel that they required uprating. It's a pretty impressive specification anyway, with big discs on all wheels (ventilated at the front), and ABS anti-lock. The latter, as usual, imparts a rather mushy feel to the pedal operation in normal use, but retardation is certainly effective. Repeated heavy braking from well over 100mph during our testing at Millbrook induced a small degree of fade, but the system soon came good again, and this kind of treatment is most unlikely unless you're trying to give the Law the slip on the outskirts of Milton Keynes. An uprated braking system will soon be available, anyway.

The interior is unchanged apart from a smaller-diameter steering wheel and the use of white-faced instruments with black lettering. We weren't keen on the appearance of the latter, although they do give the benefit of eradicating stray reflections altogether, not that this is a major problem with the usual white-on-black dials. The steering wheel is a big improvement on the Titanic wheel of the standard car.

The Wide Body offers all the practical benefits of the original design – a coupé that can accommodate four adults in comfort, which has a highly effective air conditioning system that provides a good bi-level split, and a large boot. As usual, however, despite the superb driving position, the leather-trimmed seats are too firm for most British tastes and not sufficiently shaped to compensate for their slipperiness.

Whether or not you think the Wide Body looks beautiful or

vulgar will depend on your point of view. We felt that it overstated its case somewhat. Also, while there was no denying the excellence of the paint finish and of the quality of the widened arches, we have been more impressed by add-on spoilers and lower exterior door trims on less expensive conversions.

It is untrue to suggest that what Alpina is to BMW, AMG is to Mercedes-Benz. Alpina's conversions are generally subtle, mostly under-the-skin jobs, designed to smooth out the rough edges, to do what the factory does, only better. It has been suggested that the only reason BMW do not adopt Herr Bovensiepen's

modifications for production is the widespread 'Not invented here' syndrome.

AMG's approach is quite different. What they do is take a harmless and inoffensive object, in this case a 500SEC, and make it spit flames. More than that, they make it look as if it spits flames. The man who buys a BMW 735 might be tempted, if profits were looking healthy, to trade it in for a 735 B10. The man who buys a 500SEC will no more trade it in for an AMG Wide Body than turn up in the City wearing skin-tight leather trousers. AMG's customer is more likely to be someone who is considering an Aston Vantage or a Ferrari as alternatives.

However, the suspension certainly does not disguise the fact that this is a big, heavy car and although it corners securely, we canot help feeling that a bit more tuning of suspension to tyres is required to give it a bit of extra poise.

Mostly, like the standard car, it will understeer mildly on turn-in, but there are two major changes in behaviour: one is that when it does make the transition to oversteer, either through backing off in mid-bend or under power, it does so in a more controlled manner (with one exception, which we shall come to shortly), and the other is that, when you reach that point you are travelling a great deal faster, on dry roads at least.

The exception is when you get full kickdown, and it simply isn't worth trying to use more than about 50 per cent of the performance on damp or greasy roads. Full kickdown comes in abruptly, and clumsily, totally upsetting the car's balance. This car would be much better suited to a manual gearbox, which is available for an extra £3,781 (five-speed), either close-ratio or with overdrive top).

In standard form, a 500SEC has a 2.24:1 final drive. Our test car was fitted with an effectively higher 2.65:1 ratio

AMG
MERCEDES-BENZ 500SL

Taking Mercedes one step beyond

STORY & PHOTOS BY JOE RUSZ

T HERE IS NOTHING wrong with a Mercedes-Benz. It's distinctive (in its own sort of way) and reasonably exclusive (not everyone can afford the fairly stiff price of admission). It's reputed to be one of the safest cars on the road. Overengineered, say the pundits. But unlike other luxury cars, a Mercedes, even the sporty 500SL, has none of the elan of, say, a Porsche or Ferrari. The Merc is a car for the, ahem, "mature." Especially in Europe. In the U.S., particulary in affluent areas such as Beverly Hills, Newport Beach, the Hamptons and Palm Beach, the M-B 2-seater is a kind of 4-wheel Vespa. Chic, of course, but no different than any other 500SL on the block. In places such as these, there are a lot of them. Pity the poor parking lot attendant. But more than that, pity the poor individualistic

soul who just bought one.

Fortunately, there's a cure for the cookie-cutter car syndrome—and when a Mercedes is involved, it's called AMG. Europeans call this kind of automotive specialty shop a tuning firm, but there's more to it than that. What AMG and other like facilities do is rebuild cars to suit the owner's needs or tastes. They modify the suspension, add side skirts and spoilers and other aerodynamic aids, hop-up the engine, reupholster the interior and add unusual wheels. And paint the car when they're through. In Affalterbach, West Germany, the automotive patients are Mercedes-Benzes. In our case, they are 500SLs, the personal Mercedes that is both a hardtop coupe and open convertible.

Because AMG has representatives in the U.S., it's possible

to buy an AMG-prepped Benz without ever setting foot in *der Vaterland.* But let's fantasize a bit and mentally transport ourselves to the outskirts of Stuttgart.

It's a sunny, autumn morning and we're in one of the many cozy public rooms of the Waldhotel Schatten, an inn located alongside a road that was once part of the Solitude Ring. The breakfast dishes have been cleared and as we sip our coffee, a rumble is heard outside the leaded-glass windows. A maroon 500SL, lowered, skirted, fitted with distinctive star-spoked wheels, glides into the curved driveway. Judging by the exhaust note, there's more there than meets the eye. A well-dressed, dark-haired gentleman climbs out of the driver's seat and in moments is striding toward us. He is Werner Alfrecht, founder of the firm and

'...there's a cure for the cookie-cutter syndrome... it's called AMG.'

the A in AMG. Herr Alfrecht has been gracious enough to deliver our car, knowing that without suitable transport, picking up our Merc at his shop would be difficult.

"I thought you would like me to tell you a little about your auto. Perhaps you will have questions. Then, if I could impose on your kindness, a ride to my store in Affalterbach would be appreciated. I'll buy lunch when we get there. I know a nice *Gasthaus* with an excellent kitchen . . ."

With that request, we are off, headed southeast on the *Autobahn*. There's construction outside the Stuttgart area to slow traffic, but when the red-bordered speed-limit sign shows a crossed-out 100, we bury the throttle. The VDO rev counter begins its frenzied climb past 4000, 5000, 6000 rpm before the limiter stops the needle at the engine's 7200-rpm redline. Even in the high-speed lane, the Merc is one of the fastest cars, a member of an elite class made up of Porsche Turbos, exotics and large sedans with anything but normal engines. The speedometer reads 255 km/h, 155 mph. We nod toward the dash. "Is this possible?" we ask.

"Yes, when you have 286 horsepower such speeds are possible," our host assures us. Where the *Autobahn* curves gently, the lateral forces become apparent. The adhesion of the tires—225/50VR-16s on 8-in. wheels—is impressive, as are the stability and balance of the chassis. Not only does the AMG ride on heavy-duty springs and shock absorbers, but also the car has been lowered. Up front, one spoiler keeps air from slipping beneath the car; at the back, another spoiler keeps the rear end glued to the pavement. In less than one hour, we exit the *Autobahn* and travel the last few kilometers on rural roads to Affalterbach—at what seems like a crawl. We are right on time for lunch.

In the afternoon, we tour AMG's 80,000-square-meter auto facility. Through the machine shop, the engine building room, past the dyno cell, through the showroom where components are displayed like jewels . . . peering outside, we see complete cars, all Mercedes-Benzes, all in AMG livery.

The sun casts long shadows when we finally say, *'Auf Wiedersehen'* to Werner Alfrecht. He has mapped out an interesting return route for us, one that takes us along twisty mountain roads that challenge our driving skills. But not the Merc's sure-footedness and brisk performance. It is dark when we slip into Stuttgart. Time for dinner at the Schlosshotel Am Park. Pulling under the marquee at the entrance, we're met by the parking attendant. We ask, *"Guten abend,* ah, perhaps you could park our car?" The young man bows. "This is not necessary. It will be our pleasure to have you leave your AMG just where it is."

One day when I'm sitting at my desk in our Newport Beach offices, I receive a memo: "Andy Cohen, president of Beverly Hills Motoring Accessories (the west coast outlet for AMG), has a car you should look at. It's an AMG Mercedes 500SL." I'll have to call him. And tell him about a great little *Gasthaus* in Affalterbach.

QUITE A few people running around in Mercedes-Benz sports cars would probably prefer to drive something else – a Ferrari or an Aston Martin perhaps.

They chose the Mercedes because in the case of most successful businessmen, the brain dominates the heart. A Mercedes will hold its value like no other car (except perhaps a Porsche), it will be efficient, quick and immensely reliable. If it lacks a bit of style, panache or character, then these are but romantic trifles, shaded out by the cold light of economic reality, *ja wohl*. Your pulse may not pummel at the thought of a midnight dash in your 500SL, for example, but you can be sure it will always start first time. Rather like a buxom German wife – a little unexciting, but hugely efficient.

But here we have something different. Our drab spouse has a new set of designer clothes, and more, she's been down to the AMG health farm too, returning much fitter and even brawnier. Our familiar 500SL has a larger engine, stiffer suspension and bigger wheels and tyres. Its four-speed automatic gearbox changes up later and there's a clever 'thinking' limited-slip differential to distribute the extra power through the back wheels.

In short, this is a bold attempt to be all things to all men, reliable and efficient on one hand, characterful and stylish on the

other. It's a joint effort between the technicians at Mercedes and AMG to produce a 'Ferrari' of the Fatherland.

This particular car is owned by a 26-year-old London businessman, and was manufactured in 1982. The specification of new 500SLs is virtually identical, though – the same 231bhp V8 engine, the same 0-60mph acceleration in 7.6sec, top speed of 137mph and removable hardtop for full open-top motoring.

It also has the most primitive of current Merc chassis, one descending directly from the 350SL of the early '70s. At the front there are double wishbones with semi-trailing arms behind. It's a formula which worked well with the original six-cylinder engines of the day, and has been modified surprisingly little to cope with engine size and power outputs which have constantly risen, culminating in the latest huge V8s.

Few tuning companies can have had as much experience with Mercedes-Benz as AMG. This company began life in 1967, concentrating on competition with such cars as a 300SEL with a massive 6.8-litre V8. Today the company, based at Affalterbach, near Stuttgart, is less concerned with competition, focusing instead on the modification of Mercedes-Benz road cars: engines, transmission, exhausts, chassis, wheels and tyres. There are also several inevitable 'body

styling' alternatives, of dubious aesthetic worth, including spoilers, skirts, colour coding and the blacking of chromework. Interiors can be altered too – leather or buffalo seats and trim, rootwood panelling, flashier instruments, steering wheels *und so weiter* . . .

This car, with personal number AK47, has had just about every expensive item from the AMG catalogue 'lavished' on it – some worthwhile, and some, like the red-on-white instruments, pure frippery. The car was bought for £23,000, and conversion work in Germany cost another £16,000. In addition there is a cellular telephone (£2,500) a Nakamichi hi-fi system (£2,500) and twin electric-powered Recaro seats (£2,000) which bump the car's value up to a horrifying £46,000. You could buy a similarly powerful Porsche 928S and still have enough left over to buy a 190 Mercedes . . .

There's no mistaking AK47 for an ordinary 500SL. Like an automotive Zebra, it's just two colours (apart from its alloy 'hooves'), red and black. Surprisingly this creates quite a pleasing effect, blending in pretty well with the car's original and dainty lines. It's certainly not subtle, it could be stylish, but, *mein Gott*, it's certainly distinctive.

Up front there's a deeper front spoiler, there are slightly flared

sills along the flanks and a rear under-bumper valance to bring the rump into line. Two huge chrome tail pipes protrude, each complete with tiny AMG monogram. All other chromework is anodised matt black. On the red bootlid the black numbers, 5.4, proclaim that this is no limpwrist.

Under the bonnet the engine has been enlarged from 4,973cc to 5,385. The crankshaft is toughened, the inlet manifolds polished and compression increased. Power is up to 310bhp at 5,250rpm and torque leaps from 299lb ft at 3,000rpm to 350 at a higher 4,000 revs. There's more power, here, than in any Jaguar and most Ferraris and Porsches.

The standard four-speed automatic gearbox is retained but the electronic 'brain' is replaced, forcing the 'box to hang on later before changing up. The final drive is lowered (numerically raised) from 2.23:1 to 2.27:1 to improve acceleration through the gears, and Torsen Gleason's "continuous drive" limited-slip differential improves traction for quick starts and greasy bends.

Although lowered just over an inch, thanks to harder 'chopped down' springs, the basic suspension layout is retained but with uprated dampers. The 500SL's usual wheel/tyre combination takes a jump to 225/50 × 16 tyres on the front, with massive

AMG MERCEDES-BENZ 500 SL

Mercedes' gentlemanly sports car can be tuned into something of a tearaway

if you're prepared to invest in an AMG conversion

245/45s behind. The tyres on AK47 are the new Pirelli P7 replacement, the acclaimed P700 and it's the first time we have driven a car on the public road thus shod. The alloy rims are AMG's own extremely attractive five-spoke design and have colour-matched centres.

It takes one turn of the ignition key to reveal the car's transformed character. Gone is the distinctive Mercedes-Benz hum, as the engine fires then dies to a solid tickover; instead, the unit leaps into life with a rasping boom from the tail pipes then idles lumpily at about 1,000 revs. There's no denying that this most powerful of engine conversions currently provided for the SL by AMG (there are rumours about the new 5.6-litre lump though) sounds sensational.

From a baritone grumble at walking pace, the engine becomes more and more strident as the revs rise. Although it's obvious to anyone not totally deaf that it's a V8, it has a most unusual sporty rasp, like a giant version of the Alfasud's 'boxer' four. This must be a family trait of the AMG exhaust system since it's something we

have noticed on two earlier AMG Mercedes.

At today's prices the engine conversion alone costs about £10,000, but there are two cheaper alternatives if this is beyond your Diners' credit limit. There's something called a "tune-up kit" which boosts power to 276bhp, or a smaller overbore to 5.2-litres which yields 300bhp. In each case torque is similarly increased.

The 'full-house' 5.4 conversion is certainly not bark without bite. AMG's catalogue claims a time of 6.7sec for the 0-100kph (62.2mph) sprint, and, along with a small photo of a fifth wheel attached to a car bootlid, states bravely that the performance boost can be *proved*. Well, we are happy to say that the company is spot-on with their information. On a rather windy day at Millbrook we recorded a 0-60mph time of 6.4sec, and that with a gearbox that misbehaved slightly, more of which later.

Their maximum speed claims are not quite so accurate however. Round Millbrook's high speed bowl AK47 couldn't quite reach 150mph for a full lap – 148mph was the best we could

do. Our quickest, slightly wind-assisted, quarter-mile was 150.4mph and is probably a fairer indication of the SL's straight-line ability, without the sapping effects of tyre-scrub. Nevertheless it still falls short of AMG's 155mph promise. But compare this with the stock car's top speed of 137mph, and there's a useful advantage.

If the aerodynamics could be improved further – the body addenda do reduce lift and drag a *bit* – then doubtless the 500SL would be able to pull a higher final drive. As it is, it was unable to exploit even the lower, sprint ratio provided by AMG, and ran out of puff a couple of hundred revs short of its 6,000rpm redline. The forthcoming squeezed-from-a-tube style of the new coupés could well see a genuine 160mph with help from AMG's engineers.

Whatever, the 5.4 delivers its performance with ridiculous ease. No clever clutch and stickwork is required to reproduce sub-seven acceleration times. Simply select Drive and mash your foot down. The car pauses for the torque-converter to wind up, then leaps off the line with a mere suggestion of wheelspin. Despite the new 'black box' delaying gear changes, first could not be persuaded, even with manual hold, to wait beyond 5,500rpm. This may be intentional, since an AMG 500SEC, tested in May last year, was restricted to 4,200 revs in that gear, too.

However AK47's change sometimes waited a fraction *too* long in its upper ratios bouncing unnecessarily against the rev-limiter before crashing brutally up to the next gear. To our minds the gearbox was battling to con-

trol power and torque outputs for which it was never designed. It never actually struggles, it just seems to operate on the outer limits of competence. While this never becomes apparent on the motorway, where the engine's immense strength punts it past ordinary traffic with ease, and the 'box never needs to swap ratios to deliver the goods, it is not half so happy on twisty backroads.

Unless held manually in its lower ratios (luckily the free-revving engine doesn't object to this) or controlled by a field mouse of a right foot, the auto transmission is something of an embarrassment, often depriving the driver of the precise gear he would have chosen to tackle a particular bend. This is demanding and slightly irritating on dry roads, and makes smooth fast progress very awkward.

In the wet, full kickdown (it's a rather clumsy change) upsets the car's balance to an alarming extent, making it simply not worth the bother of using more than half the accelerator's full travel. Luckily AMG do provide a manual gearbox option at about £3,800, and that would transform the car's driveability.

Despite the vintage of the chassis, the car's handling is pretty accomplished. Like the standard version it understeers mildly on turn-in (although at very much higher speeds) and corners impressively neutrally on faster bends. It prefers fast, smooth dry roads when it feels extremely secure, rolling very little, simply following the desired line. Provoked oversteer, either by backing off mid-bend, or under power, is progressive and almost self correcting.

Generally the P700 tyres provide outstanding grip. Only on wet or greasy surfaces do they seem merely par for the course, when both they and the limited-slip differential are ultimately outgunned by the engine's torque. However, on narrow, twisty roads the tyres do tend to 'whiteline' and follow every surface irregularity, making the car seem unwieldly and slightly edgy.

To its credit, though, the SL is not thrown off line by mid-corner lumps and holes. AMG's dampers still manage to soak up broken surfaces despite being very much stiffer than standard. It does give the car a 'wobbly roller-skate', feel when working hard, though, and this is one area where BMW tuners, Alpina, are clearly superior.

Although reasonably high geared, the recirculating-ball

steering feels quite removed from the action up front, especially when pointing straight ahead. Its in-use accuracy and precision do help place the car into a corner, and is some compensation, however.

If things do get out of hand, the 500SL's standard-issue brakes are well able to handle the extra power. The ABS anti-lock electronics have thieved some of the pedal's firm, reassuring feel, but the ventilated front and solid rear discs are little troubled by repeated hard use. Stopping from more than 100mph time after time at Millbrook simply lengthened pedal-travel temporarily and fractionally. A bigger disc/caliper set-up is available for the bottomless bank-account holders if required.

Despite the harder suspension, ride comfort is still quite acceptable. The going gets a bit lively and jiggly over broken surfaces, ridges and manhole covers, etc, but a surprising degree of pain is removed from the worst. Overall the ride/handling compromise is a good one, bearing in mind the less-than-ideal raw materials being employed.

Neither are the occupants assailed by excessive noise. An ill-fitting hard-top (easily curable, we understand) tended to drown out the racy Can-am-style sound of the engine, which would otherwise have dominated. Only on long trans-continental-type journeys would this ultimately become fatiguing. An annoying resonance which appears at about 3,000rpm quickly fades, too. Tyre thump-and-slap is present but reasonably muted.

Removing the hard-top (a simple four-bolt job) naturally brings the various sensations nearer home, but unpleasant buffeting and wind-thrum is not a problem at sensible speeds.

Interior modifications were restricted to a partial retrim to renew various worn pieces of

material, a smaller steering-wheel, the substitution of white-on-black to red-on-white dials (the latter including a higher-reading speedometer) and the addition of two leather-trimmed Recaro seats. Although stylishly designed and comfortable enough for motorway use, the low-friction surface highlighted shortcomings in lateral support, especially for the hips and shoulders.

Otherwise, the driver has an ergonomic and pleasing environment, with good major-control relationship and excellent visibility all round. Some switchgear though remained un-lit and proved awkward to track down at night. And while the air-conditioning was effective it is not the easiest system either to control or comprehend without detailed examination of the handbook.

In keeping with the car's perceived image, the ICE fitted, the top-range Nakamichi, with no less than *three* separate power amplifiers, is simply awesome.

For all the car's qualities – its great power, reasonable economy (15.5mpg overall, if that's of the slightest relevance to a potential customer) generally good handling, mile-gobbling pace and super finish – it would be hard for us to justify spending almost £50,000 on one. AK47 may be more 'individual' but a Porsche 928 is simply a better car.

There must also be some question marks raised over the longer-term reliability of the automatic gearbox, which, we believe would be the first major component to fail. This, in turn must cast doubts about the resale value, and suddenly two of Mercedes-Benz's great strengths are eliminated. It *is* characterful, and, as AMG will testify, there *are* plenty of customers willing to pay for this transformation. Bundles and bundles of bank-notes are quite obviously viewed in a completely different light by these people.

Above: Red-on-white dials are gaudy but cut out reflections. AMG steering wheel is craftsman-built, but costly.
Below left: Recaro seats look good, but leather trim is slippery when the going gets rough.

PERFORMANCE

Test carried out at Millbrook Test Track, Bedfordshire.

Maximum speed (lap of banked circuit)	147.7mph
Fastest quarter-mile	150.4mph

Acceleration from rest:

0-30mph	2.4sec
0-40	3.5
0-50	5.3
0-60	6.4
0-70	8.6
0-80	11.0
0-90	14.0
0-100	17.3
0-110	23.0

Acceleration in kickdown:

20-40mph	1.9sec
30-50	2.9
40-60	2.9
50-70	3.3
60-80	4.6
70-90	5.4
80-100	6.3
90-110	9.0

ECONOMY

Overall consumption	15.5mpg.
Test distance	420 miles
Tank capacity	18.7 gallons
Range*	306 miles

*Based on a touring consumption of 17mpg

WEIGHT

Unladen (with fuel for 50 miles) 31.7cwt

ENGINE

Sohc per bank, water-cooled V8, front-mounted 5,425cc (98.5/89mm bore/stroke). Five main bearings. Compression ratio 9.8:1. Light alloy cylinder heads and block. Two valves per cylinder. AMG camshaft and crankshaft, enlarged and polished ports, polished inlet manifold. Bosch mechanical fuel injection. Maximum engine speed 6,000rpm. Maximum power 310bhp (DIN)/5,250rpm. Maximum torque 350lb ft (DIN)/4,000rpm.

TRANSMISSION

Rear-wheel drive, four-speed module and torque converter. Torsen Gleason/AMG limited-slip differential. Internal ratios and mph/1,000rpm:

Top	1.00:1/28.2
Third	1.44:1/19.6
Second	2.41:1/11.7
First	3.68:1/8.3
Reverse	5.14:1
Final drive ratio	2.72:1

BODY/CHASSIS/SUSPENSION/STEERING

Unitary steel body/chassis. Glass-fibre reinforced plastic front spoiler, side sills and rear apron. Front suspension, independent by double wishbones, coil springs, telescopic shock-absorbers, anti-roll bar. Anti-dive geometry. Rear suspension; independent by semi-trailing arms, coil springs, telescopic shock-absorbers and anti-roll bar. Anti-squat geometry. Power assisted recirculating-ball steering. Three turns lock-to-lock.

TYRES/WHEELS/BRAKES

Pirelli P700 tyres, 225/50 VR 16 on alloy 8×16in AMG front rims, 245/45 VR 16 on alloy 8×16in AMG rear rims. Brakes, servo-assisted discs, ventilated front 10.9in diameter; solid rear, 11.0in diameter. Dual circuits split front/rear. Bosch anti-lock system (ABS).

DIMENSIONS

Overall length 172.8in, width 70.5in, height (with hardtop roof) 51.3in, front/rear track 57.5/57.6in, wheelbase 96.6in.

ELECTRICAL

1120W alternator, 12V 66Ah battery.

AMG MERCEDES-BENZ 500SL 5.4

Maker: AMG Motorenbau GmbH,
Daimlerstrasse 1, D-7151 Affalterbach, West Germany.
UK concessionaire: Strattons of Wilmslow, Water Lane, Wilmslow, Cheshire. Tel: 0625 532678.
Price as tested (see text) £46,000.

photography by Kent Mears

A little white lie

*This modded Merc does it not only in style,
but does it, period*

by Michael Stahl

IF LADY GODIVA had to do her stuff here in 1985, which car do you reckon she'd choose? Somehow I see a white Mercedes-Benz 380 SEL with AMG body mods and very heavily tinted windows...

And if a peeping Tom Selleck were to appear in a Ferrari 308 GTS, our fair Lady would have at least a healthy chance of keeping him at bay. Her worries would be fewer yet if she'd opted for the full-house AMG kit, with 32-valve heads, extractors, full suspension workover and the meanest wheels and tyres around.

When you drive an AMG Mercedes-Benz, you know you're in good company. Five members of the Royal Family of Monte Carlo drive AMG-improved Mercs. Coincidentally, Stefan Casiraghi, husband of Princess Caroline, happens to be the AMG distributor for Monaco. Casiraghi himself drives a bitchen, black 500 SEC with the works.

The bond between AMG and its mere 31 dealers across the world is as intimate as you'll find except, perhaps, for that which exists between the Mercedes-Benz Stuttgart birthplace and the AMG finishing school at Affalterbach. Some former members of Daimler-Benz' management team have even jumped the fence and are now working with AMG.

A survey of Mercedes-Benz 190E buyers in Europe revealed that more than 28 percent had customised their cars with aerodynamic equipment either from AMG or the few competitive manufacturers. Of those 28 percent, some 92 percent maintained that they wouldn't have bought the car in the first place had the gear not been available.

Daimler-Benz by then had fully appreciated the quality of work being done by former employee Hans-Werner Aufrecht's AMG company. Further co-operation resulted — witness the W124 series, an example of which was in the custody of AMG several months before the new car was released.

AMG's fundamental understanding of everything Mercedes tends to show in all the cars it touches. This virginal V8 from AMG Australia carried about half the gear available for it — with exhaust and suspension the only mechanical changes — but the enhancement of the 380 SEL's character was obvious.

This car's external treatment includes the front air dam, side skirts, rear spoiler and rear skirt. All are made from tough ABS RIM plastic, and are precisely colour-matched to the car. Other minor add-ons are the $400 AMG leather steering wheel and AMG boot badge. Oh, and by the way — the 500 SE badge is a little white lie...

Mechanically, the AMG angel breathed only lightly on this car, leaving it as an effectively stock 380 SEL. But even the addition of the AMG lowered suspension system, with self-levelling ride height, and an AMG exhaust system has lifted the car way above being a mere dress-up.

Despite its hefty $2500 price tag, the exhaust system has a very noticeable rub-off on top-end breathing. The car likes to rev now, and its exhaust note, while still restrained, shows just a little hint of naughtiness.

The car's balance is impeccable. It was a surprise to see body roll in the photographs of the car — barely any is discernible from behind the steering wheel. All the time the car feels like it wants to go, its fat 16x8 alloy wheels and Yokohama A-008 tyres allowing it racetrack adhesion.

Through a favourite twisty stretch of road, the big, automatic Merc felt like a car one-half its size. A well-driven Nissan 300ZX wouldn't have a chance. It continues to amaze that all this stuff simply bolts on within seven days — the bill for this car, including painting, fitting and tyres, came to a shade over $8000. And after $87,000 for the standard 380 SEL, does that matter? □

WHAT'S INSIDE THE **BLACK MAGIC** BOX?

No soft centres, that's for sure. How does 5.6 litres and 360 bhp sound . . . David Vivian opens it up

As a rule, the ribbon of heat-sensitive metallised paper spewed out by our Peiseler fifth-wheel printer isn't a very cherishable commodity. Once the relevant figures have been extracted, it's usually a one-way trip to the dark and dusty recesses of a manilla wallet file, probably never to see the light of day again.

There are two little rolls of the stuff, however, that I keep in a safe place. One rushed out of the printer so rapidly that we feared for the well-being of the dot-matrix printing mechanism. In the event it survived to record the following: 0-60 mph – 2.7 sec. The car to which this little piece of history can be attributed is the phenomenal 570 bhp 4wd X-Trac Escort driven by John Welch: quite simply, the fastest-accelerating car *Motor* has ever tested. The tape is dog-eared now, but it still gets shown to disbelievers.

The other is relatively pristine, the digits a little crisper. The important ones are these: 0-30 mph – 1.5 sec, 0-60 mph – 5.0 sec, 0-100 mph – 12.6 sec, 120 mph – 18.3 sec. Standing start statistics for road cars don't come much better than these. A Ferrari Testarossa, for instance, trails by 0.8 sec to 60 mph, 0.1 sec to 100 mph and 0.2 sec to 120 mph. A Porsche 911 Turbo is 0.8 sec behind at the 120 mph marker. Look at it another way. This car reaches 130 mph in 22.2 sec – the sort of time in which a top-league fast hatch would struggle to reach 100 mph. Standing quarter mile? A 13.3 sec sprint beats the Ferrari's 14.2 sec and the Porsche's 13.4 sec.

But the most startling thing on the tape is scrawled on the top in black felt-tip. It reads "AMG 560E". An AMG 560E, for those of you who don't know, has four seats and four doors. It also has four forward speeds, all of them automatic. That tape is special. It's the record of the most rapid automatic – with the exception of a 1000 bhp T-bucket dragster called Andromeda – that has ever passed through our hands.

You may remember that in November we tested AMG's 320E – a Mercedes 300E with a Rambo injection – courtesy of the famed German tuners and body kit specialists. That car had an expanded (3208 cc) version of the standard model's sohc straight-six with gas-flowed cylinder head and manifolds, a high-lift cam, a twin-pipe exhaust system and an additional 57 horses giving a total of 245. Hot stuff in the light and slippery 300-series body – even with AMG spoilers and skirts, enough to crack 60 mph in six seconds dead – but about as spicy as a bowl of semolina when you start to consider the double-vindaloo-with-extra-chilli 560E.

This car is to shoe-horning what Cyril Smith is to Levis 501s. You have to look to America back in the 'Sixties to unearth a more severe exposition of the muscle car principle. In this case, the silky 190 bhp 3-litre straight-six is dumped altogether to make way for Mercedes' big-gun 5.6-litre V8, an engine which even in standard form pushes the Stuttgart company's 560 SEC flagship to a top speed in excess of 150 mph. Quite powerful enough, you might suppose, to convert Mr Pirelli's most expensive rubber into a swirling mist, the like of which hasn't been seen since the Plague. But the people at AMG don't quite see it that way.

They see the big V8 with four high-lift cams, four valves per cylinder, a 9.8:1 compression ratio and 360 bhp at 5500 rpm (the standard unit develops 299 bhp), and that's the way they build it. Maximum torque is a stump-pulling 358 lb ft at 4000 rpm. The only trouble is that the engine doesn't naturally fit. Stratton, sole agents for AMG in the UK, have to completely rework the bulkhead and engine bay, making countless sheet metal changes. This is one of the reasons that even if you start off with a 230E, as Stratton did, the total bill for the 560E won't be far short of £55,000. That said, the conversion does include a long-striding 2.24:1 final drive, a Gleason Torsen differential, a suspension kit with shorter coil springs and Bilstein dampers, 8×17 in alloy wheels wearing ultra low-profile 215/45 and 235/45 Pirelli DT88s front and rear, and a mild spoiler and skirt body kit.

That 2.24 final drive is significant – it gives 29.5 mph/1000 rpm in top and a top speed, according to the AMG catalogue, of around 180 mph. Stratton don't believe that and neither do we, but consider this: the 560E lapped Millbrook's high-speed bowl at an average of 162.7 mph with a best quarter of 164.0 mph, and that was on the second lap. The third lap didn't happen for fear of the tyres giving out – a not unreasonable precaution at a speed higher than any car we've tested has achieved round the Millbrook bowl.

More admirable still, the 560E delivers its mighty performance with a complete lack of temperament or fuss. Its mid-range slam is almost paralysingly savage – a sensation of gathering pace that makes even the Porsche Turbo's exponential thrust seem tame, cushioned. Yet, at the same time, the Mercedes'

performance delivery is seductively silk-gloved, the engine hauling cleanly and evenly from as little as 2000 rpm. From 3500 rpm, the hollow, bellowing V8 exhaust note takes on a harder, more rasping edge as the engine climbs on to its four cams, then yowls remorselessly all the way to the 6500 rpm change-up point. A genuine 140 mph can be held with a sense of ease only the most rapid of supercars possess. Going for it sees peak-

COSTS

Overall price depends on the base car, but the conversion costs are as follows:

5.6-litre, quad-cam, 32-valve V8	£25,000
Body kit	£1496
Wheels and tyres	£2710
Suspension kit	£776
Black wood	£750
Sports exhaust system	£816
Gleason Torsen differential	£2000
Colour-coded radiator grille	£100
"560E" boot badge	£23
Total plus VAT	**£38,919.45**

PERFORMANCE

MAXIMUM SPEED

	AMG 560E mph	560 SEC mph	Porsche Turbo mph	BMW Alpina B9 mph
	162.7	155 est	160.1	140 est

ACCELERATION FROM REST

mph	AMG 560E sec	560 SEC sec	Porsche Turbo sec	BMW Alpina B9 sec
0-30	1.5	2.8	2.2	3.1
0-40	2.4	3.9	2.7	4.2
0-50	3.7	5.4	3.7	5.1
0.60	5.0	7.1	5.3	7.2
0-70	6.4	8.9	6.4	9.1
0-80	8.0	10.9	7.8	11.4
0-90	10.1	13.5	10.3	14.2
0-100	12.6	16.6	12.3	17.8
0-110	15.3	19.7	15.0	—
0-120	18.3	24.0	19.1	—
0-130	22.2	—	—	—
Overall mpg	17.4	15.6	15.9	18.7

rev shifts at 48, 73 and 123 mph, the tautly set-up auto power-shifting like an Indy racer.

Dynamically, the 560E is both forgiving and masterful. Most of the traditional handling shortcomings of its exotic mid-engined rivals – strong understeer in tight turns, snap oversteer on lift-off – don't apply here. The 560E turns in with agility and precision yet is blessed with superb balance, staying

neutral for far longer than anyone would have any right to expect. Yet the tail can be powered out in a progressive and easily held or corrected manner. In steady state cornering on perfectly dry tarmac, the sheer bite of the supersquat P700s is virtually impossible to overcome. Vices are few – a mild tendency to follow cambers and white line: small chinks in the Mercedes's all-but-impregnable

heavy-duty armour. Certainly, the 560E's massive all-round ventilated discs are beyond criticism, capable of hauling the car to a standstill from three-figure velocities time after time without any signs of fading.

The 560E, then, is driving satisfaction personified. But has the Mercedes' essentially suave character been ruined in AMG's quest for Porsche and Ferrari domination? The original 230E

seats – yet to be supplanted by something more suitable in Stratton's evolving demonstrator – are well-shaped and comfortable, but not really up to providing the sort of specific support needed in a car capable of generating such relentless acceleration, braking and cornering forces. And despite the extensive use of glossy black wood cappings, the rest of the cabin is surprisingly standard.

A firm yet supple ride with closely controlled high-speed damping is more good news, though the suspension and tyres thump and rumble over ridges and rough surfaces with uncompromising disapproval. Wind noise is adequately suppressed, however, and if the engine gets loud when worked hard, the quality of its vocalisations can hardly warrant anything but indulgence.

The 560E's instruments feature no additional gauges to monitor the activities under the bonnet, but the display is more than adequate with large, clearly marked dials under a single, reflection-free glass. The rest of the cabin is a business-like, no-frills affair in the clinical Mercedes tradition and the overall effect, while failing to arouse any strong feelings, at least prompts the usual respect for Swabian efficiency. AMG, of course, can change all that with appropriate injections of cash, good taste guaranteed. The 560E's fuel consumption isn't so much surprising as shocking: 17.4 mpg for a large automatic saloon capable of outdragging a Porsche Turbo almost defies belief but speaks volumes for the efficiency of the W124 body's shape and the innate benefits of a huge power/weight ratio plus long gearing.

After experiencing the 560E, there is only one reasonable conclusion. There is nothing, repeat *nothing*, to compare with the kick of driving a big, mean V8 in a light, fat-tyred saloon. For all its sophistication, subtlety and lavish engineering, the 560E is the Hemi-Cuda re-born. But just a final word to any Hemi-Cuda owners out there. If you come across a black W124 hugging the tarmac, rocking gently from side to side and bearing the number plate "1 AMG", do yourself a favour and leave it well alone. You can tell your friends its driver chickened out. **The AMG 560E is available from Strattons (Wilmslow) Ltd, Water Lane, Wilmslow, Cheshire SK9 5BQ. Tel: 0625 532806.**

Europe 1987

AMG Mercedes Hammer

The hottest passenger sedan in history.

• Don't ask, "What's in a name?" *Hammer* means in German precisely what it means in English, and this car's name says exactly what it is: a hard-hitting tool. AMG crafts it to pound everything else flat.

The Corvette, the 911 Turbo, the Testarossa, and the Countach may be a wee bit quicker in a category or two, but no cigars. They may also take the cake for sex appeal, a highly prized attribute in this speedy league. But this four-door German hot rod utterly flattens them all on comfort, on practicality, and, most important, on the absolutely unadulterated, instantly available ability to rocket across the face of the earth. The Hammer we tested leaped from 0 to 60 mph in five seconds flat. It hurtled through the quarter-mile in 13.5 seconds at 107 mph. And it pounded down a long, flat straightaway to a top speed of 178 mph.

Like the Corvette, the 911 Turbo, the Testarossa, and the Countach, the Hammer covers ground so quickly that you swear you can feel the earth's curvature racing to meet you. Yet the Hammer is different. This AMG-modified sedan keeps you completely at ease as you pierce the atmosphere like a horizontal bolt of lightning. All that's lacking is the stench of scorched sulfur from the shocked aftermath of your receding thunder.

We have watched AMG, Germany's famed Mercedes-Benz tuning firm, tap an ever wiser and wider range of experience.

Always high on horsepower, the company has now come to grips with handling and aerodynamics as well. Hans-Werner Aufrecht, its owner, and Richard Buxbaum, his henchman at AMG of North America, in the Chicago suburb of Westmont, are moving quickly to expand their market. How better than by offering the fastest sedan available anywhere?

Before you auction off the family Countach, however, we have a disclosure to make: the Hammer pictured here is a rough prototype. According to Buxbaum, the performance of the finished products will be nearly identical to our test car's, but a number of alterations to the blueprint are planned before the conversion of customer cars begins. Instead of starting with a European-specification 230E, as AMG did in the case of our test car, future Hammers will be based on U.S.-spec 300Es. (The 230E, which is not available in the U.S., is essentially a 300E with a 2.3-liter four-cylinder instead of a 3.0-liter six.) High-performance three-way catalysts will be added, and KE-Jetronic fuel injection will replace the K-Jetronic of our prototype. Two bodywork pieces that on our test car were fiberglass prototypes will be fabricated from more permanent materials: the front air dam will be made of reaction-injection-molded polyurethane, and the ducktailed deck lid will be steel. Together with the safety hardware on the U.S.-spec 300E, these changes will in-

crease the Hammer's weight. AMG expects no loss of horsepower, however, because the U.S.-specification fuel injection is more sophisticated than the equipment in our test car and should more than make up for the exhaust restriction caused by the addition of catalysts.

AMG is also considering the use of stronger driveline components as a result of a failure that occurred during the final stages of our testing: a CV joint and a rear-axle half-shaft broke. AMG views this as a freak occurrence—no such troubles have cropped up in European Hammers—but it also realizes that a carefully nurtured reputation is at stake, so appropriate measures are under discussion. The Mercedes S-class four-speed automatic transmission and differential assembly have proved quite reliable to date in this application, and neither suffered a moment's hesitation during our tests.

Thanks to Mercedes-Benz's original efforts, the car that AMG begins with is thoughtfully designed, usefully packaged, exceptionally comfortable, and wonderfully practical. It gladly carries four adults, plus luggage. And with a little help from the mechanical midwives at AMG, it is reborn to buffalo those who buy megabuck cars more for brazen trolling than for brilliant driving.

The heart of the matter is a brawny V-8 stuffed into the hole left by the removal of the standard Mercedes in-line engine. The

PHOTOGRAPHY BY RON STRONG

Hammer conversion begins with the disassembly of a brand-new 5.5-liter powerplant from the S-class line. After polishing, blueprinting, and balancing the all-aluminum engine's gleaming guts, AMG swaps the stock single-cam, two-valve-per-cylinder heads for its own free-breathing twin-cam, four-valve-per-cylinder units. Each engine is carefully reassembled and tested on a dynamometer for eight to ten hours.

The payoff is 388 pound-feet of torque at 4500 rpm and 355 horsepower at 5500 rpm. That's 60 hp more than a stock European 5.5-liter Benz, and 125 hp more than America's hoo-boy 5.7-liter Vette. Just as important, the AMG engine in our test car whirred with no nasty quirks. Around town

or flat out, it always slathered its ferocity with imperturbable smoothness.

The Hammer is more than just an expensive engine swap. AMG's striking 8.0-by-17-inch alloy wheels look both aggressive and aerodynamic, and they wear Pirelli P700 215/45VR-17 rubber up front and 235/45VR-17s in back. A set of shorter, stiffer springs lowers the car, and the inner fender lips are pruned slightly to provide clearance for the huge tires. Snugly valved shock absorbers retain the famed Mercedes ability to keep the chassis off its bump stops, even under duress. In fact, AMG has made its greatest strides in suspension tuning. The firm ride comes up a little thumpy over potholes, but not harsh. Over relatively smooth surfaces, it borders

on silky, presuming you like your silk over a touch of muscle tone.

Either of two sets of bodywork finishes off the package. The more extreme choice consists of extra-low front, side, and tail skirts, said to cut the European 300E's drag coefficient from 0.29 to 0.25. The aero package applied to our Hammer hugs the ground less tightly, producing a claimed 0.27 Cd and few scrapes against tall curbs and steep driveways. Thanks both to its aerodynamics and to its tall final-drive ratio (2.24:1), the Hammer's thirst for premium fuel can be limited to a gallon every twenty miles or so when cruising, but only beneath the throttle foot of a saint.

The stabilizing effect of AMG's ducktailed deck lid, which does away with the 300E's beveled trunk line, feels as ducky as the lid looks. Even at very high speeds, we noticed no gusty winds until we stopped. Overall, the chassis never wavers, the interior remains free of wind noise at all speeds, and only when the big V-8 has its way with the world do the wondrous guttural snarls of the exhausts make themselves known.

That shoehorned V-8 is shorter than the Benz six but heavier. AMG's various alterations make the Hammer about 400 pounds heavier than a 300E, but the extra mass is at least equitably distributed. The battery is relocated to the trunk to clear space under the hood, and rear floorpan

Building Hot Rods the AMG Way

Hans-Werner Aufrecht has his own ideas about motoring in a Mercedes-Benz.

• Hans-Werner Aufrecht, the principal partner of AMG, has the style you expect of a man who invented the high-tech look of Mercedes-Benz hot rods. He wears expensively tailored suits and does business in Stuttgart, Beverly Hills, Tokyo, and Sydney. But when he discusses his company, founded in 1967 in an old mill near the village of Burgstall in Württemberg, it is clear that his interests run deeper than monochromatic paint schemes. Aufrecht built sports-car engines in the Mercedes racing shop in the early fifties, and he still has an insatiable passion for performance.

"AMG is different because we are twenty years old next year," Aufrecht says. "Also, from 1967 to 1977 we did only engine and suspension development work, so we are coming from the *Technik* way. And last, we have always been involved in racing. We now have a 190E sixteen-valve that is second in the German championship. The important thing is that we are always coming from the sports and *Technik* way, and we show it at the racetrack."

AMG is now based in Affalterbach,

just outside Stuttgart. Its 135 employees work in a four-building complex that includes an installation center, a paint shop, upholstery facilities, and an elaborate machine shop. AMG did its magic on 6000 cars around the world last year, of which 1500 were shipped to the U.S.

This year, however, Aufrecht and Richard Buxbaum, the president of AMG of North America, have concentrated on expanding the U.S. operation. Five warehouse distributors and 75 subdistributors are being established, and the ultimate goal is a nationwide chain of installation centers with AMG-trained personnel. "We are now prepared to install the whole program we have in Germany," Aufrecht says. "We do the whole car; we make the *Technik,* the *Optik,* and also the interior."

Andy Cohen, the president of Beverly Hills Motoring Accessories, believes the U.S. market has extraordinary potential for AMG. His company signed on as AMG West and opened an installation center last fall. Cohen observes that the decline of the gray market leaves AMG with little competition. In addition,

AMG can now offer professional installation and warranty coverage, making the hardware even more attractive to both individuals and Mercedes dealers.

The outlook for high-tech European hot rods here appears to be brighter than ever. First, the collapse of the lucrative Arab market due to falling oil prices has forced European tuners to pay more attention to the U.S. And second, the new exhaust-emissions laws in Germany have led to a generation of high-performance engine hardware that also meets U.S. emissions requirements. AMG is simply the first to realize the dimensions of this new market. Aufrecht hopes soon to equip five percent of Mercedes-Benz's annual 80,000 U.S. imports with his products each year.

The U.S. market may have its own priorities, but Aufrecht says his standards of performance will not change. He is a hard, serious man, and he emphasizes that his company's reputation is founded upon its technical expertise. For example, "we went from design to production of our four-valve cylinder head in one year," he says. "A big firm needs

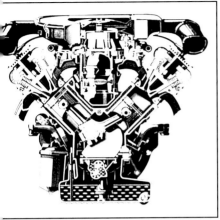

reinforcements are added to accommodate the S-class final-drive assembly. As a result, the Hammer actually boasts better weight distribution than the 300E.

The Pirelli P700 tires specified for the Hammer were in short supply during our time with the prototype, so AMG asked us to substitute other rubber for our cornering and braking tests: a set of sixteen-inch Goodyear VR50 S tires with shaved treads. The modified gatorbacks didn't run as smoothly as the Pirellis, but their gluey adhesion helped the Hammer pound around the skidpad at a punishing 0.85 g, neck-stretching with the swoopiest of supercars. Judging by our tire tests, we doubt that the Hammer would be able to exceed that figure on P700s.

In stopping from 70 mph, the stock Mercedes ABS disc brakes clamped Doktor Hammer to a halt in a thrillingly short 165 feet—a performance only one foot longer than the best-of-the-best, that of the ABS-equipped Corvette. Both cars easily outstop the Testarossa and the Countach. An all-out stop from top speed would probably be too much to ask, but on hill-bent, forest-wrapped roads, the Hammer's brakes never faltered. Slowing from a ripping 160 mph on weaving lanes down to 50 mph for blind corners, we found only modest fade. Bigger brakes are on the way for those who need even more stopping power.

AMG prepares the 300E's four-speed automatic for life behind a more powerful engine with a special hydraulic valve body and revised modulator-pressure settings. The first combination we tried was performance-oriented; it produced 30-to-50-mph and 50-to-70-mph bursts of 2.8 and 3.1 seconds, the fastest we have ever recorded. But it also made the gearbox shift jerkily and often refuse to upshift at part throttle until the pedal was feathered. When we questioned the need for such harsh action, AMG reset the modulator pressure, and our test car promptly shifted more smoothly. This one small adjustment transformed the Hammer's charac-

four or five years. In one year, maybe they have the drawings ready, but not the engine."

As for the kind of cars his company is likely to produce, Aufrecht often tells the story of testing a big Merc V-8 with AMG four-valve heads at the Nürburgring. He found himself behind a Ferrari GTO, one of his personal automotive favorites. He blew past the exotic turbocharged sports car, reaching down as he went by to turn on the Merc's radio. That, Aufrecht says, is his idea of luxury motoring. —*Michael Jordan*

ter from ball peen to hard rubber.

For all its power, the Hammer applies its blows superbly. The moment you move away from rest, the chassis action meshes. The power-assisted steering winds up taut, linear, and informative. Its firm grasp loosens just enough at high speed (*really* high speed) to keep the car from twitching when the road turns lumpy or changes camber. The chassis absorbs the road's upsets with none of its own. The Hammer's basic cornering mode is slight understeer, just enough to keep you square. Power puts the tail wherever you want it. The driver's job is to hew to the one true line and to look *way* ahead, because that's where the car will be in a flash. Squeezing down from full flight and drifting through a 120-mph corner, you can press the throttle just hard enough to skate all four tires a little wider in a classic four-wheel drift—or you can kick the automatic down to third (good to 141!), slewing the tail out to sweep you to the fine edge of the corner's exit in a deliciously syrupy swoop of power oversteer. The amount of syrup you pour is strictly up to your foot. The mighty Hammer asks only that you pay close attention, because, one way or the other, it is going to pump your scrawny hide into the next county like a shot. The low-drag shape encourages flights from 70 to 170 as if the wind had been canceled due to lack of resistance.

Thanks to the solid packaging provided by Mercedes, this mid-sized sedan proves an exceptional mega-performance platform, easy to see out of, tidy to wheel, and a whiz to place. The stiff structure lends itself to the Hammer's high-load dynamics, and its roominess makes it inviting. The optional bolstered rear seats match the new power Recaro CSE sport models up front. The Recaros' inboard thigh bolsters bulge with fifteen control buttons apiece—far too many—but include three memory settings for saving the magic positions once they've been found.

We slipped out of state for a hot date, and our favorite blonde harrumphed that she liked Porsches and, besides, these seats were too hard. (Indeed, they feel like boards at first.) Duly buckled in, however, she savored her Recaro's abiding support during a demonstration of the Hammer's stunning athletic abilities. In a trice, Porsches were the last thing on her expanding mind; this car may be the best import since Dr. Ruth.

Given the Hammer's $125,000 base price, takers will be among the chosen few. AMG will build no more than two a month.

COUNTERPOINT

• Specialty-car builders are the artists of the aftermarket, a group of kindred spirits seeking expression in the search for automotive perfection. For all who try their hand, few have the purity of purpose or crystal-clear vision of Hans-Werner Aufrecht and his staff. It might embarrass the AMG guys to be called the Rembrandts of the industry, but their Hammer is certainly a 178-mph masterpiece.

Like many artists, the AMG staff feels that its masterworks are never really finished. In the Hammer's case, bigger brakes and a more compliant suspension may be brushed in at a later date. But even in its present form, the Hammer is the ultimate expression of the automobile's promise.

Yes, the Hammer is ridiculously expensive—but have you priced any van Goghs lately? I'll never buy a Hammer, but I'm thankful that the loosely wound enthusiasts at AMG have built this wundercar to delight and inspire everyone who loves automobiles. What more could you ask of a work of art than for it to be the stuff of dreams? —*Rich Ceppos*

Our test car was black-on-black, but think of the AMG Hammer as the great white shark of the auto kingdom— uncommon, unchallenged, unafraid. Its presence alone is enough to end most confrontations before they start. Indeed, just seeing one can be counted an experience in itself.

Certainly, driving the Hammer is an experience like no other. You want speed? Press the accelerator pedal and you can have as much as you want. You want room? Don't forget: this is a four-

door Mercedes sedan. You want refinement? Try Mozart at 165 mph. The Hammer does it all with effortless, purposeful grace.

Unfortunately, the Hammer is a voracious creature, too: ours lunched on fuel and driveline bits with abandon.

Tread lightly if you're ever lucky enough to spot a Hammer cruising through traffic. If you're so foolish as to press your luck against AMG's beast, you'll quickly get a rough idea of how it feels to be bitten by a great white.
—*Arthur St. Antoine*

Thanks to AMG, it's now somewhat easier to separate go-fast poseurs from serious hyperperformance addicts. You'll still have to look closely to determine if the person behind the wheel of a low-slung, twelve-cylinder macho-missile is driving it to go fast—or merely to look fast. The buyer of a Hammer, however, doesn't purchase the waist-high lines that are essential to curbside sex appeal. And there's not a penny to be saved by choosing a Hammer instead of a Countach or a Testarossa. There's only one reason to buy a Hammer, and that's to stay high on speed on a steady basis.

The Hammer makes speed easier than ever. With its automatic transmission, it demands only the slightest effort to send its speedometer spinning toward dizzying heights. And with its spacious four-door body, the Hammer's blasts need not be reserved for weekend recreation, but can be enjoyed with a full load of passengers.

Beware of this car. It means serious business, and I'll bet most of its drivers do, too. —*Csaba Csere*

Bargain shoppers can show up at AMG of North America with their own 300Es and cut the tab to a low $90,000.

The Hammer is the most scintillating sedan we have driven. The *C/D* staff drools as one. Even after federalization, AMG's

meanest should match pure speed with any factory's wildest—and make such speed more usable to boot. Not even Dr. Ruth can tell you how to wake up with a Hammer-sized grin for only 90 grand.
—*Larry Griffin*

Vehicle type: front-engine, rear-wheel-drive, 4-passenger, 4-door sedan

Price as tested: $137,000

Options on test car: base AMG Hammer, $125,000; full leather interior, $7500; Recaro CSE seats, $3500; rear bucket seats, $1000

Standard accessories: power steering, windows, seats, locks, and sunroof, A/C, rear defroster

Sound system: Blaupunkt Bamberg AM/FM-stereo radio/cassette, 8 speakers

ENGINE
Type . . . . V-8, aluminum block and heads
Bore x stroke . . . . 3.80 x 3.73 in, 96.5 x 94.8mm
Displacement . . . . 338 cu in, 5547cc
Compression ratio 10.0:1
Fuel system . . . . Bosch K-Jetronic fuel injection
Emissions controls . . . . none
Valve gear . . . . chain-driven double overhead cams, 4 valves per cylinder
Power (SAE net) . . . . 355 bhp @ 5500 rpm
Torque (SAE net) . . . . 388 lb-ft @ 4500 rpm

DRIVETRAIN
Transmission . . . . 4-speed automatic
Final-drive ratio . . . . 2.24:1, limited slip

Gear	Ratio	Mph/1000 rpm	Max. test speed
I	3.68	8.9	45 mph (5000 rpm)
II	2.41	13.6	84 mph (6200 rpm)
III	1.44	22.7	141 mph (6200 rpm)
IV	1.00	32.7	178 mph (5450 rpm)

DIMENSIONS AND CAPACITIES
Wheelbase . . . . 110.2 in
Track, F/R . . . . 58.9/58.6 in
Length . . . . 186.6 in
Width . . . . 68.5 in
Height . . . . 54.1 in
Ground clearance . . . . 3.4 in
Curb weight . . . . 3636 lb

Weight distribution, F/R 53.3/46.7%
Fuel capacity . . . . 18.5 gal
Oil capacity . . . . 8.5 qt
Water capacity . . . . 13.7 qt

CHASSIS/BODY
Type . . . . unit construction with 1 rubber-isolated crossmember
Body material . . . . welded steel stampings

INTERIOR
SAE volume, front seat . . . . 50 cu ft
rear seat . . . . 40 cu ft
trunk space . . . . 15 cu ft
Front seats . . . . bucket
Seat adjustments . . . . fore and aft, seatback angle, front height, rear height, lumbar support, upper side bolsters, thigh support
General comfort . . . . poor fair good **excellent**
Fore-and-aft support . . . . poor fair good **excellent**
Lateral support . . . . poor fair good **excellent**

SUSPENSION
F: . . . . ind, strut located by control arm, coil springs, anti-roll bar
R: . . . . ind, 2 lateral links and 3 diagonal trailing links per side, coil springs, anti-roll bar

STEERING
Type . . . . recirculating ball, power-assisted
Turns lock-to-lock 3.4
Turning circle curb-to-curb . . . . 36.7 ft

BRAKES
F: . . . . 11.2 x 0.9-in vented disc
R: . . . . 10.2 x 0.4-in disc
Power assist . . . . vacuum with anti-lock control

WHEELS AND TIRES
Wheel size . . . . 8.0 x 17 in
Wheel type . . . . cast aluminum
Tires . . . . Pirelli P700, F: 215/45VR-17; R: 235/45VR-17
Test inflation pressures, F/R . . . . 38/42 psi

---

CAR AND DRIVER TEST RESULTS

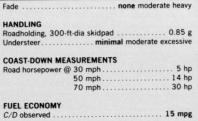

ACCELERATION — Seconds
Zero to 30 mph 2.2
40 mph 3.0
50 mph 3.9
60 mph 5.0
70 mph 6.5
80 mph 8.1
90 mph 10.1
100 mph 12.0
110 mph 14.7
120 mph 18.3
130 mph 22.8
Top-gear passing time, 30–50 mph 2.8
50–70 mph 3.1
Standing ¼-mile . . . . 13.5 sec @ 107 mph
Top speed . . . . 178 mph

BRAKING
70–0 mph @ impending lockup . . . . 165 ft

Fade . . . . **none** moderate heavy

HANDLING
Roadholding, 300-ft-dia skidpad . . . . 0.85 g
Understeer . . . . **minimal** moderate excessive

COAST-DOWN MEASUREMENTS
Road horsepower @ 30 mph . . . . 5 hp
50 mph . . . . 14 hp
70 mph . . . . 30 hp

FUEL ECONOMY
C/D observed . . . . 15 mpg

INTERIOR SOUND LEVEL
Idle . . . . 56 dBA
Full-throttle acceleration . . . . 81 dBA
70-mph cruising . . . . 70 dBA
70-mph coasting . . . . 70 dBA

CURRENT BASE PRICE dollars x 1000
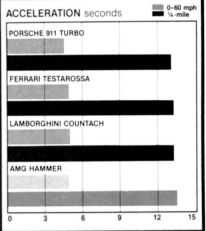

ACCELERATION seconds
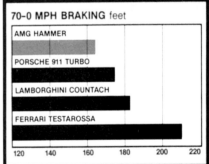

70–0 MPH BRAKING feet
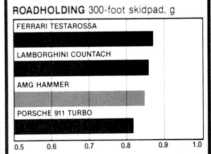

ROADHOLDING 300-foot skidpad, g

TOP SPEED mph
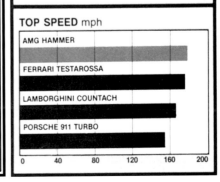

AMG
HAMMER

A Mercedes 4-door that runs like a Ferrari Testarossa? Eat your heart out, Sonny Crockett!

BY JOE RUSZ

PHOTOS BY JOHN LAMM

W HEN THE RED 4-door pulled out to pass his slow-mov-
ing tractor-trailer rig, the trucker shook his head.
There was no way a sedan, even a Mercedes-Benz
300E, could get out, around and back into the proper lane in
what little space this short stretch of straight highway provided.
Shoot, he'd probably have to get on the binders and let that
lunatic tuck in ahead of his big rig. Imagine the truck driver's
surprise when the Merc blasted by, then almost as quickly slot-
ted itself into the queue as if it had been there all along. Sedans
aren't supposed to be able to do that. Sports and musclecars,
maybe. But family 4-doors, even Mercedes? Never. Alas, what
the fellow didn't know was that this was no ordinary Benz but
an AMG Hammer, the family sedan that doesn't just think it's
an exotic; it runs like one. Zero to 60 in 5.3 seconds, top speed
180-plus mph, just like the Ferrari GTO or Testarossa without
any sacrifice in comfort, room or quietness.

Obviously, the Hammer is not exactly your mass-produced
Merc. It's a selectively equipped 300E impeccably turned out
by AMG, the German tuning firm specializing in those other
cars from Stuttgart. For those of you who don't know, AMG is
to Mercedes what Alpina is to BMW, Ruf to Porsche, Treser to
Audi. The firm was founded in 1967 by Hans-Werner Aufrecht and Erhard Melcher, two former Daimler-Benz engineers, and its name comes from the initials of their last names
and of Grossaspach, Aufrecht's birthplace. AMG supplies a
full line of show-and-go components to followers of the→

3-pointed star who seek to enhance the appearance, handling and performance of their Mercs. It also sells complete cars including an extensively modified 300E known as the Hammer, its most outrageous model.

At first glance it's tempting to dismiss this sedan as nothing more than a Mercedes-Benz W124 with cafe racer bodywork. That's understandable. Every fly-by-night automotive fiberglass shop is into aero, and the Hammer's swoopy front and rear spoilers, side skirts and fender flares are out of the same mold, or so it would seem. However, AMG assures us that its aero aids have been wind-tunnel tested and give the Hammer its remarkably low 0.25 C_X (says AMG) that enables the 4-door to slip through the air like a phantom to achieve top speeds normally associated with the world's fastest exotic cars.

You say those highly polished flat spoke wheels look a bit garish? Maybe so. But these 8-in. wide, 17-in. tall alloys are a perfect fit for those 215/45VR-17 front and 235/45VR-17 rear Pirelli P700 tires that give the Hammer lateral acceleration equal to the stickier sports cars and (when combined with stiffer springs, re-valved shocks and stiffer anti-roll bars) endow it with handling comparable to that of the best GTs.

Of course, all of this is just frosting on the cake because what makes the Hammer unique is AMG's mind-bending V-8 that churns out an impressive 365 bhp even after it's been sanitized to meet U.S. emissions standards. Designed by Melcher (no longer part of AMG but under contract to the firm), the KE-Jetronic-equipped powerplant is based on a 5.6-liter Mercedes aluminum V-8 that's been bored out to 6.0 liters, fitted with special 9.8:1 pistons and topped off by Melcher's 4-valve, double overhead-cam cylinder heads. Such a pretty sight. Also, a pretty hefty package especially when shoehorned into the W124 engine compartment where M-B's longer but skinnier sohc 3.0-liter 177-bhp six usually reposes. Not only is the V-8 fatter than the inline-6, but also it's about 100 lb heavier. Normally, this would upset weight distribution a tad. But with the installation of a stronger rear subframe and heftier W126 components, springs, suspension bits, disc brakes, transmission, driveshaft and rear differential, that extra 800 lb (for the total package) is spread more equitably throughout the chassis, so that the car's balance is better than the stock 300E's. If that's not enough, the battery has been moved to the trunk in a further attempt to restore front-to-rear balance. One more thing: The metal spoiler that's an integral part of the rear deck lid adds a few extra pounds to the back end.

Inside, the AMG influence is minimal. But it includes a custom steering wheel, wooden shift knob, wooden dash and door panel trim, deep-pile floor mats emblazoned with the AMG logo and (best of all) a gorgeous AMG speedometer that reads up to 190 mph. Gilding the automotive lily? Not in the Hammer. Granted, you may never see the speedo's needle reach 5 o'clock. But with 360 or so ponies on tap, you'll find yourself whistling up to 2 or 3 o'clock without even trying . . . as we discovered after spending several exciting days dashing about Southern California in our bright red test car. It was provided →

Filling the Hammer's engine compartment, the AMG-built powerplant is based on a Mercedes-Benz V-8 that has been bored out to 6.0 liters and fitted with dohc heads with 4 valves per cylinder. KE-Jetronic-injected, it develops about 365 bhp in federalized trim.

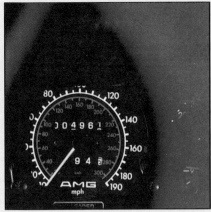

AMG's 190-mph speedometer is more than just an affectation. The Hammer goes almost that fast, thanks to its excellent aerodynamics and a ground-pounding dohc V-8.

for us by Andy Cohen, owner of Beverly Hills Motoring Accessories, AMG's West Coast distributor (200 S. Robertson Blvd, Beverly Hills, Calif. 90211; 213 657-4800). In addition to being the only Hammer in America, our car had the distinction of being the first to be built in the U.S. Although the engine and components came from Germany, the conversion (of an American-spec 300E) took place at AMG of North America (233 W. Ogden Ave, Westmont, Ill. 60559; 312 971-2002).

The big V-8 fires up easily and shakes the ground as it goes. Dual 928S 4 catalytic converters emit a melodious burble—when the engine is loafing. Put it to work and the exhaust note becomes a roar as the revs climb to the 4-cam's 6000-rpm redline. Although AMG has built about 170 dohc V-8s, this is one of the few 6.0-liter powerplants in existence. The added displacement provides an increase in torque while four valves per cylinder allow the engine to breath more freely—and to rev.

Working the shifter of the Hammer's 4-speed W126 automatic deftly through the gears is fun, but not really necessary. With 400 lb-ft of torque almost any gear is a good one, especially if you leave the selector in Drive and let D-B's minions (or is it, pinions?) do the work. That's the lesson we learned after running the Hammer at the dragstrip. We tried low-gear starts, moving the stick to the side of the Lo gate to engage D1, but found that wheelspin was excessive and that we couldn't shift fast enough to avoid overrevving the engine and causing the governor to kick in. We tried starts in D2 and still got a lot of wheelspin but not the stumble caused by overrevving. Finally, we simply left the lever in Drive and found that, all things being equal, the Hammer still managed some mind-boggling-tire smoking elapsed times—5.3 sec from 0 to 60, 13.5 sec to the quarter mile. Oh, we did find a way to avoid wheelspin in the Hammer: racing slicks. By locking up the brakes and spinning the rear wheels in a puddle of water to get 'em good and hot, we got the Hammer to "hook up" and shaved about 0.5 sec of our best 0 to 60 and quarter-mile elapsed times.

Okay, so the Hammer's a rocket. But how does it handle? Lateral acceleration is reasonably good, the torque of the big V-8 enables you to squirt from turn to turn in a flash, and ABS allows you to late-brake deep into every corner—at speeds most enthusiast drivers are accustomed to, let's say, 7/10ths. But at 9/10ths or 10/10ths the AMG gets a bit nervous because there's more engine than chassis. Power is a 2-way street: Applying it gently but progressively in a corner can cause the car to understeer, probably because the rear wheels, assisted by the limited slip, are getting a better bite than the front wheels; on the other hand, applying it suddenly and excessively in a turn can break loose the rear wheels and induce oversteer. Of course, most musclecars do this, and we love them for it. So we should love the Hammer, right? Yes. And we do, in that context. But the Hammer is no Camaro or Mustang, and considering the company this car is expected to keep, handling could be better or at least more manageable.

So who needs handling when all most people want to do is whistle along at, how fast was that again, 180 mph? Yes, that's the top speed all right. Actually, it's a bit more. Or so say the folks at AMG who clocked a European 5.6-liter Hammer at 303 km/h (187 mph) on the *Autobahn*. We never had the chance to probe the car's upper limits although we did spend a lot of time at 130 mph where our red sedan proved to be rock steady and impressively quiet—save for the rumble of that magnificent AMG 32-valver.

You'll probably never see another one like it because more than likely you'll never see a Hammer. Unless you buy one of your own. Turnkey ready, a Hammer costs $161,422, but if you already own a 300E and want to have it converted into a Hammer, deduct $39,000 from that figure. That leaves only $122,422, which breaks down like this: Mercedes-Benz 5.6-liter engine with KE-Jetronic $17,000; modification to 6.0-liter dohc, $39,950; Hammer conversion package (heavy-duty rear subframe, W126 rear differential with Gleason-Torsen limited slip), $33,302; AMG suspension kit, $1495; AMG wheels with Pirelli P700 tires, $5050; AMG aero body kit, $4125; installation and painting of body and parts, $3500; labor, $18,000.

At full pop or at the discount price, you're buying exclusivity. There are only 13 Hammers in the world including this car, the only one of its kind in America. But more than exclusivity, you're buying the fastest Mercedes in the world, an automobile with the body of a 4-door sedan and the soul (and performance) of an exotic.

Why die the richest man? You certainly can't take it with you. Even as you read this, there are incredibly expensive homes, boats, planes, and cars being built to help alleviate this problem. Granted, not all of us have such a concern, but the possibility does exist of winning the lottery, discovering oil in your backyard, or inheriting an anonymous $50 million.

Of the automobile companies that have elected to build for the cost-be-damned market, Mercedes-Benz is the most prolific. Unlike many of its contemporaries, Mercedes-Benz offers a wide range of models from which to choose, starting at a mere $30,000 for the little 190 to its near-$75,000 560SEC Coupe.

Priced around three times the average national family income, the Mercedes' top-of-the-line coupe must be heaped into the dream-car category. And in this high-rent neighborhood, the SEC gets some very high marks. Though maybe not as ferocious as a Testarossa nor as sleek as a Countach, the Coupe handles well, is fairly quick, is handsomely styled, and stops on a dime. And, unlike most of its exotic cousins, it's quiet, comfortable, and practical (seats four and has a trunk), plus you can get it

Mercedes-Benz 560SEC AMG

Four cams and 32 valves equals high performance for high dollars

by Michael Brockman

PHOTOGRAPHY BY MARK CLIFFORD

fixed almost anywhere. Try that with a Countach!

If this is beginning to sound a little too sane and mundane for your ultimate dream car, fear not, the solution is near at hand. AMG, the German aftermarket wizard that started the monochromatic craze, has created its version of the SEC, which should satisfy even the most extravagant of Robin Leach's interviewees.

The full-boat AMG conversion you see on these pages is ultra high-tech and sells for a meager $143,500. If you want to save $43,500, you *could* have AMG prep an SEC for approximately $100,000, which includes car,

chassis, and appearance packages. But why not go all the way and spend the 43 Gs so you can pass your neighbor at 180 mph on your way to the beach house?

As you probably know, AMG tunes Mercedes-Benz products with an emphasis on performance. In the 20 years AMG has been in business, engine and chassis tuning has always been its credo, and, in the past eight years, its execution in packaging the product (single-color scheme) has snowballed into a worldwide cliché. AMG products are engineered, designed, and developed in Affalterbach, West Germany, then shipped to its U.S. distributor in Westmont, Illinois, for finish, assembly, and delivery.

When we first heard about the AMG engine conversion for the SEC, we called AMG's West Coast outlet, Beverly Hills Motoring Accessories, which graciously gave us the Coupe for the day.

First stop, the Beverly Hills Hotel for lunch. This is one of the true tests: If the parking valet leaves the car out front instead of parking it in back, you know you have a winner. Well, it passed the first test and lunch was great—now, to the racetrack. If only this envious mob waiting for their valet-parked cars knew what little money we make.

The AMG engine conversion in our

The AMG convert seems like a stock 560—until you actually get into it

test car is actually a 6-liter version of M-B's 5.6-liter engine with AMG-designed 32-valve chain-driven double overhead cam heads, producing 375 hp at 5500 rpm and 407 lb-ft of torque at 4000 rpm, compared to 238 hp at 5200 and 287 lb-ft at 3500 in the stock model. To handle the extra 137 hp and additional torque, a Gleason-Torsen limited-slip differential is used, as well as a re-valved 4-speed automatic for positive upshifts and downshifts. Other than a rough idle and a throatier sound, the AMG convert seems very much like a stock 560, until you actually get into it. The first

time off the line at the dragstrip was a real surprise; the extra torque makes a big difference. And a 5.79-sec 0-60 isn't bad for a 3900-lb car with a 2.65:1 gear that's advertised to run at 180 mph flat out.

Braking was better than we have seen before on the SEC—60-0 in 123 ft. The brakes are the same as the standard 560SEC, but we reckon the 17-in. 235/45ZR Pirellis were the reason for this excellent stopping distance. Over the road, the car transmits a little more feel due to the revalved Bilsteins, shorter springs, and 45-series tires. It's not a rough ride, but you definitely feel the difference. And with this kind of performance, the price is well paid.

Adorned with AMG's front airdam, side and rear skirts, and rear spoiler, a 3.4% decrease in front lift and a whopping 37% decrease in the rear is claimed. We weren't able to verify this in our testing, but AMG says it's wind-tunnel proven, and, if you're going to drive this 32-valve conversion anywhere near its potential, it will come in very handy.

If you are in a position to buy this car, you probably couldn't care less about the price breakdown. But we thought it might be interesting to list them in approximate figures.

TECH DATA

Mercedes-Benz 560SEC AMG

POWERTRAIN
Vehicle configuration	Front engine, rear drive
Engine configuration	V-8, DOHC, 4 valves/cylinder
Displacement	5953 cc (363 cu in.)
Max. power (SAE net)	375 hp @ 5500 rpm
Max. torque (SAE net)	407 lb-ft @ 4000 rpm
Transmission	4-sp. auto.
Final drive ratio	2.65:1

CHASSIS
Suspension, f/r	Independent/independent
Brakes, f/r	Disc/disc, power assist, ABS
Steering	Recirculating ball, power assist
Wheels	17 x 8.0 in., cast alloy
Tires	235/45ZR17

DIMENSIONS
Wheelbase	2885 mm (112.0 in.)
Overall length	5060 mm (199.2 in.)
Curb weight	1765 kg (3890 lb)
Fuel capacity	103.0 L (27.1 gal)

PERFORMANCE
Acceleration, 0-60	5.79 sec
Standing quarter mile	14.37 sec/100.9 mph
Braking, 60-0	123 ft
Lateral acceleration	N/A
EPA rating	15 mpg
BASE PRICE	$74,960
PRICE AS TESTED	$143,500

The 4-cam 32-valve heads look right at home in the 560's engine bay.

The often-copied AMG skirts and spoilers make a subtle but striking difference.

560SEC base price	$ 74,960
AMG conversion	39,950
Body package: airdam, side skirts, rear spoiler	2,215
Painting body package, strip and paint chrome	2,350
Headers	1,695
Exhaust and catalytic converter	3,895
Gleason-Thorsen Differential	2,395
Shocks and springs	2,295
Wheels and tires	5,125
Labor	7,000
Mats, emblems, etc.	1,620
Total:	$143,500

The bottom line is that the Mercedes-Benz 560SEC Coupe is an incredibly good car, although it *is* expensive. The AMG engine conversion is a well-executed refinement of that automobile, even though it's *incredibly* expensive.

So, if you're on Robin Leach's list, have just won the lottery, discovered oil in your yard, or inherited millions, give the folks at AMG a call. They'll be glad you did. Ⓜ

AMG

BABY HAMMER

Prodigious power in a
pint-size package

BY RAY THURSBY
PHOTOS BY JEFFREY R. ZWART

BIOLOGICAL IMPERATIVES apply in all sorts of situations. Big birds spawn baby birds; big bees are inevitably followed by little bees. Now, the AMG Hammer has sired a Baby Hammer. Parents and progeny, we're happy to report, are doing just fine. ▪ AMG is one of those companies that rate the cliché of needing no introduction. Hans-Werner Aufrecht's firm has specialized in the manufacture and marketing of appearance and performance parts for

Mercedes-Benzes since 1967. Most of AMG's offerings have been more than enthusiastically received; success has allowed Aufrecht to expand his facilities in Germany and open a center in the U.S., where AMG products destined for North American sale are built. Erhard Melcher, Aufrecht's former partner and now a supplier of some AMG engine components, and Aufrecht's home town, Grossaspach, are respectively the "M" and "G" of the company name, by the way.

Complete makeovers are performed on customers' own cars, new or used, at the Westmont, Ohio AMG plant, or, as an alternative, individual parts can be purchased for installation on any recent Mercedes. By referring carefully to the catalog, those so inclined can make a Baby at home.

No AMG car has generated more excitement than the Hammer. The automotive press has taken to the current AMG centerpiece in much the same manner

as tabloid newspapers have embraced UFOs, though the Hammer's traits and performance are easier to identify and evaluate.

Big Hammers, for those who need reminding, are 300-series Mercedes-Benzes (coupe, sedan or station wagon) that have had their factory-issue 6-cylinder engine unceremoniously yanked out, to be replaced by a Mercedes V-8 with AMG modifications (4-valve twincam cylinder heads, an increase from 5.6 to 6.0 liters displacement, etc). The

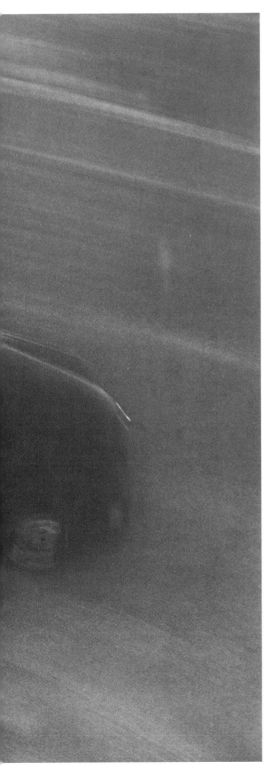

swap, when coupled to the kinds of chassis and body modifications one might correctly demand as companions to the much-augmented power, results in a very serious motorcar, one whose circa-185-mph maximum speed exceeds its price (in thousands of dollars), but not by all that much. Gives you something to think about if your lottery ticket wins, doesn't it?

BABY HAMMERS are something else again. These get their basic structure from 190-series Mercedes, and the modifications are somewhat less extensive—and less expensive—than those applied to the larger Hammers.

AMG did not, as I simultaneously hoped and feared when first confronted by the car, create the Baby Hammer by stuffing a big M-B V-8 under the 190's hood. That's been done by another German tuning firm, with spectacular results, but AMG has chosen to resist the temptation. Wisely, I think, though I'll admit that a 190 so equipped would be a tempting package to try. Once. On a wide, dry road. When nobody's watching.

Instead, motive power comes from a derivative of the 2.6-liter, sohc 6-cylinder engine that Mercedes installs in top-line 190s. In standard form, it's good for 158 bhp and adequate, if not sparkling, performance.

Externally, the AMG-modified engine looks much the same as the unit it supplants. But if its appearance isn't destined to rack the citizens, listing the internal modifications that make a 76-bhp difference in output ought to make up for the lack of visual flash.

From the top, the engine gets a reworked

A glint of sunlight off a highly polished wheel is all that's needed to fire an enthusiast's heart. These lovely wheels, shod with grippy Goodyears, work in harmony with AMG-spec springs and shocks to up the limits of the 190E's chassis a couple of clicks.

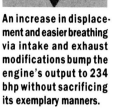

An increase in displacement and easier breathing via intake and exhaust modifications bump the engine's output to 234 bhp without sacrificing its exemplary manners.

cylinder head with larger valves, gas-flowed inlet and exhaust tracts and a different camshaft. What alteration AMG makes to the intake system, if any, is not specified, but special headers are applied to the exhaust side. These bolt to AMG's own tailpipe/catalyst/muffler assembly, said to be worth 7 bhp all by itself.

By comparison, very little is done to the block. A boring bar is applied, raising displacement to 3.2 liters, but that's about it. New pistons are installed, raising the compression ratio from 9.2 to 10.0:1. The owner's manual for the 190E calls for premium fuel; same goes for *Hammerchen*.

Two groups of numbers sum up the AMG 3.2: 234 (bhp *and* lb-ft torque) and 15,450 (how many dollars AMG gets for the conversion, plus exchange engine).

Behind the single most expensive part of the Baby Hammer package, either a 5-speed manual or a 4-speed automatic can be applied. In either case the factory gear ratios remain unchanged, but the automatic (from a 300E) gets different valving, tailoring its shift points to the bigger engine's power curve.

A limited-slip differential is installed, and each corner gets an AMG-spec coil spring and shock absorber, 16 x 7½-in. cast alloy wheel (two designs, a 5-spoke and the "aero," as seen here, are available) and 245/45VR-16 Goodyear Gatorback tire. All other suspension components, including front and rear anti-roll bars, are standard 190E fare.

Horsepower and handling are the major ingredients in the Baby Hammer recipe. But the most visible ones are the air dams, side sills and trunk-lid spoiler. These pieces, more than anything else, define the car's character to casual onlookers.

Except, of course, for the monochromatic paint scheme, which has become *the* AMG trademark. Paint any Mercedes a solid color—white and black appear to be the favorites at the moment—from radiator shell to trunk-release button, not forgetting badges, window moldings, door handles and all the other bits originally destined to be chrome-plated, and presto! *An AMG Mercedes.* Even if it really isn't. That shows how well AMG's concept has caught on with people who wouldn't know a Koenig from a kangaroo.

Like everything else that goes in or on an AMG conversion, the monochrome look was a carefully thought-out response to a perceived need for individuality. And, at least in the case of our black test car, the add-on pieces and the one-color-covers-all paint scheme drew positive response from everyone. Hardly anyone bothers to look at a 190; the sinister *schwarz* AMG version could pull crowds in the Gobi Desert.

It's a little less successful at attention-grabbing in Beverly Hills, simply because AMG Mercedes and their paint-alike generic imitators are not unknown in local driveways and valet parking lots. Another reason for the reduced response is the presence of Beverly Hills Motoring Accessories (209 S. Robertson Blvd, Beverly Hills, Calif. 90211), west coast AMG distributor and supplier of our test car.

BEFORE WE get into driving impressions, a few caveats: First, and most important, the Baby Hammer, like all AMG Mercedes, is essentially the sum of a great many individual items, which each purchaser may order or not, according to taste and budget. Thus, it's possible that anything that disappoints in this subjective

appraisal might not apply to other Baby Hammers. Probably won't, in fact.

Second, our subject car had been sold not long before we were due to take it away. In deference to its new owner, a certain extra measure of restraint was in order.

Exercising restraint, as this lucky purchaser may have already found out, is the hardest part of driving a Baby Hammer. From the first turn of the ignition key, it's ready to go as far and as fast as its pilot could wish. Farther and faster, maybe.

Once the Baby Hammer gets past a grumbly idle, all impressions are positive. The tachometer needle climbs swiftly, especially after 4000 rpm, which is only 500 rpm shy of the 3.2's torque peak. What little smoothness may have been lost in the hop-up process isn't missed because all that extra eagerness more than compensates.

Moreover, drivers with long memories will take extra pleasure from the distinctive sound emerging from the twin tailpipes (each with its own chrome AMG-logo tip); it bears an uncanny resemblance to that of another fuel-injected sohc Mercedes six, as installed in the 300SL. Just right for the car.

It's a good thing the exhaust note is pleasing, because a Baby Hammer equipped with automatic transmission, as this one was, runs at fairly high revs most of the time. A steady 60 mph takes just under 3000 rpm; that's rather short gearing by today's standards. While not ideal for maximum speed (I'll estimate 140 mph), low ratios do wonders for acceleration (0–60 mph should take about 7–7.5 seconds when you're not worried about burning up someone else's Goodyears); that's more useful in this country anyway. Manual-transmission versions, according to (believable) AMG figures, should be good for a 152-mph maximum and a 6.2-sec 0–60 time.

Shifts in the automatic are more authoritative than unobtrusive and, under

Interior options are many, ranging from a leather-wrapped AMG steering wheel to Recaro articulated power seats. Owner of this car opted only for a dashboard wood trim kit.

full-throttle conditions, occur just as the rev limiter cuts in at 6500 rpm.

Stiffer springs and shocks coupled to super-wide tires don't do much for the Baby Hammer's ride; low-speed travel over pavement of indifferent quality comes close to being unpleasant. On smooth roads, at higher speeds, things are much better, but some harshness is always there.

That, however, is the inevitable trade-off for exceptional cornering ability. The car goes exactly where you point it, thanks to its precise steering and grippy tires, maintaining a resolutely neutral stance at speeds that might amaze you. This is a great way to travel, and it gets better with practice.

Get-in-and-go drivers are liable to be in for some surprises. This is a car that requires a high level of competence from its driver at very high velocities. Mid-course alterations in trajectory, for example, must be approached with care, lest all that tire adhesion turn them into undesirable major direction changes. Bump steer is present in moderate quantities, too, but any lump in the road large enough to cause problems may bring the outside front tire into contact with its fender lip.

In all probability the simple cure for these problems is to avoid the use of springs intended for the lighter 4-cylinder 190. These were installed on our car and, while the lower ride height they provide looks wonderfully racy, using them on the 3.2 may not suit the most energetic drivers.

But, minor correctable problems aside, it doesn't take long to get comfortable with the Baby Hammer's high-speed behavior; after that, it's all fun. Pick out a challenging road and attack with confidence, letting the suspension, steering and brakes (the last with ABS, naturally) do the hard work. The combination of well developed underpinnings and a responsive engine adds up to torpedo-fast exits from hairpin turns and sweeping bends alike. Who needs *Autobahnen*?

While all this is going on, driver and passengers are being cosseted by all the requisite Mercedes luxury touches: excellent ventilation and air conditioning, lots of leather and myriad thoughtful details, all assembled with typical M-B quality. The driver gets well placed positive-acting controls and an easy-to-read instrument board as well. AMG offers a variety of upgrades for the 190 interior, from special steering wheels, instruments and Recaro seats to floormats, shift knobs and wood trim kits (finished in the same ultra-glossy manner as Mercedes' own lumber); our example had only the wood.

If I had a Hammer, the Recaro seats would head the option list. Standard Mercedes 190 seats are fine for everyday driving, but a Baby Hammer's cornering abilities make additional lateral support a must. A substitute steering wheel (bye bye, airbag) would be nice, too. And, I'd definitely call for the 5-speed.

It is said that an increasing number of AMG customers are ordering the engine and suspension modifications without the exterior treatment, giving up the delights of extrovert paneling and monochrome paint for the pleasure of having a genuine Q-ship. That would be a hard choice to make; the AMG pieces all match their factory M-B counterparts in fit and finish, and they are eye-catching. Of course anonymity does have its rewards . . .

Fully dressed or traveling incognito, the AMG transformation of the 190E scores high marks on the desirability scale. As it comes from Stuttgart, the baby Benz is just another kid from a good family, but in Baby Hammer guise, it's rambunctious, bouncy and ready for a good tussle with almost any opponent.

A great candidate for adoption.

U.S. SPECIFICATIONS

Price	est $62,255
Curb weight, lb	2835
Wheelbase, in.	104.9
Track, front/rear	57.3/56.3
Length	175.1
Width	66.1
Height	53.5
Fuel capacity, U.S. gal.	16.3

ENGINE

Type	sohc inline-6
Bore x stroke, in./mm	3.54 x 3.31/90.0 x 84.0
Displacement, cu in./cc	196/3205
Compression ratio	10.0:1
Bhp @ rpm, SAE net	234 @ 5750
Torque @ rpm, lb-ft	234 @ 4500
Fuel injection	Bosch KE-Jetronic III

DRIVETRAIN

Transmission	4-sp automatic
Gear ratios: 4th (1.00)	3.27:1
3rd (1.49)	4.87:1
2nd (2.41)	7.88:1
1st (4.25)	13.90:1
Final-drive ratio	3.27:1

CHASSIS & BODY

Layout	front engine/rear drive
Brake system	10.2-in. vented discs front & rear; vacuum assist, ABS
Wheels	cast alloy, 16 x 7½
Tires	Goodyear Eagle, 225/45VR-16
Steering type	recirculating ball, power assist
Turns, lock-to-lock	3.3

Suspension, front/rear: modified MacPherson struts, lower A-arms, coil springs, tube shocks, anti-roll bar/5-link, coil springs, gas-pressurized tube shocks, anti-roll bar

PERFORMANCE

0–60 mph, sec	7.0
Standing ¼ mile, sec @ mph	15.5 @ 93.7
Top speed, mph	est 140

The latest number from AMG—a baby Hammer that perhaps should have been called a Mallet—is the trendy way to mess with the minds of BMW M5 owners. Your $59,500 buys a full load of AMG aero aids, not to mention 245 bhp under the hood.

AMG 190E 3.2

Attention, BMW owners: Beware of sneaky men with little Hammers.

Beverly Hills—

The speed-crazed technicians at AMG's installation centers have been making headlines recently by yanking the six-cylinder engines out of Mercedes-Benz 300Es and installing DOHC V-8s in their stead to create the Hammer 6.0. Apparently, this has left a bunch of 3.0-liter in-line sixes with nothing to do. Hey, why not pump them full of AMG horsepower and stuff them into the 190E, the littlest Benz?

That's all there is to AMG's 3.2-liter 190E. It's kind of a baby Hammer, available for the cut-rate price of $59,500, which doesn't even make you breathe hard compared with the big Hammer's $175,000 price tag. Maybe it won't do 180 mph, but you could be happy with

152 mph, right?

AMG does its usual thorough massage on the Mercedes-Benz six before installing it into the 190E, giving it 90mm pistons and a compression ratio of 10.0:1. A big-valve SOHC cylinder head, new cam timing, Bosch KE-III Jetronic fuel injection, and a new exhaust system do the rest. The result is 245 bhp (as much as a Corvette has) at 5750 rpm—an increase of 38 percent.

Although the chassis improvements are not as elaborate as those for the Hammer 6.0, they include new springs and Bilstein high-pressure gas shock absorbers. A limited-slip differential with a shorter ratio (3.27:1) feeds the power to the sixteen-inch alloy wheels and the 225/45VR-16 Goodyear Gatorbacks. A full complement of AMG aero aids reduces the bodywork's lift at high speed (Cd is said to be 0.33) and also gives the little Benz a suitably tough look.

Once it's stuffed with horsepower, the AMG 190E really rips and the power band is broad and deep. Zero to sixty is accomplished in 6.2 seconds.

In the corners, the car heels over with its inside front wheel on full rebound, like a standard 190E, but once you pick up the throttle, the AMG settles down and works all four tires nicely. The baby Hammer also isolates you efficiently from bumps, and there isn't a trace of shimmy from the steering wheel to betray the low-profile tires.

For all this car's speed and style, however, it feels a little too tightly wrapped. The exhaust tone is a little too insistent, and the freeway ride is a little too choppy. Somehow, the AMG 190E 3.2 doesn't have the same breezy, long-legged confidence of the bigger car. Of course, that impression might be just a side effect of the stock 190E's cramped interior and tacky trim, not to mention a symptom of withdrawal from

AMG 190E 3.2
Base price/price as tested
$59,500/$59,500

GENERAL:
Front-engine, rear-wheel-drive sedan
5-passenger, 4-door steel body

POWERTRAIN:
SOHC 6-in-line, 196 cu in (3205cc)
Power SAE net 245 bhp @ 5750 rpm
4-speed automatic transmission

CHASSIS:
Independent front and rear suspension
Power-assisted recirculating-ball steering
11.2-in vented front disc, 10.2-in rear disc brakes
Anti-lock system
225/45VR-16 Goodyear Gatorback tires

MEASUREMENTS:
Wheelbase 104.9 in
Curb weight 2840 lb
Fuel capacity 16.3 gal

the big Hammer's miraculous 375 bhp.

Horsepower addiction aside, the AMG 190E 3.2 is still a pretty sneaky way to mess with the minds of BMW M5 owners. Think of it as a satisfying way to mark time until you have an additional $100,000-plus for a full-size Hammer.

—Michael Jordan

CIVI

OWNING A top-model BMW or Mercedes is beyond the means of most people. But for some, possession is only the start of a crazy dream. For those who are never satisfied – who always crave for more – specialists like Alpina and AMG have the solutions.

Each carries on where the car maker leaves off, adding muscle and beauty until their creation is unique. Their targets may be opposite, but hot their quests for perfection.

Alpina consider themselves car manufacturers, preferring to sell fully modified BMWs built to order – whereas AMG offer a more flexible approach, supplying a range of engine tuning and body parts to suit means and taste.

These companies are the Harley Street specialists of the car conversion world, and their *clientèle* are dealt with in the kind of secrecy kept for royalty – though it is known that Beatle George Harrison was one of the UK's first Hammer customers.

To give you a sample of their activities, we brought their finest works together. It's a mouthwatering conflict, with Alpina's mighty B12 – the epitome of discreet elegance and carefully honed good taste – lined up alongside the menacing, almost sinister-looking AMG Mercedes. Together they boast 11 litres, 20 cylinders and a tarmac-melting 735bhp. The pair could be yours for around £200,000.

You might think that the standard V12 engined BMW 750i represents the pinnacle of Munich's achievement. Alpina think not. They regard it as merely the starting point from which the B12 is built.

When they're finished, the result is a subtly altered Seven series, whose only real giveaway is the enormity of its rear tyres – 265/40 ZR 17s.

With raised compression, bigger valves and cam lobes, and a carefully doctored Bosch engine management system, the tuned "12" turns out 350bhp, 50bhp up on standard. It's also catalyst-equipped and stripped of the governor that holds the standard car to 155mph.

Fast? You bet it is. Even with the encumbrance of automatic transmission, the B12 is claimed to go beyond 170mph.

AMG's most potent Mercedes is a hot-rod called "The Hammer". It's based on the mid-range W124 saloon, coupé, or even the estate, but with the original four or six cylinder engine exchanged for a thumping quad-cam V8. There's a choice of 5.0, 5.6 or 6.0-litre versions to suit your own particular fancy, all coupled with modified S-Class transmission.

Naturally the suspension, wheels, tyres and brakes are all changed or substantially altered. Even the speedometer is replaced, presumably to avoid 'over-revving' the original – the new one reads to 320kph! By the time AMG have finished, few Mercedes parts remain, body apart.

The Germans prefer the Hammer to look completely standard. It's a wickedly fast Q-car if ever there was one. But there's a whole cata-

logue of body and interior parts available if you want some visual enhancement.

For this contest, we had to have the ultimate! We chose a wolf in wolf's clothing, a six-litre body-kitted coupé, with 385bhp and enough torque to pull a house down.

Of course AMG will sell you the parts to build a look-alike for a fraction of the cost – but without the 32-valve V8, that 'Benz could not be called a Hammer.

Common ground is that both cars have four leather seats, automatic transmission and enough wood to have felled a forest. And they're very, very quick. Each can gobble up a 911 Turbo on the autobahn and qualify on the shortlist for the world's fastest four-seater.

Unfortunately, no UK test track is suitable to unleash their full speed potential, but we suspect that the AMG – timed at over 180mph by *Car and Driver* – would win a 'maxing' contest.

You know what to expect from it the moment you twist the key. Its shoehorned V8 thumps into life, shaking and rumbling as it idles. Blip the throttle and the whole car twists in brutal reaction, letting you know that it's not for show.

From outside, the AMG is probably as loud as German TUV regulations will allow. The deep toned decibels hint at what's in store, and the note assumes a hard-edged yowl as the engine climbs onto its four cams.

But this Mercedes is not uncouth. There's a docile side to its make-up: slide the gearbox switch to E (for economy?) and the torque will ooze the car along with the tacho needle barely above tickover. The throbbing exhaust note recedes to a quiet burble when cruising, aided by gearing set at around 30mph/1,000rpm in top. Don't think this is an overdrive though, it's just that the AMG needs long legs.

When BMW launched their new 12-cylinder engine, they claimed that "smoothness and low noise levels are to a standard never before achieved in automobile engineering".

Alpina have made it more efficient and more tuneful – and just a shade more vocal. Gone is the flat and soulless sound of the stock 750i. With the Alpina, a gentle hum gives way to a muted wail under assault, but it's never loud enough to offend. It sings a glorious tune.

And it idles as smoothly as an electric motor, glued to a rock-steady 600rpm by Bosch Motronic engine management. The loudest sound is the whirring electric fuel pump.

Amazingly, the engine's crankshaft seems to have no inertia, such is the way it responds to a touch of the throttle. But there's a sense of disappointment in the acceleration. The car's quietness doesn't help: it fools the senses into thinking not much is happening. Neither does its weight of nearly 37cwt, or a bottom gear good for nearly 60mph.

Truth is, the B12 doesn't feel that much quicker than a run-of-the-mill 750i – though a stopwatch would confirm the extra 50bhp. It is

claimed to reach 100kph in 6.9sec (approx 6.4sec to 60mph) compared with 7.4sec for a 750i.

Things are different once the car is rolling, almost as if the energy is being conserved for greater things higher up the speed range. Like an aircraft on take-off, the B12 gives the impression of linear acceleration, unhindered by upward gearshifts. It passes 100mph barely into its stride – and only just into third gear – and will cruise at an easy 140mph gait when conditions allow.

WAR

When five litres of Alpina BMW takes on six litres of AMG "Hammer" Mercedes, the result is bound to be exciting. Lance Redhead investigates the ultimate super saloons, and finds a *svelte* executive jet in conflict with a full-blooded fighter

s standard but mighty V12 is 50bhp richer

Few roadgoing manual gearboxes can handle the torque this pair can muster. Automatic transmission suits them, because neither is meant as a track racer. It's all part and parcel of their gentle giant nature.

AMG can supply a manual 'box for the Hammer, but until the BMW 850i (which may be sold as a manual) appears, Alpina cannot . . .

Each automatic has the refinement of "Sports" and "Economy" programmes, which influence their part-throttle kickdown response – though it doesn't matter which setting is used when you floor the pedal.

The BMW's engine breezes well into the red when the pressure's on, a telling sign that the ZF auto has been got at. The 'box is very good when you suddenly kick down and demand lots of power. Put your foot down at 70mph and it will smoothly and decisively shift down two ratios.

But it's not so good when the driver needs a gradual increase, say when exiting a corner: here it can be clumsy and hesitant, sometimes downshifting brutally, then changing up a second or two later.

While the Alpina's transmission is almost very good, the AMG's is perfection. Quite simply the S-Class transmission does a masterful job in harnessing so much horsepower so smoothly. There's no jerking even when power-shifting on full throttle, while kickdown is quick and clean.

Abort the flow of power, and the 'box seems to disconnect the drive before softly engaging a higher gear ratio. Few drivers can shift a manual as capably.

Both 'boxes shy away from first gear, perhaps as a precaution against dispatching too much 'grunt' to the back wheels, through excessive torque multiplication.

It is possible manually to select first in the AMG, but be warned: an indiscriminate prod of the right pedal will 'light up' the rear tyres.

You can't do this with the Alpina. It's fitted with Automatic Stability Control (ASC), which shuts down the engine as soon as there's any sign of slip – it's easily accomplished, since the cableless electronic throttle lends itself to modulation.

But even if you override the ASC system – by pressing a button on the facia – those enormous rear tyres are more than equal to the torque on tap, so long as the road is dry. You get the feeling that the B12 has been engineered to stay on the road, irrespective of its driver's ability.

Having fatter tyres at the back than at the front (where 235/45s are fitted) cures any waywardness brought about by the extra power. Even so, there's enough attitude movement to let you know when cornering grip is fading. The tail will edge out long before a full-blooded slide develops, so the driver can feel exactly what the car is going to do before it happens.

Handling balance feels neutral, with no tendency towards premature understeer or oversteer: what the car does is largely up to the driver. An unwanted downshift powering round a greasy bend might upset this equation. . .

The BMW's steering is almost fingertip light at parking speeds, but Alpina have altered the Servotronic power assistance to firm up more quickly as speed builds. It's a good thing: the extra weight coaxes smooth and deliberate inputs from the driver.

Huge steering wheels are the norm behind the three-pointed star, so it's nice to drive a Mercedes with a chunky four-spoke AMG wheel. It's a pity that the rim obscures the instruments and you have to search for the horn buttons hidden in the spokes, though.

Despite this improvement, the steering could benefit from less assistance – it's too light a touch to guide such a serious missile. Thanks to that mass up front, the AMG runs straight and true. It also steers quickly and accurately.

But don't be fooled. This car is a beast, which has to be mastered. You must grab it by the scruff of the neck and show it who is the boss – but it needs to be done with a degree of caution.

Against predictions, the Hammer doesn't feel nose-heavy in corners. Rather, it turns in strongly displaying little stabilising understeer. As you'd expect, its behaviour is dominated by the driver's right foot – but even in steady-state cornering, the back end feels 'loose' – squirming about over bumps, and tightening the line unex-pectedly when you turn the power on or off.

In truth it does feel overpowered, as if the suspension and tyres are not up to the task of taming the big-gun V8. Gone is the user-friendliness and delicate balance that the Mercedes once had – replaced instead by something more ferocious, and altogether more demanding.

This is a car for the skilled enthusiast capable of taming nearly 400 horses.

Large diameter disc brakes haul these cars down from speeds they were never originally designed for – and each has ABS.

But whereas the Alpina uses the standard braking system, right down to the pad material, the AMG's brakes are purpose designed. They inspire more confidence, needing much less pedal effort than the heavy BMW calls for.

Alpina have yet to decide on suspension settings for the B12. Our test car – the first right-hand-drive car built – had German spec Alpina dampers which Sytner believes are too firm for UK roads. British B12s may retain the standard 750i's electronically-controlled dampers, which allow two quite different settings – though in our experience, neither would be ideal.

We prefer the tauter set-up, since it better complements the B12's sporting nature. It keeps you in touch with the action, yet it's never really uncomfortable.

The Hammer is even more firmly sprung. It's lumpy, almost brutal at times – yet oddly there are times when control feels weak. In particular, the back end 'looseness' seems to be induced by under-damping. There's room for fine-tuning.

Both cars' wide tyres thud like a machine gun when you drive over cat's eyes – this is the price you must pay for their extra grip and steering accuracy. But neither car suffers from tramlining over white lines.

Obviously the B12 has a lot more room inside than the AMG coupé. Even a short-wheelbase 7-series can accommodate five in comfort. Of course, the Hammer engine can be supplied to fit an S-Class Limousine – but with its lessened power-to-weight ratio, it's not the no-compromise machine we are looking at here.

Opulence is the only word to describe the interior of these cars. With the B12, the walnut and leather trim is all that's supplied with a normal 750i. The only change being that the test car was fitted with BMW's excellent sports seat option. There's some texture and colour difference between leather and plastic, but the wood veneer tastefully lifts the interior without dominating it as in the AMG.

Enthusiasts might bemoan the lack of instruments, for the binnacle contains no more dials than you'd find in a Sierra. But there are no complaints about the control layout, the fully-linked heating/air conditioning system or the equipment supplied.

The only Alpina hallmark is – or should have

been – a facia mounted plaque showing the car's serial number.

There is no fixed specification for the Hammer's interior. You can mix and match according to your taste of what's offered in the AMG catalogue. Our car had the full polished-walnut treatment, a pair of Recaro Classic sports seats and the previously mentioned steering wheel.

Equipment stretched to air conditioning, electric adjustment for the seats and the steering column fore and aft – and of course Mercedes's unique motorised seat belt arms.

heavily modified. Cornering quickly requires caution

It's a pity that some of the leather resembles the perforated vinyl material found on some older Fords, though.

The common denominator between this pair is that these are 'alternative supercars'. They're bought by film stars, hard-charging company directors and hare-brained connoisseurs. Their role is when something less ostentatious than a Testarossa is needed, faster and more practical than a Bentley.

Predictably they cost a lot. Most of us would have to win the pools or sell our homes to contemplate either.

The Alpina will set you back £68,000, including the £48,000 that a short-wheelbase 750i costs. By any standards £20,000 is a lot to pay for fancy wheels, an extra 50bhp and some careful tuning to the gearbox and steering characteristics.

But it is a superbly honed sports saloon, more appealing and more driveable than the car on which it is based. It impressed us most for its refinement and civilised ways – it just happens to be one of the world's fastest big saloons as well. And it will be very exclusive, for Sytner of Nottingham only assemble about 120 cars in

total, few of these being the flagship B12.

With the AMG, the price depends on what you start with and what you want to end up with. But when the engine alone costs £45,000 it's not difficult to spend more than £80,000 on the total conversion. Then you have to buy a Mercedes.

AMG concessionaire, Strattons of Wilmslow, say that using a £25,200 Mercedes 230CE as a "base", a Hammer Coupé could be assembled for about £112,000 (almost double the cost of the B12).

The result is a complete transformation of the original vehicle – a six-litre rocket that just

happens to reside in a Mercedes bodyshell!

It's an aggressive animal whose handling is on the wild side – perhaps an inevitable consequence of trebling the power. Such a specialised motor cannot offer the value you get with off-the-peg Mercedes.

But value considerations have no place in a comparison of absolutes. Some must have the best, the most, the fastest – irrespective of the financial burden. And so long as that is the goal, there can be no substitute for the AMG.

What else can compare with such an adrenalin-pumping monster?

	Alpina BMW B12	**AMG Hammer**
Price	£68,000	£112,000

ENGINE

Cylinders	V12	V8
Capacity, cc	4,998	5,953
Bore/stroke, mm	84/75	100/94.8
Camshaft	Sohc per bank, two valves per cylinder	Dohc per bank, four valves per cylinder
Compression ratio	9.5:1	9.8:1
Fuel system	Bosch Motronic M1.2 injection	Bosch KE-jetronic injection
Max power, bhp/rpm	350/5,300	385/5,500
Max torque, lb ft/rpm	347/4,000	417/4,000

TRANSMISSION

Type	Four-speed automatic	Four-speed automatic
Internal ratios and mph/1,000rpm		
Fourth	0.73/32.0	1.00/29.5
Third	1.00/23.4	1.49/19.8
Second	1.48/15.8	2.41/12.2
First	2.48/9.4	4.25/6.9
Final drive	3.15:1	2.44:1

SUSPENSION-STEERING-BRAKES

Front	Double joint-spring strut axle, coil springs, Bilstein gas-filled dampers, anti-roll bar	Double wishbones, coil springs, Bilstein gas-filled dampers, anti-roll bar
Rear	Independent via semi-trailing arms, coil spring Bilstein gas-filled dampers, anti-roll bar	Independent via Mercedes multi-link system, coil springs, Bilstein gas-filled dampers, anti-roll bar
Steering	Recirculating ball with power assistance	Recirculating ball with power assistance
Brakes, front/rear	11.9in ventilated discs/ 10.2in ventilated discs	11.2in ventilated discs/ 10.2in ventilated discs

WHEELS-TYRES

Wheels	Alloy 8.5J × 17 front 10J × 17 rear	Alloy 8.5J × 17 front and rear
Tyres	235/45 ZR17 front 265/40 ZR17 rear	235/45 ZR17 front and rear

PERFORMANCE

Maximum speed	152.1	185*
*Manufacturer's claimed figure		

Acceleration through gears, sec

	0-30mph	0-40mph	0-50mph	0-60mph	0-70mph	0-80mph	0-90mph	0-100mph	0-110mph	0-120mph
Alpina BMW B12	2.9	4.2	5.6	7.0	8.5	10.4	13.0	15.8	18.8	22.8
AMG Hammer	1.5	2.4	3.7	5.0	6.4	8.0	10.1	12.6	15.3	18.3

Acceleration in kickdown, sec

	30-50mph	40-60mph	50-70mph	60-80mph	70-90mph	80-100mph	90-110mph	100-120mph
Alpina BMW B12	2.7	2.8	2.9	3.4	4.5	5.4	5.8	7.0
AMG Hammer	2.2	2.6	2.7	3.0	3.7	4.6	5.2	5.7

DIMENSIONS

	Length, in	Width, in	Height, in	Wheelbase, in	Front/rear track, in	Fuel tank, gall	Kerb weight, cwt
Alpina BMW B12	193.3	72.6	54.8	111.5	60.6/60.4	22.4	36.6
AMG Hammer	186.5	68.5	56.8	110.3	60.6/60.2	15.4	33.2

FUEL CONSUMPTION

Government test figures, mpg		
Urban cycle	14.6	Fuel figures not available
Steady 56mph	32.1	
Steady 75mph	26.4	
Maker/Importer	Sytner of Nottingham, 165 Huntingdon Street, Nottingham NG1 3NH. Tel: 0602-582831.	Stratton of Wilmslow, Dean Way Business Park, Wilmslow Rd, Handforth, Cheshire SK9 2JT. Tel: 0624-532678

AMG HAMMER COUPE

JUST NAIL IT

BY RAY THURSBY

PHOTOS BY BILL KELLER

OF ALL THE thousands of adjectives and superlatives available for use in the English language, Steve Millen chose a single word to sum up his impressions of a drive in AMG's Hammer Coupe. To some, that feat of verbal miniaturization may seem akin to inscribing the entire Bible on the head of a pin, or working through an income tax form in five minutes; that's all it took him, though. One word. This one: "boring."

Boring?!?!

Yep. Of course, Millen has driven just about every kind of race car that ever touched the ground with four wheels, in every kind of racing event that sanctioning bodies can dream up. And he *was* driving Joe Galdi's Hammer around Nissan's Arizona Test Center track, a 5-plus-mile oval on which 150 mph or more can be a real snooze. But . . . boring?

Guess what? *He's right.* At high speed on a straight piece of road (at 150 to 180 mph or so), the Hammer is so relaxed and confidence-inspiring that you can easily begin to wonder what all the fuss about full-throttle travel really means. In other words, Millen wasn't putting the

Hammer down when he put the hammer down.

Thank goodness top speed has little to do with the Hammer's unique character. In every other respect you'd care to name, AMG's wonder of Teutonic hot-roddery is probably the most exciting exotic car available to mortal man. If it doesn't offer thrills on a nice safe closed course, that's something its owners will just have to cope with.

On the other hand, if plain old brute horsepower is what captures your attention, the Hammer has it in ample quantity. Enough to break those big 17-in. Goodyears loose from the asphalt in 1st gear. And in 2nd gear. Probably 3rd as well.

There's more to be said for the Hammer. It's a beautifully built product from a well-established tuner, one with close ties to Daimler-Benz. AMG's concept has been proven in numerous Hammer conversions performed on M-B's 300-series sedans and station wagons.

B UT A basic Mercedes-Benz 300 CE is not exactly an inexpensive car to begin with, and AMG of Affalterback, West Germany, has done more than just kit it out with monochrome paint and wider tires to make a Hammer Coupe. For the extra money, AMG replaces almost everything but the body panels and interior; even those areas get their own lesser alterations. I hesitate to suggest that any $185,000 car can be termed a bargain; this one's very close, though.

A 300 CE comes standard with a lovely 3.0-liter 6-cylinder engine. Producing 177 bhp, it's enough for reasonable performance combined with glassy smoothness. Hammers get something a little stronger: a powerplant based on that found in larger Mercedes coupes, sedans and roadsters. In factory-fresh form, the all-alloy sohc V-8 develops 238 bhp from 5.6 liters. For Hammer use, AMG fits its own 4-valve dohc cylinder heads, applies a boring bar to the cylinders and makes smaller modifications; the result is a 375-bhp, 6.0-liter fire-breather.

Installing this monstrosity in an engine bay designed for an inline-6 takes some doing. The firewall must be cut away, then reconstructed and re-insulated. New engine mounts are made, ancillary components and wiring are remounted and a new exhaust system is put in place. At job's end, the V-8 takes up virtually every inch of available space under the hood, but looks like it belongs there.

(As even Mercedes-Benz seems to think it does. The parent company will soon offer its own V-8 300 with 4-wheel drive and electronic traction control. Imitation is the sincerest form of flattery, after all.)

A complete new exhaust system goes under the Hammer's floorpan. At low speeds, this keeps the Coupe quiet, but loses its effectiveness (exactly as it should) at high revs. The unmistakable sound of the AMG/Mercedes V-8 is well worth hearing, as anyone within half a mile of a Hammer being driven flat-out will be able to attest. In line with German regulations, the system is *mit Katalysator* and the Hammer is designed to run on *Super Bleifrei*; everywhere but in California, that is, where Hammers, even with catalytic converters and unleaded premi-

PHOTO BY SCOTT DAHLQUIST

PHOTO BY SCOTT DAHLQUIST

sign, are part of the Hammer package. Normally, these are of 16-in. diameter, with a 7½-in. rim, though the aero is available in a 17 x 8-in. size, as seen here. These can be left in their natural finish, plated or painted body color. In most cases, Goodyear Gatorback tires are supplied in the U.S, but these, too, are subject to the customer's wishes.

The pieces work together with the precision of Count Basie's Band. It's possible to conduct the Hammer at a nice steady tempo and then, by unleashing that big brass section under the hood, get things swinging.

A sense of rhythm is as important to a Hammer driver as it is to a bandleader, lest the swinging get out of hand. Too much use of the Coupe's prodigious torque will break the back end loose, despite the best efforts of the Torsen differential and wide tires to keep it in line. A $185,000, 3700-lb coupe traveling sideways is an awe-inspiring sight.

But tangential travel in the Hammer is as safe as it can be. The power-assisted steering gives you accurate information about direction and traction levels, just as the precise throttle link-

um fuel, aren't supposed to run at all.

Other components are beefed up to withstand the rigors of Hammer use. A 4-speed automatic transmission—also from the larger 5-series cars—gets revised valving for more precise shifting and a Gleason Torsen limited-slip rear differential (with any one of five ratios installed according to customer preference) replaces the standard M-B differential.

Suspension changes, while extensive, leave certain stock parts (such as front and rear anti-roll bars) in place, supplementing them with AMG's own coil springs and gas-pressurized shock absorbers; the latter are built to AMG specifications by Bilstein. Braking chores are handled by 11.2-in. diameter discs—equipped with 4-piston calipers—in front, and 10.2-in. discs in the rear. The anti-lock circuitry and sensors are standard M-B pieces.

Alloy wheels, in either a 5-spoke or aero de-age lets you constantly modulate power levels to keep the car balanced in its chosen attitude. The choice is yours alone: incredibly fast travel between and through corners with no outward signs of speed, or a CinemaScope spectacular of Hammer-tossing and -catching, complete with lots of smoke from rapidly evaporating tires.

Even straight-line acceleration can be plenty dramatic, and just as hard on the rubber. Full throttle at 20 mph in 1st gear brings on instant wheelspin; so do the 1-2 and 2-3 shifts. The latter aren't just the little between-gears "erks" you can experience in some other high-powered cars, but are detectable momentary losses of traction. Get the procedure down, however, and the Hammer will vanish into the sunset with a boring alacrity few other street cars can match.

With the aerodynamic add-ons and the flat, almost plain-Jane wheels, the Hammer looks comfortable at any speed.

wheels (17 x 8½s in front, 17 x 10s in the rear) can be accommodated.

The Hammer Coupe has a wide array of positive attributes, but its best is not immediately obvious: unless you're well versed in Hammer-ology, or have access to an AMG parts catalog, it's virtually impossible to tell where Mercedes-Benz left off and AMG began.

In its balance of speed, handling, comfort and build quality, the AMG Hammer Coupe has no rivals. It's a guaranteed head-turner, whether at rest or in (fast) motion, and a genuine joy to drive. This is a car that begs to be driven hard; the return is sheer pleasure.

Boredom has never been so exciting.

The 200-mph speedometer isn't just there for show—a hefty foot will push the Hammer to more than 180 mph.

N O MATTER how fast the Hammer's going, its occupants will travel in comfort. The standard Mercedes seats are excellent for touring if a hair short on lateral support for hard driving. If the customer directs, AMG will reupholster them, in anything from cloth to Connolly leather to buffalo hide. Or remove them and bolt in a set of Recaros. Trim carved from exotic woods can be installed on request, as can instrument faces in body color (or any other hue). A speedometer with numbers that reflect the Hammer's enhanced performance comes standard.

Naturally, the basics are retained. M-B's superb air-conditioning system is present, as are airbags for the driver and passenger. On a happier note, there's the fine standard Becker radio that M-B supplies, though this can be supplanted according to the buyer's taste.

AMG uses just 13 plastic exterior pieces to change the 300 CE into a Hammer Coupe. Eight of these replace the utility-gray lower body sides on the stock CE; the rest are side skirt and front/rear spoiler additions. Combine these with the now-inevitable monochrome paint, and the result is a purposeful appearance that is worlds away from the conservative sweetness of the production-line coupe.

Frankly, the solid paint scheme is getting a bit old, especially when it has even worked its way onto various production cars of minimal sporting quality. The time has come for AMG to start a new trend of some sort.

One step toward that new trend might be the Wide Body package which AMG lists as an option for all 300-series Mercedes. This adds pushed-out fenders (plastic in front, steel in back) to the normal Hammer pieces. Some people may find the resulting chipmunk-cheek look excessive, but there's one undeniable benefit: under those expanded wheel arches, wider

AMG Hammer Coupe

U.S. SPECIFICATIONS

Price	$185,000
Curb weight, lb	3710
Wheelbase, in.	106.9
Track, f/r	59.5/59.1
Length	183.3
Width	68.5
Height	53.9
Fuel capacity, U.S. gal.	18.5

ENGINE & DRIVETRAIN

Type	dohc 4-valve V-8
Bore x stroke, in.	3.94 x 3.73
Displacement, cc	5953
Compression ratio	9.2:1
Bhp @ rpm, SAE net	375 @ 5500
Torque @ rpm, lb-ft	407 @ 4000
Fuel injection	Bosch KEIII Jetronic
Transmission	4-sp automatic

CHASSIS & BODY

Layout	front engine/rear drive
Brake system, f/r	11.2-in. vented discs/10.2-in. vented discs, vacuum assist, ABS
Wheels	cast alloy, 17 x 8
Tires	Goodyear Eagle, 235/45ZR-17
Steering type	recirculating ball, power assist
Suspension, f/r:	MacPherson struts, lower A-arms, coil springs, tube shocks, anti-roll bar/5-link, coil springs, tube shocks, anti-roll bar

PERFORMANCE[1]

0–60 mph, sec	5.0
Standing ¼ mile, sec @ mph	13.2 @ 109
Top speed, mph	185

[1]Factory claims

na means information is not available

WIDE BOY

Take one of the world's best coupes, add 30 per cent more power, then stretch the lowered body over massive race tyres. The result is a 146mph AMG Mercedes. By Martin Vincent, photography by Peter Burn

AMG corners flat and fast. Treated with respect, limits of adhesion are high

AMG is an organisation dedicated to planting the party spirit in an otherwise sober soul. The small but respected German engineering and design facility from Affalterbach near Stuttgart makes Mercedes macho, melting the traditional icy reserve with warmed up engines and an immodest line in seductive body curves. It's an unashamedly radical approach, calculated as much to transform as to enhance but, more than that, to exploit concealed potential in a wholly extrovert and explicit way.

From past experience, we know that AMG has the tools and the talent to transform an urbane and restrained businessman's express into a snarling, tyre-scorching monster with the road presence of a full-blooded supercar. The company's *piece de resistance* for the Mercedes 124-series range is a 400bhp 6-litre 32-valve V8 crammed under the bonnet of a flare-winged 300CE shell with impossibly wide wheels and tyres. Read 180mph and 0-60mph in 5secs. That's one for serious speed merchants with fat wallets.

Only slightly less outrageous, however, is the 3.2-litre six-cylinder 245bhp wide-bodied coupe you see here. The immediate benefits of this conversion are well over a second sliced off the regular 300CE's standing quarter time and a top speed tantalisingly close to 150mph. But at £70,000, it's no snip.

Situated close to Daimler-Benz headquarters and enjoying even closer links with its

engineering and development staff, AMG has access to vital technical information.

Armed with this background data and 20 years of Mercedes tuning experience, its staff of 120 makes full use of AMG's modern and impressive technical facilities. Automated CNC machines produce the special AMG cylinder heads; body alterations are shaped with the help of wind-tunnel development; and each completed engine is subjected to a full dynomometer trial in a computerised test facility. This is no garden shed tuning firm.

For AMG in the UK, Strattons of Wilmslow, Cheshire, is the company to see. Using only parts supplied from AMG in Germany, Strattons undertakes all the conversion work involved in creating an AMG Mercedes. Engines are supplied complete from AMG but bodywork, trim and suspension mods are all executed in-house.

AMG has extracted an extra 57bhp from Mercedes' M103 3-litre six, but you'd never guess it from lifting the bonnet. The engine looks absolutely stock. But beneath the plain black twin cam cover and massive air filter housing, there's evidence of extensive internal modification. A longer throw crankshaft and bored out block raise the capacity to 3205cc and new lightweight pistons increase the compression ratio from 9.2 to 10 to 1. Cylinder head breathing is improved while the polished valves open wider and for longer duration thanks to AMG's own, specially profiled camshaft. Finally, a performance exhaust system aids the flow of burnt gases without sapping power.

Output rises from 188bhp at 5700 to 245bhp at 5750rpm. Torque is boosted by a smaller but still telling margin, from 192lb ft at 4400rpm to

'The harder you drive it, the better the AMG becomes'

PERFORMANCE
MAXIMUM SPEEDS

Gear	AMG 320CE	300CE
	mph	
Top (Mean)	146	135

Standing ¼ mile 15.4secs (16.6), 91mph (86)
Standing km 27.8secs (30.1), 116mph (109)
(Merc figs in brackets)

ACCELERATION FROM REST

	AMG 320CE	300CE
True	Time	
mph	(secs)	
30	3.0	3.3
40	4.2	4.8
50	5.7	6.3
60	7.3	8.5
70	9.5	11.1
80	12.2	14.4
90	15.1	18.3
100	18.9	23.8
110	24.3	31.3

ACCELERATION IN EACH GEAR

mph	Top	3rd	2nd
10-30	—	—	—
20-40	—	—	—
30-50	—	—	3.4 (3.0)
40-60	—	—	3.2 (3.7)
50-70	—	—	—
60-80	—	5.1 (5.9)	—
70-90	—	5.5 (7.2)	—
80-100	—	6.5 (9.4)	—
90-110	9.8 (13.0)	—	—
100-120	11.5	—	—
110-130	14.2	—	—

Figs in brackets show times for Mercedes 300CE.

FUEL CONSUMPTION Overall mpg: 18.5 (22.1)

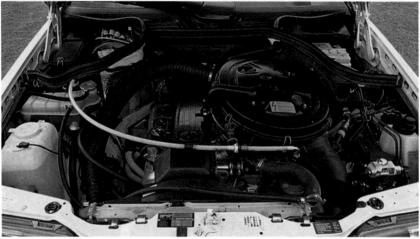

Split-rim forged alloys help distinguish AMG. Bored-out six produces 245bhp

239lb ft at 4500rpm. The changes boost performance and sharpen throttle response.

At idle, the engine has a deep, waffly and not unattractive beat. Under duress, the engine note deepens and hardens perceptibly without becoming much louder. Either way you want to keep listening. From rest, 100mph comes up in under 19secs — nearly 5secs quicker than the regular 300CE. All out, the AMG is good for 146mph — more than 10mph up on the 300CE. The increased urge is apparent throughout the range but is most obvious at higher speeds. Powering from 80-100mph in third takes just 6.5secs, nearly three seconds better than the standard car's best shot.

All this is achieved with no loss of tractability or refinement. Effective sound insulation ensures that the engine isn't intrusive. The only glitch in the otherwise smooth power delivery comes if you suddenly back off the accelerator — an undignified lurch begs a smoother approach next time. Also, the 6500 ignition cut-out comes in with a bang.

The price of all this performance is fuel consumption of around 18.5mpg — not unreasonable for a large and fast four-seat coupe but hardly economy run material.

The test car was equipped with Benz's super four-speed automatic gearbox. The gearshift pattern is a masterpiece of design. Slick and smooth, its slot pattern is cleverly designed so that you always know the position of the lever and never have to move it too far when changing gear manually. Upchanges are smooth but slurred, allowing the revs to flare slightly during the transition between gears.

Downchanges, however, are less refined and, for kickdown, the throttle needs to be planted firmly to the floor. One annoyance of the way the gearbox is set up is the way it can kick down to a lower gear to use up the 250 revs or so before the red line before changing up again — a somewhat frenetic and futile exercise. An economy programme allows gearchanges to take place at lower speeds but judicious use of the manual override can achieve better results still.

The AMG's wide-bodied look is achieved by the addition of flared front and rear wings. These are expertly crafted in steel so that it is impossible to tell where Mercedes metal ends and AMG's starts.

Not so professional are the plastic spoilers. They don't look as integrated as those on other AMG conversions and, on our test car, some of the retaining screws were poorly fitted. The bootlid spoiler hides the Mercedes badge but re-christens the car as an 'AMG'. Colour coding for the radiator shell, headlamp wipers and three-pointed-star complete the body building.

Those bulbous wheelarches are filled out by massive 17ins diameter split rim wheels, 8.5ins wide at the front, 10ins at the rear. Each of the forged alloy split-rims is clamped together by 35 aircraft quality bolts, a visual reminder of the fine engineering that lies beneath the smooth body shape.

Inside, the test car had gloss black lacquered door cappings, facia and centre console panels. Concert pianists might be attracted to the Steinway piano-type finish but many would prefer the burr walnut option. The lacquer was poorly applied anyway; wood grain showed through the finish close to the edges.

Add a smaller diameter four-spoke leather-

'No Mercedes without a V8 can rival the charisma of the AMG'

Leather seats over-firm, black woodwork oppressive, legroom vast

covered steering wheel and AMG-adorned light-grey instruments and the transformation is complete.

The already taut Mercedes suspension is made less compliant but more responsive with stiffer and shorter coil springs and replacement Bilstein dampers. A massive footprint at each corner comes from Dunlop D40 ultra-low profile rubber, 235/45 front, 255/40 rear.

For the first few miles, it is hard to appreciate any benefits of the AMG suspension mods other than increased chassis responsiveness and precision and sharper turn-in. Certainly, the bone-hard ride and constant humming from the tyres aren't hugely endearing.

But the AMG demands to be driven hard and fast over the most challenging roads you can find. Then you understand. It will flick through S bends with a poise and balance that belies its considerable bulk.

Although the limits of adhesion are very high once the tyres are warm, cold tyres or a wet road can precipitate a tail slide of alarming suddenness, a timely reminder that 245bhp must be treated with the utmost respect. And this is despite the efforts of an electronically controlled limited slip differential.

And yet the harder you drive it, the better the AMG becomes. On the right road it can be taken by the scruff of the neck and you know that it won't bite back. The AMG feels safe and secure, always rock steady and endowed with a great feeling of integrity.

But there are flaws. Gun the AMG fast through a bumpy dip and the sound of metal scraping against tarmac assaults the eardrums as the centre silencer box touches down. At least it has a skid plate at its front edge to prevent it being wiped off altogether.

Another area where the AMG falls below expectations is its ride suppleness. The stiff tyre sidewalls and firm springing don't absorb surface imperfections with much enthusiasm and speed-related vibration affecting the test car could also be clearly felt as the speed rose above 80mph, although it disappeared beyond 100mph.

More serious is a tendency for the brakes to fade under sustained heavy use. Generally the unmodified all vented disc arrangement is superb, with a short, firm pedal action and plenty of bite. But drive the car really hard and the pedal action slowly becomes mushy as the braking distances rise. Next, a whiff of brake smoke comes as a warning that everything under the wheelarches is not as it should be. The culprit would seem to be the front spoiler that starves the brakes of cooling air. There can be no excuse for this in a £70,000 car.

It is hard to justify the cost of any Mercedes coupe. At double the price it is even harder to justify the cost of this AMG. That said, the AMG 320CE has the sort of performance and charisma no Mercedes without a V8 under the bonnet can rival. Even the 560SEC — which sells for less than the AMG 320CE and offers similar performance — can't compete for presence.

But you don't need to spend £70,000 on an AMG. If you want the pep without the pose, or vice versa, Strattons can oblige. As a rough guide, the 3.2-litre 245bhp engine costs around £6000 on exchange with another £1128 for the exhaust system. The wide body conversion works out at just over £9000, with a further £1100 for the suspendion mods. Wheels and tyres are about £1000 a corner. AMG's prices may be outrageous, but then so is the car.■

'AMG's prices may be outrageous, but then so is the car'

AMG 300TE 6.0

Not a Hammer, but a mighty muscular mallet.

BY JOHN PHILLIPS III

• Tampering with a well-known adage, Adlai Stevenson once observed, "Power corrupts, but *lack* of power corrupts absolutely." It's too bad that Mr. Stevenson never met Hans-Werner Aufrecht, the power broker behind the world's best-known customizer of Mercedes-Benz automobiles, AMG. For two decades, Aufrecht has clung tenaciously to statesman Stevenson's theory, ensuring that approximately one Benz per week would never lack for spleen-rupturing power. In the process, Aufrecht and company—including his Chicago-based AMG agent

in the U.S., Richard Buxbaum—have been corrupting buyers with such muscle-bound machines as the 181-mph AMG Hammer that we tested in our December 1987 "Gathering of Eagles."

But forget about Hammers. Instead, let us review a more practical, somewhat more subtle AMG offering. One that will carry five people, two bags of golf clubs, three pieces of Gucci luggage, and one medium-sized golden retriever. This automobile began life as a stately and serene Mercedes-Benz 300TE wagon. Now it's called the AMG 300TE 6.0—not

a Hammer, exactly, but something closer, perhaps, to Hercules' club or Thor's industrial-strength mallet.

"It is just a *nice* car," says Buxbaum. "Something for around town."

A "nice" car for people with more money than God.

Nail the throttle in this nice, $99,500 wagon and you and your golf clubs will be transported to 60 mph in (hold on to your spleen) 5.7 seconds. Hang on for another 8.5 seconds and you'll smash through the 100-mph barrier. Cruise at that speed and the wagon's engine will

PHOTOGRAPHY BY AARON KILEY

tick over at an I'm-so-bored 3700 rpm—not yet into the real power range. If your golfing pals aren't impressed, point out that these acceleration figures are nearly identical to those of a Porsche 911 Club Sport. Or if your pals lean more toward bowling than golfing, point out that your 3636-pound family wagon reaches a 4-mph-higher speed in the quarter-mile than a Corvette Z51. And that its top speed of 153 mph bests both the Porsche *and* the Chevrolet.

Some *nice* wagon.

To obtain that ripping speed, AMG's Buxbaum simply yanks out the 300TE's standard 177-hp in-line six and replaces it with the engine and drivetrain from a wrecked, low-mileage Mercedes 560SEL. Alterations to the SOHC, all-aluminum V-8 are minimal. After it has been bored out to displace 6.0 liters, the two-valve V-8 is balanced and blueprinted, and its cylinder heads are ported and polished. The camshafts are unaltered. Even the 560's engine-management system is left intact.

The whole works then drops neatly into the 300TE's engine bay. The result is a docile, tractable powerplant that is perfectly content—providing you feed it a gallon of fuel every fifteen miles—to

churn out about 310 hp at 5200 rpm and 320 pound-feet of torque at 4000.

The power threads its way to terra firma via a four-speed automatic transmission whose hydraulic valve body has had its modulator-pressure settings revised by "a small German gentleman who works like a clockmaker," says Buxbaum. "He takes the valve bodies home at night, then brings them back in the morning. That's all we know."

Whatever necromancy is involved, it's fine by us. Launch the AMG wagon from a stoplight—an exercise guaranteed to warp the frontal lobes of onlooking Corvette owners—and only moderate wheelspin ensues. But the engine rushes urgently to its 6000-rpm redline, and under full throttle the transmission upshifts with a driveline-shuddering *ka-POW!*, as

if you'd just made a George Hurst powershift in a Pro Stock Hemi 'Cuda. The final *ka-POW!*—the upshift from third to fourth—comes at 114 mph, and even there the acceleration is still fierce enough to flop the front floor mats in half. To the German clockmaker's credit, the NHRA-style shifts occur only under full boot.

"So," you're asking, "if this wagon is so fast, how come it isn't a Hammer?" Because "real" Hammers sport four-valve heads (which deliver an additional 50 horsepower) and require an extra 200 hours of labor to produce. Hammers also carry a price tag that is heavier by some $65,500.

"See," Buxbaum explains, "the customer's assignment for this car was 'Make it fast, and make it cost less than

mph top speed (which is 27 mph higher than a stock 300TE's), the AMG's chassis goes into an odd corkscrewing motion. The car doesn't wander badly—steering corrections are minimal—but the unpredictable tracking prompted us to hold the AMG some distance from the guardrail during our top-speed runs, lest we return Herr Vader to Buxbaum with a Darlington stripe.

What is the culprit? The wheels on this car are an inch wider than the stock 300TE's, the nose—stuffed chockablock with V-8—is heavier than a stock 300TE's, and reducing the number of coils in a coil spring inevitably increases spring rates. Tinker with German suspension geometry and you have to expect a surprise or two.

Driven hard into corners, the AMG wagon initially heels over in typical Mercedes fashion, its inside front wheel on full rebound. And just when you reckon you'd better back off, the car assumes a firm, controlled set. Push harder, while holding a rock-steady throttle, and the AMG tends toward moderate understeer. Lift off the gas mid-turn, however, and the rear end departs instantly for Kalamazoo. The trick is to feed in throttle and induce a smidgen of power over-

$100,000.' So we went the two-valve route, and it worked so well that we may see a lot of these babies." (A lot for Buxbaum isn't *a lot*—he's talking maybe 50 cars in 1990.)

To lessen costs, AMG laid on only the barest of cosmetic gewgaws: white instrument faces, an Alpine 7903 AM/FM/compact-disc player, and new wood dash inserts—"pickled bird's-eye maple" in this case, which looks to us like the sort of fake travertine marble you'd find in the honeymoon suite of a Las Vegas motel.

Outside, the 300TE is gussied up with AMG's special skirts and spoilers. And every square inch of sheetmetal—from the three-pointed star on the radiator to the three-pointed star on the tailgate—is slathered with ebony paint, as if the car had fallen into a vat of boiling tar.

Suspension modifications are few. The customer didn't want the low-profile Yokohama tires looking lost in the cavernous wheel wells, so Buxbaum cut one coil from each coil spring, lowering the Benz 1.5 inches and giving it the menacing countenance of, say, Lyle Alzado on his hands and knees.

Typically, lowering a car in that method plays hell with suspension geometry and also degrades the ride. Surprisingly, however, the wagon's ride—even with the inflexible sidewalls on the Yokos—is nearly as good as a stock 300TE's. Plenty of wheel travel remains, and road impacts are more an affront to your ears than to your backside.

The modified suspension *does* have one delinquent trait, however. Beyond 100 mph, and right up to the car's 153-

steer—fun and evidently the fast way through turns, but a path safely trodden only by a driver whose right foot is practiced and masterfully disciplined.

Indeed, with practice we were able to hustle the AMG wagon around the skidpad at 0.82 g—a performance identical to that of a Mazda MX-5 Miata and nearly as good as a Porsche 911 Carrera 4's 0.83 g. What we have here is a 3636-pound wagon that is door-handle deep in sports-car territory.

Of course, the superb skidpad performance can be attributed largely to the nearly treadless Yokohama tires and to AMG's five-spoke, 7.5-inch-wide wheels (polished to a luster that would make them a welcome addition in the Hall of Mirrors). A dandy combination. *Until it rains.* You can't grasp the meaning of sweaty palms until you've driven a 310-hp AMG 300TE 6.0 in the rain and felt its rear end break loose under acceleration at 65 mph. Buxbaum usually insists on Pirelli P700s, and we can see why.

Of greater concern, however, is that the AMG 300TE 6.0 displays the flaws, fissures, faults, and foibles so often resident in conversions of this sort. During the wagon's two weeks with us, its cruise control began to surge maniacally. The heater steadfastly refused to deliver a single British thermal unit. AMG's unique exhaust resonator broke free and crashed to the asphalt. Two warning lights blinked intermittently for no obvious reason. The power-steering pump stopped pumping. The unique AMG speedometer was 13 mph optimistic at top speed. And from the moment we took delivery, our AMG wagon idled as if it were a decrepit Cummins diesel, ticking, rattling, and gasping in decidedly unrefined fashion.

We love the AMG 300TE 6.0, even though it is 49 percent more obscenely expensive than the car that initially rolled into Buxbaum's garages. Strangers pull alongside and shout, "Wow, is it a Hammer?" ("Yes," we always replied, lying.) But we also love the stock 300TE (*C/D*, August 1988), which costs a "mere" $50,880 and certainly would *not* have exhibited eight defects in the first 5000 miles of its life.

Moreover, what will AMG do in 1991, when the Mercedes-Benz factory itself builds a 300E fitted with the luscious 322-hp, DOHC V-8 that currently nestles under the hood of the new 500SL? That supersedan won't cost anything like $99,500, and it may slap a hammerlock (forgive us) on Aufrecht and Mister B.

Be heedful, AMG, lest you corrupt power absolutely. ●

Vehicle type: front-engine, rear-wheel-drive, 5-passenger, 5-door wagon

Price as tested: $99,500

Options on test car: base Mercedes-Benz 300TE with AMG discount, $42,739; AMG modification package (includes 6.0-liter engine and driveline with 2.65:1 final-drive ratio and limited-slip differential, suspension tuning, Hammer-style side and rear skirts and front spoiler with driving lights, chrome Aero 7.5-x-16-inch wheels, Yokohama AVS 205/55VR-16 tires, white-face instrument cluster with 200-mph speedometer, gray bird's-eye maple trim kit, Alpine tuner and compact-disc player, AMG floor mats, Mitsubishi Diamond cellular telephone), $56,761

Standard accessories: power steering, windows, seats, locks, and sunroof, A/C, cruise control, rear defroster and wiper

Sound system: Alpine 7903 AM/FM-stereo tuner and compact-disc player, 4 speakers

ENGINE
Type	V-8, aluminum block and heads
Bore x stroke	3.94 x 3.73 in, 100.0 x 94.8mm
Displacement	363 cu in, 5956cc
Compression ratio	9.2:1
Fuel system	Bosch KE-III-Jetronic fuel injection
Emissions controls	3-way catalytic converter, feedback fuel-air-ratio control, EGR
Valve gear	chain-driven single overhead cams, hydraulic lifters
Power (C/D estimate)	310 bhp @ 5200 rpm
Torque (C/D estimate)	320 lb-ft @ 4000 rpm
Redline	6000 rpm

DRIVETRAIN
Transmission .... 4-speed automatic
Final-drive ratio .... 2.65:1, limited slip

Gear	Ratio	Mph/1000 rpm	Max. test speed
I	3.87	7.1	42 mph (6000 rpm)
II	2.25	12.1	73 mph (6000 rpm)
III	1.44	19.0	114 mph (6000 rpm)
IV	1.00	27.3	153 mph (5600 rpm)

DIMENSIONS AND CAPACITIES
Wheelbase .... 110.2 in
Track, F/R .... 58.9/58.6 in

Length	188.2 in
Width	68.5 in
Height	58.8 in
Frontal area	22.5 sq ft
Ground clearance	5.4 in
Curb weight	3636 lb
Weight distribution, F/R	49.8/50.2%
Fuel capacity	19.0 gal
Oil capacity	8.5 qt
Water capacity	13.7 qt

CHASSIS/BODY
Type .... unit construction with 1 rubber-isolated subframe
Body material .... welded steel stampings

INTERIOR
SAE volume, front seat	50 cu ft
rear seat	40 cu ft
luggage space	42 cu ft
Front seats	bucket
Seat adjustments	fore and aft, seatback angle, front height, rear height
General comfort	poor fair **good** excellent
Fore-and-aft support	poor fair **good** excellent
Lateral support	poor **fair** good excellent

SUSPENSION
F: .... ind, strut located by a control arm, coil springs, anti-roll bar
R: .... ind, 2 lateral links and 3 diagonal trailing links per side, coil springs, automatic-leveling shock absorbers, anti-roll bar

STEERING
Type .... recirculating ball, power-assisted
Turns lock-to-lock 3.3
Turning circle curb-to-curb .... 36.7 ft

BRAKES
F: .... 11.2 x 0.9-in vented disc
R: .... 10.9 x 0.4-in disc
Power assist .... vacuum with anti-lock control

WHEELS AND TIRES
Wheel size .... 7.5 x 16 in
Wheel type .... cast aluminum
Tires .... Yokohama AVS AV1-55W, 205/55VR-16
Test inflation pressures, F/R .... 30/30 psi

CAR AND DRIVER TEST RESULTS

ACCELERATION — Seconds
Zero to 30 mph	2.1
40 mph	3.1
50 mph	4.3
60 mph	5.7
70 mph	7.4
80 mph	9.5
90 mph	11.8
100 mph	14.2
110 mph	18.0
120 mph	22.4
130 mph	28.1
Top-gear passing time, 30–50 mph	2.9
50–70 mph	3.8
Standing ¼-mile	14.2 sec @ 100 mph
Top speed	153 mph

BRAKING
70–0 mph @ impending lockup .... 175 ft

Fade .... none **moderate** heavy

HANDLING
Roadholding, 300-ft-dia skidpad .... 0.82 g
Understeer .... minimal **moderate** excessive

COAST-DOWN MEASUREMENTS
Road horsepower @ 30 mph	6 hp
50 mph	15 hp
70 mph	32 hp

FUEL ECONOMY
C/D observed fuel economy .... 15 mpg

INTERIOR SOUND LEVEL
Idle	50 dBA
Full-throttle acceleration	79 dBA
70-mph cruising	71 dBA
70-mph coasting	71 dBA

AMG
500SL 6.0

Hot metal sunshine on a field of green

BY THOS L. BRYANT
PHOTOS BY JOHN LAMM

I t was the warmest, sunniest day of early summer in Central Europe. Photographer John Lamm and I set out from the Hotel Steigenberger Graff Zeppelin, just across from the main railroad station in downtown Stuttgart, headed for the small village of Affalterbach, about an hour's drive from the city. There, nestled in a less-than-grand-size industrial park is the works of AMG, one of Europe's finest specialty tuners/manufacturers. Specializing in Mercedes-Benz automobiles, AMG has come a long way from the two-

man shop of Hans-Werner Aufrecht and Erhard Melcher, established in 1967. Now the company has official ties with Mercedes, and employs more than 400 people to turn Benzes into barnstormers.

Our mission this fine day was to drive and photograph the top-of-the-line AMG, the 500SL 6.0. Not to be confused with the 600SL with the 6.0-liter V-12 powerplant, the AMG 6.0 is the V-8 from the 500 with the displacement increased to 6.0 liters. When they wheeled this spectacular beauty out of the showroom for us, John began to mumble about f-stops and all that photographic jargon. I just stood there with my mouth slightly agape, thinking I was seeing the most brilliant shade of yellow that had ever been seen. A yellow so sharp that it hurt your eyes to stare directly at it in the sunlight. A yellow that made me think of the

Though its top speed is limited to 155 mph...the 6.0 V-8 is working athletically at speeds near that upper limit.

tartest lemon bar I'd ever eaten, the hottest desert day I'd ever sweated through.

We drove the car away from the factory, enjoying the massive torque of the 6.0-liter engine, the throaty rumble of the exhaust. On a tiny country lane, barely one-car wide, we found the spot John deemed perfect for photos. Close by on each side of the road were green fields of some crop or other, offering a marvelous backdrop for the screaming yellow AMG. Bees hummed their way past on their pollinating journeys among the fields, while large, black flies zoomed in on the yellow hood of the car, once again proving that flies love yellow cars just as much as photographers do. I stared at the car, thinking about its 381 horsepower and, even more impressive for acceleration, its 413 lb-ft of torque.

Imagine yourself behind the wheel of this supercar, top down, warm German sunshine flooding you with warmth, as you meander through the rolling hills of Swabia. Passersby on the streets of the little villages stare with unabashed envy. Other motorists run the risk of collision in their efforts to get closer. And all the while you coolly cruise along, secure in the knowl-

■ A warm summer day in Germany and a sensational AMG SL is a combination that's hard to beat. The mostly yellow interior is eye-popping in its brightness, but those who seek something more subdued can order the black interior with just a few touches of yellow wood, as seen in the bottom photo. Either way, the AMG is hot!

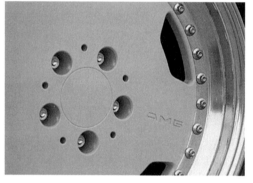

■ Beneath the daunting black AMG engine cover lurks the 6.0-liter V-8. With horsepower approaching the magic 400 zone, the AMG SL boasts stout acceleration and superior high-speed cruising.

edge that you could mash your right foot down on the throttle and rocket away.

Or perhaps your fantasy is more in tune with a high-speed run down the *Autobahn*, snuggled securely beneath the hardtop and gobbling up huge chunks of German real estate as this AMG sails past the merely mortal cars. Though its top speed is limited to 155 mph through an agreement with the German transport ministry, the 6.0 V-8 is working athletically at speeds near that upper limit, no strain, no sweat. Acceleration to pass other cars is instantaneous. Handling to accomplish lane changes and tackle curves in the road is characterized by vault-like stability.

Hour after hour, the AMG Mercedes tracks on, never tiring. Its power is hypnotizing. Eventually you begin to think

that the world is moving past while you sit securely in the bucket seat, controlling the movements of the traffic around you. Unfortunately, just as you enter that sort of dream world, some guy in a Trabant usually pulls out to pass a smog-making truck that's clearly hauling half of Eastern Europe at a speed of about 10 mph. At that point, you thank your lucky stars for big disc brakes and anti-lock capability. And should the road surface turn less friendly, traction control is also part of the equation. Nothing has been overlooked in making this a road car that cossets its occupants, keeps them safe, and delivers them to their destination in the quickest manner possible.

In addition to the work done by AMG to the engine, modifications are also made to the suspension, with the fitting of an adaptive damping system with self-leveling on both the front and rear of the car. Light alloy wheels highlight the side view of the SL, as well as carry the 235/45ZR-17 front tires and the 255/40ZR-17 rears. All of this adds up to a wheel-tire-suspension package that is a treat for the driver. While there is no denying that the Mercedes SL is a weighty car, the enthusiast driver will find it delightfully docile in the moderately fast going, and eminently predictable when

you truly put the hammer down. For me, the non-paying borrower of the car, the hardest part is to convince myself that it's okay to throw a $170,000 or so car into the twisty bits with a vengeance. Once that reluctance is overcome, however, the AMG rewards the driver with an unbridled willingness to perform.

AMG has a high regard for the styling of Mercedes-Benz cars, so bodywork changes are subtle and in keeping with the original design character. New front and rear end caps along with rocker-panel additions give away the AMG heritage, but not by shouting. Inside, in the case of this particular car, AMG did a complete reupholstery job to meet the customer's wishes, matching the screaming-yellow-zonker exterior color to the leather. And the match is nearly perfect, leaving you with a feeling that you are sitting in a sea of yellow that demands very dark sunglasses, even at night.

During our photo shoot, the AMG 500SL 6.0 drew spectators to our narrow little country lane like bees to flowers. As the afternoon wore on and we watched a thunderstorm make its way across the valley to the west of us, I thought about this AMG and its place in the world of exotic cars. As someone who has driven a great many of the world's most exciting cars over the past 20 years, I find this to be a superb everyday exotic. By that I mean a car that you could usefully drive to work, to the concert, to the country club or to the market. It has the driveability and reliability for which Mercedes-Benz and AMG are both famous. It is comfortable, safe and secure. It is fast, it handles well and it stops like a boat anchor.

All in all, the AMG 500SL 6.0 is a prime investment in driving excitement, backed up by a guarantee of long-term

durability. And when you're plopping down money in the six digits to buy a car, you want to be damn sure it isn't going to let you down. Rest assured, this one won't.■

AMG 500SL 6.0

SPECIFICATIONS

Curb Weight	3894 lb
Wheelbase	99.0 in.
Track, f/r	61.7/61.3 in.
Length	176.0 in.
Width	71.3 in.
Height	50.9 in.
Fuel capacity	21.1 gal.

ENGINE & DRIVETRAIN

Engine	dohc 32-valve V-8
Bore x stroke	100.0 x 94.8 mm
Displacement	5956 cc
Compression ratio	10.0:1
Horsepower, SAE net	381 bhp @ 5250 rpm
Torque	413 lb-ft @ 4000 rpm
Fuel injection	mechanical/electronic
Transmission	4-speed auto
Final-drive ratio	2.65:1

CHASSIS & BODY

Layout	front engine/rear drive
Brake system, f/r	vented disc, vacuum assist, ABS
Wheels	3-piece aluminum alloy, 17 x 8.5 f, 17 x 10.0 r
Tires	Bridgestone RE71, 235/45ZR-17 f, 255/40ZR-17 r
Steering type	recirculating ball, power assisted
Suspension, f/r	upper and lower A-arms, coil springs, tube shocks, anti-roll bar/5-link, tube shocks, anti-roll bar

PERFORMANCE[1]

0-100 mph	5.8 sec
Standing 1/4 mile	14.0 sec
Top speed	155 mph

[1]Manufacturer's claims

Teutoni

TITAN

BY GREG KABLE

PHOTOGRAPHY BY BURKHARDT HELLWIG

JUST WHEN IT LOOKED LIKE BMW HAD THE FOUR-DOOR PERFORMANCE CROWN SAFELY LOCKED AWAY WITH THE STUNNINGLY EFFECTIVE M5, MERCEDES-BENZ HAS UPPED THE STAKES WITH THE STORMING E60 AMG — THE WORLD'S FASTEST FACTORY-BACKED SPORTS SEDAN. WE SCORE AN EXCLUSIVE DRIVE

It's nothing special to look at, Mercedes-Benz's E60. Clothed in familiar E-class sheetmetal and without any external add-ons to grab your attention, it does very little to visually convey its abilities. But don't let this fool you because in just about every other area it is sensational. Based around the Mercedes-Benz E500 — a stunningly quick luxury express assembled by Porsche and sold exclusively in left-hand-drive European markets, the recently-introduced E60 establishes lofty new standards which lift it well above the current crop of factory-backed sports sedans and, in pure performance terms, place it alongside some of the world's most exotic supercars . . . the likes of which all fail to match the Stuttgart stormer's outstanding levels of comfort and practicality.

You can forget about the BMW M5. For while it is seriously quick, the big-hearted Bavarian just isn't in the hunt when this latest and possibly final variation of the W124 series E-class has built up a full head of steam and has an open stretch of autobahn on which to furiously lay it all down through whopping great Bridgestone Expedia rubber. The E60 AMG, you see, can edge out any factory-backed four-door you'd like to name with a stomping 0-100 km/h time of just 5.40 seconds. Even more impressive are its 0-400 metre and 0-1000 metre times which, at 13.56 and 25.00 seconds respectively, make it the fastest car in Mercedes-Benz's vast model line-up — SL600 included!

Top speed, like all factory-backed Mercedes-Benzes, is electronically-governed to an unfulfilling 250 km/h . . . unfulfilling because there's little doubt the E60 would rocket all the way to 300 km/h if given the chance.

The key to the E60's chilling open-road performance is its tremendously-effective V8 engine which has been given a thorough going over by Mercedes-Benz's highly-credentialled AMG motorsport offshoot and performs to the strict emission regulations of Germany's transport authority.

With a don't-argue capacity of 6.0-litres along with four overhead camshafts and 32-valves, the hi-tech V8 musters a mighty 275 kW of power at 5500 rpm and a Trojan-like 580 Nm of torque at an easily accessible 3750 rpm.

Another triumph by Mercedes specialists, AMG. Bored and stroked to 6 litres, the V8 plant (RIGHT) offers brutish acceleration.

Word has it that when AMG set about winning BMW's four-door crown they initially toyed with the idea of shoehorning the SL600's 6.0-litre V12 into the engine bay of an E-class in a move not dissimilar to that undertaken by a number of Germany's aftermarket tuners. But the extra length of the 12 would have necessitated expensive front-end modifications that, as well as adding weight, just couldn't be financially justified given the small production numbers forecasted.

Subsequently, a decision was made to boost the capacity of the E500's excellent 5.0-litre V8 by extending both the bore (96.5 mm to 100.0 mm) and stroke (85.0 mm to 94.8 mm). Other significant changes include the adoption of reprofiled camshafts, lightweight pistons and reprogrammed Bosch fuel-injection system . . . all of which add up to a tantalising spread of V8 performance, the likes of which make the 215 kW delivered by HSV's new Commodore appear comparatively weak-hearted.

Not content with simply upping the performance of the engine, AMG has also brought some significant changes to the E60's automatic transmission in a bid to further increase its accelerative ability and lift it on to an altogether higher performance plane than the fast-accelerating BMW M5 which, in its latest guise introduced at March's Turin motor show, has gained a six-speed manual transmission and an upgraded brake package.

The E60's slick-shifting automatic retains the power and economy modes of the standard transmission but gets four closely spaced ratios (3.87, 2.25, 1.44 and 1.00), remapped computer chips and a lower final drive ratio (2.82).

When trundling along with the hordes around town there is precious little about the E60 that heralds its world-beating ability. That is until you make your first hearty exploration of the throttle and liberate the mechanical beast that lurks underneath its familiarly sculpted bonnet. It is here, in the split second it takes the E60 to draw breath and swap ratios, that the very essence of AMG's purposeful tinkering makes its presence felt. And don't for a minute think the result is subtle.

Adhesion can be broken on certain surfaces if you dial up the "sport" mode on the four-speed automatic transmission and really lay into the long-travel throttle while hauling along in a low gear. But the E60's traction control device quickly ensures expensive rubber trails are not included in its heightened dynamic repertoire.

This initially suppresses any tyre screeching excitement you might have expected. But this wayward distraction rapidly vanishes as the extraordinary acceleration provided by the seemingly endless reserves of torque brings the horizon racing forward at a furious pace.

Remember that 0-100 km/h sprint of just 5.4 seconds? Add another 15.2 seconds and you're looking at the E60's brutish 0-200 km/h time . . . all achieved safely within a standing kilometre!

On the run the E60's kickdown performance is frightfully efficient. There's no hesitation as the powerful engine management computer selects a lower gear and the transmission's converter loads up with great wads of torque before dispatching you with Exocet-like proficiency.

In the race to red-figure revs there is a wonderful linearity and compelling urgency about the power delivery . . . traits that are genuinely reflected in the E60's impulsive 60-120 km/h third gear split of 5.9 seconds.

The exhaust note has to be heard to be believed. It begins silently from idle with little hint of what is to come, and grows into a slightly raspy growl through the mid-range as the full effects of AMG's engine modifications are just beginning to be felt. And finally tops out with a full-blooded howl at its 6200 rpm red-line leaving you and anyone else within earshot with little doubt about its race-bred commitment.

What also sets the E60 apart from the four-door crowd is the consummate ease with which it can be whipped up to 200 km/h and comfortably held there for extended periods without any apparent strain. Out on the autobahn it exhibited wonderful stability on the straights and tracked faithfully through sweepers at speeds well in excess of 200 km/h, its rock solid composure

only beginning to wane when the concrete surface threw up ill-placed expansion seams.

For all its bitumen-burning potency the E60's big V8 is not overly thirsty. We managed a respectable 12.8 L/100 km on a long autobahn cruise interspersed with numerous surges into the 200 km/h bracket. A severe caning on the Mercedes-Benz test track saw this rocket to a predictably high figure of 16.9 L/100 km.

With a combination of 245/45 ZR17 rubber and Mercedes-Benz's universally-praised E-class chassis you'd expect the E60 AMG to be an impressive handler. Driven vigorously across winding backroads, it provides a good deal more feedback, both

through steering and suspension, than any other E-class variants we've driven, and with masses of front-end grip it tempts you to push through corners at speeds that belie its considerable size and 1700 kg kerb weight.

Turn-in feel is positive rather than electric due to a rather lazy 3.0 turns across the bump stops and the amount of rubber being dragged across the bitumen. Nonetheless, the speed-sensitive power steering weights up well on a quarter turn of lock with a nice progressive feel that leaves you in little doubt about the action of the big Bridgestones working away at the front end.

At anything below racetrack cornering

class models. Not that this detracts from the driving experience in any way. Rather, the shorter spring travel, uprated damping and unforgiving nature of its competition-grade rubber provide it with the sort of underlying firmness that is inherent in all great Mercedes-Benz sporting sedans — secure and

speeds the E60 AMG remains beautifully balanced with a steadfastly neutral stance that perfectly reflects Mercedes-Benz's renowned chassis expertise.

Body roll, a predominant trait of lesser E-class models, is kept well in check thanks to a number of detailed suspension tweaks, including a lowered ride height and uprated spring and damper package.

Diving into tight corners at very high speeds can loosen the E60 AMG's prodigious front-end grip and induce faint understeer, but this is very quickly tempered by the aforementioned traction control device which detects tyre slippage and employs the brakes to haul the car to a more subdued speed before any dramatic action has a chance to unfold.

This makes for safe and unflustered handling whatever the road conditions and however demanding the terrain, something Mercedes-Benz says fully justifies its decision to retain full-time traction control rather than offer a switchable device like that found on BMWs.

It's a rather convincing argument in these safety conscious times of ours. Still, the E60 AMG felt too clinical and uninvolving for us to really become intimate with it in the way we might have with a BMW M5 — a pure and unadulterated driver's car if ever there was one — over the same roads.

The sublime feeling of man and machine working as one fails to fully materialise in the E60 AMG in the same way it does in the M5. It's as if Mercedes-Benz has purposely suppressed the car's potentially colossal excitement factor in the interests of retaining its responsibility toward world-leading safety.

The suspension modifications AMG has brought to the E60 in a successful bid to elevate its handling also deliver a noticeable change in the ride compared with other E-

compliant with a delicious feel. The ability of the E60's multi-link suspension to communicate faithfully is tremendously rewarding and keeps the driver in touch with the bitumen at all times whatever the surface conditions, and on all but the worst pot-hole ridden roads it sponges away irregularities with an iron-fisted authority that could only come from a car wearing the three-pointed star.

Equally as effective is the E60 AMG's upgraded braking package that, with monstrous 320 mm ventilated discs from the SL600 at each corner and an advanced four-channel anti-lock braking system from Bosch, provides unstinting stopping security under most conditions.

Despite its hefty kerb weight the E60's brakes proved flawless after continual high-speed braking at Mercedes-Benz's test track just outside Stuttgart, with nary a hint of fade and without any deterioration in overall pedal feel.

We did, however, discover one dramatic shortfall in the E60 AMG's braking ability. Under extreme loads the front-end has a tendency to tramline quite severely on broken surfaces, something that is obviously brought on by its unyielding rubber and heavily damped suspension.

This peculiarity and the question mark that hangs over the E60's strangely detached handling are the only real glitches in its otherwise superb dynamic behaviour. When spirited hard across country it possesses a tremendously secure feel with a degree of balance and poise that belies its luxury car origins. And in terms of straight line pace it leaves the BMW M5 trailing well in its wake.

If we could just convince Mercedes-Benz and AMG to provide the E60 with a switchable traction control device it would be as close to perfect as we could wish for. **M**

Mercedes-Benz E60 AMG
6.0-litre, 4-speed automatic

ENGINE

Location:	front, longitudinaly-mounted
Cylinders:	90˚ V8
Capacity:	5956 cm³
Valve gear:	chain-driven double ohc per bank four-valves/cyl
Bore and stroke:	100.0 mm x 94.8 mm
Compression ratio:	10.0:1
Induction:	electronic multi-point fuel-injection
Power:	275 kW at 5500 rpm
Torque:	580 Nm at 3750 rpm
Maximum rpm:	6200
Specific power output	45.83 kW/litre
Driving wheels:	rear

SUSPENSION

Front	Independent by MacPherson struts with coil springs and anti-roll bar
Rear	Independent by multi-links with coil springs and anti-roll bar
Wheels	alloy, 8.5 J x 17
Tyres:	Bridgestone Expedia 245/45 ZR17

BRAKES

Front	320 mm ventilated discs
Rear	320 mm ventilated discs
Anti-lock	yes

STEERING

Type	power-assisted rack and pinion 3.0 turns lock-to-lock

DIMENSIONS

Wheelbase:	2800 mm
Front track:	1538 mm
Rear track:	1529 mm
Length:	4750 mm
Width:	1796 mm
Height:	1408 mm
Kerb weight:	1700 kg
Weight to power (kg/kW)	6.18

FUEL CONSUMPTION (claimed)

90 km/h (constant)	9.9 L/100 km
120 km/h (constant)	11.9 L/100 km

EQUIPMENT

Adjustable steering	yes
Air-conditioning	yes
Alloy wheels	yes
Central locking	yes
Cruise control	yes
Driver's footrest	yes
Folding rear seat	yes
Intermittent wipers	yes
Power steering	yes
Power windows	yes
Radio/cassette	yes
Compact disc player	yes
Remote outside mirror adjust	2 elec
Sun roof	no
Tachometer	yes
Trip computer	yes

PERFORMANCE

0-100 km/h:	5.4 secs
0-200 km/h:	20.6 secs
Standing 400m:	13.9 secs
Standing 1000m:	25.0 secs

PRICE (ex Germany)

List price:	DM156,400 (SA190,000)

Not a white interior in sight: restrained, leather seats a tasteful option

MERCEDES-BENZ AMG E36 COUPE

'Cheap' Porsche 911 alternative

The tuned Mercedes can conjure up all the wrong images — boomerang TV aerials, owners with more jewellery than sense and all manner of unsavoury goings on behind those blacked-out windows.

Thankfully, the first factory-endorsed hot E-class elegantly sidesteps all things tacky and comes direct from Unterturkheim with a warranty and not a white leather interior.

You will know of AMG. The famous German tuning company successfully

campaigned Mercedes' fearsome C-class DTM cars this year and produces a breathed-on version of the little C-class called the C36 AMG. Logically enough, the same 3.6-litre engine from this car is used to fatten out the model options and finds its way into all the current E-class models including the estate.

So what is it like in the wonderfully elegant coupe, a car hardly short of poke with the stock 3.2-litre, 24-valve, 220bhp straight six? If you want a sizeable dollop more go (48bhp

to be precise) and can afford the £8100 extra it will cost you over an E320 coupe then it's the car for you.

Discretion is the watchword here. Only AMG badging and huge single-piece AMG 7.5x17in wheels with broad 225/45 ZR17 Bridgestone tyres give the game away (unless you go for the full bells and whistles AMG styling kit at £3800). Leave those lovely lines alone and only those in the know will be able to tell it's something special.

Tickle the throttle butterflys open, however, and everyone will know the score. 'ASR' traction control keeps 284lb ft of torque in check, the rear end squats and the E36 will rocket you to 60mph in about 6.8sec and on to an electronically policed 155mph. Fast enough, Mercedes says, for the 40-pluses who buy this sort of car.

The engine is an absolute delight, being both torquey enough to waft you past traffic in top gear without kicking down through the four-speed, two-mode auto 'box into third, and having the top end fight of a goodish race engine. Push on towards the 6400rpm red line and the creamy engine note curdles into a full-on twin-cam scream.

Handling builds on the safe, predictable nature of the standard car. You will find the power-assisted steering pleasingly weighty, linear in its response with lock applied but rather short on feel.

AMG uprates the springs and dampers to give you a

Read 3.6 litres, 268bhp and 284lb ft

For Performance, damping, classy, low-key looks, engine note, build
Against Price, ride, tyre rumble
Price £48,700
On sale here Now
0-62mph 7.0sec*
Top speed 155mph*   *claims

beautifully controlled but expectedly firm ride (harder than the Sportline sports suspension option offered by Mercedes-Benz UK on lesser models). Potholes are therefore best avoided and there's a little tyre thrum to put up with as well.

Wonderfully supportive (and electrically adjustable) seats, a fabulously solid interior and good passenger and luggage space more than compensate. The E-class coupe has always been a sensible tool for the style-conscious two-door buyer who wants usable rear space.

What you have, then, is a very potent engine in a lovely looking coupe. See it as a classy, cheaper alternative to a Porsche 911 because it's about as far removed from a 'tuned special' as you can get.
James Thomas

The **best** of Benz

It would be nice if the dash flashed up a message telling me I'd won a couple of million on the pools. But that would be greedy. The info it's displaying now will do just fine. The outside temperature is 31 degrees, and we're holding a steady 6,000rpm.

Our speed is a bit more tricky to work out, though, because the needle went off the clock at 260kph, which is around 160mph. This sort of speed, in

anywhere else but Germany, would get you locked up until your trousers went out of date.

It's not big, it's not clever, but hammering across Europe at top speed is an awful lot of fun. And we've got to use a lot of the AMG SL60's amazing ability to get from Stuttgart via Metz and Verdun to Reims, the legendary race circuit east of Paris. And after that – with little time to spare – we're headed to England's counterpart, Brooklands. Another track where Mercedes, or Benz, ran classic fast cars at incredible speeds. But we're now

doing the same sort of speed in a true ancestor of those record-breakers, the new AMG Mercedes-Benz SL60.

AMG is the official tuning company to Mercedes-Benz. Previously, British Mercedes dealers were only able to sell AMG suspension and tuning kits, but now they can supply fully-built cars.

AMG has a simple recipe for making SL60s. Get one range-topping Mercedes SL600 V12, replace the engine with a heavily modified V8 and beef up the suspension. Only a few are likely to be imported into the UK, at less than the SL600's £96,400, but still

not by any means cheap. But why replace the V12 with a V8? The V12 has 384bhp on tap, the AMG-tuned V8 only 378. But the V8 is lighter, torquier, and produces its grunt more quickly at the lower part of the rev range. The result is the fastest-accelerating Mercedes – 0-60mph in 5.6secs.

We know, because after driving it home from Stuttgart we checked it out at Millbrook Proving Ground. If you wanted to use all that power all the time, though, you'd have to go and live at Millbrook and drive around the two-mile banked circuit all day. Not

If Reims were in England, it would be surrounded by barbed wire. But it's in France, off the N31. You can just stop and marvel at the slowly crumbling grandstand

A gleaming piece of '90s high technology glows gently in the evening sun. And that's just Angus's hat. The SL60's impressive and highly-tuned V8 engine has even more cubic capacity than said cap and produces loads of torque. The hat produces loads of laughs

even on German autobahns can you sit flat out for long; there's always someone pulling out in front of you. Even if it's a mile up the road, you've got to lift off at 150mph. Heading out of Stuttgart we managed a couple of uninterrupted flat-out runs, but for the most part our progress consisted of a series of stop-start drag races.

It's easy work in an SL thanks to an automatic gearbox and massively strong brakes. Make sure the gearbox is in sport, not economy, mode and you're guaranteed near instant kickdown acceleration whenever you want.

Floor the accelerator and the V8 bays into life and gets on with some serious horizon-seeking. Acceleration begins instantly, the needle sweeping around the speedo dial. There are no holes and no gaps in the engine's repertoire; it just punches the big Merc through the air with brutal efficiency.

When the inevitable car or lorry pulls out in front, you ease off, squeeze the brake and the speed vanishes. Wait until the obstacle's gone, floor the throttle and off you go again. The Merc can take this all day long without a hint of brake fade.

The only thing to slow you are pee and petrol stops. You might be able to hold on, but the SL won't. When it's got to go for fuel it's got to go, and in sport mode it's got to go all too often.

Once over the border into France we

ease the pace a little. The midday sun is fearsome and even with the hood down at speed, the air conditioning is left firmly on. With the rear windbreak and the side windows up, the SL's cabin is almost turbulence-free. Holding a normal conversation – or a map – is not a problem. Anyway, our route's easy enough. We think.

But finding the old circuit at Reims doesn't prove easy. The people at the tourist office haven't got a brochure. Only one person seems to know of it, but their hand-written directions prove wrong. At last we find the main road that runs past what remains of pits and grandstand. We pull off the road and park the SL in the early evening sun.

The first race was held at the road-based Circuit de Reims in 1925. The final French Grand Prix ran there in 1966 and the last race ever in 1969.

But 1938 was the year for Mercedes-Benz. The Grand Prix de l'Automobile Club de France was won by Manfred von Brauchitsch in a W154, with team mates Rudi Caracciola and Hermann Lang second and third. And today we have brought another fast Mercedes-Benz to the circuit to pay tribute.

It's an eerie place. No railings stop you falling from the crumbling steps in the main three-storey building. But the old grandstand's fantastic – you can almost hear the crowd roar.

An hour spent driving around the old

circuit shows that the SL is more suited to straight-line work than stringing a series of bends together. Permanent traction control and an automatic gearbox mean that it's never going to be the perfect driver's car, but even fitting a smaller steering wheel would improve matters. There's no questioning the grip from the 17-inch Bridgestone tyres or the car's outright cornering ability, but there's little feel or flair.

Back on the autoroute the SL is a happier beast. Here it can work its old magic again. No matter what the speed it feels rock solid. Yet the ride comfort is also superb. It's all so effortless.

But the sun has faded away. To drive all night on these perfect roads would

be good, but by 3am we've crossed the channel and are back in Blighty.

The next morning we head to Brooklands, but there's no magic on these roads. The A3 has sprouted a fresh crop of cones and there are roadworks to crawl through. The SL isn't very happy either. British tarmac isn't to its taste. Where it felt smooth and relaxed on French and German roads, here it feels nervous and fidgety.

Parking it on the Brooklands banking is the scariest part of the trip. It feels like the whole thing is just going to fall over and roll back down. Trying to open that heavy door against gravity takes an awful lot of muscle power.

Brooklands would never have existed

first**steer**

The Brooklands banking is
almost scarily steep; it's
nearly impossible to walk up
it, so the thought of racing
improbable vintage cars there
sends shivers up the spine

if it hadn't been for Hugh Fortesque Locke King returning from an ill-fated trip to the 1905 Coppa Florio in Italy in a very bad mood. He'd damaged his car, he'd missed the race – and, to add insult to injury, no Englishman had entered. It was time to do something about it. It was time to start proper motorsport in Great Britain.

It took one year, 2,000 navvies and 200,000 tons of concrete to complete the circuit. Then it took men and women with nerves of steel to race there; among them V Hemery and LG Hornsted who set records with Benz cars in 1909 and 1914.

But, like Reims, Brooklands outlived its usefulness. The cars simply got too

fast. Unlike Reims, though, part of it has now been restored and there's an excellent museum on site. But there's hope for Reims too; their people have been in contact with Brooklands to ask about setting up a restoration project.

Finally, we thread the SL through North London backstreets to the office. Here it doesn't make so much sense. Sure, you can pose in it, but you can't use it like it ought to be used.

But that shouldn't detract from the SL60's speed and glory.

It's the perfect indulgence for storming across Europe in – it makes you believe that the motor car's golden years aren't over yet.

It will be a sad day if, like Reims and

Brooklands, the world no longer has a place for cars like the Mercedes-Benz AMG SL60 □

Story: Angus Frazer
Photography: Richard Newton

IN DEPTH	
0-60mph	5.6 secs
0-100mph	12.9 secs
50-70mph thro grs	2.5secs
engine	V8, 32v dohc per bank
capacity	5,956cc
max power/rpm	378bhp/5,500rpm
max torque/rpm	428lb ft/3,750rpm
transmission	4sp auto/rwd
price	£85,000 (approx)

And you thought that personalised number plates were just for sad estate agents from Plaistow. No, the Germans have them as well. The SL's abilities, however, enable you to make a quick escape from anyone with a personal plate

87

AMG HAS PUT MERCEDES' RATHER PUNY C-CLASS ON A BODY BUILDING COURSE, MICHAEL BROWNING TOOK THE STEROIDAL BENZ FOR A WORK OUT.

1995 AMG C180 MERCEDES

▲ Muscular style

▲ Tuning kit

▲ Definite style plus

Despite muscular looks of AMG body kit, and tuning kit on engine, our C180 was not a tarmac burner ... but it is a great tourer.

For all its undeniable style and *savoir faire*, there's one thing the Mercedes-Benz C-class has been tight on in the lower model echelons ... testosterone.

Like the 180E and 190E before, its prime Australian targets have been the upwardly mobile mother and the retiring male executive, with scarcely a thought for the younger male with a bulging wallet ... until now.

Enter Hans Werner Aufrecht, the boss of Germany's AMG — the man who single-handedly has transplanted more hairs on the chest of Mercedes-Benz over the past quarter century or so than anyone else.

At first his body-building 'additives' were officially ignored by 'Benz marketing executives in the 1970s, then subtly synthesised into new models in the '80s.

However since 1990, when he signed a contract of co-operation with Mercedes, Hans has officially been one of the boys from 'Benz and his extended personality panels are now offered as dealer-fitted options on all C-class models in a bid to stem the younger executive tidal wave to BMW.

Those at the recent IndyCar Grand Prix will have admired the AMG-kitted C280 models that were the event's official pace cars. The same muscular look is also available on every

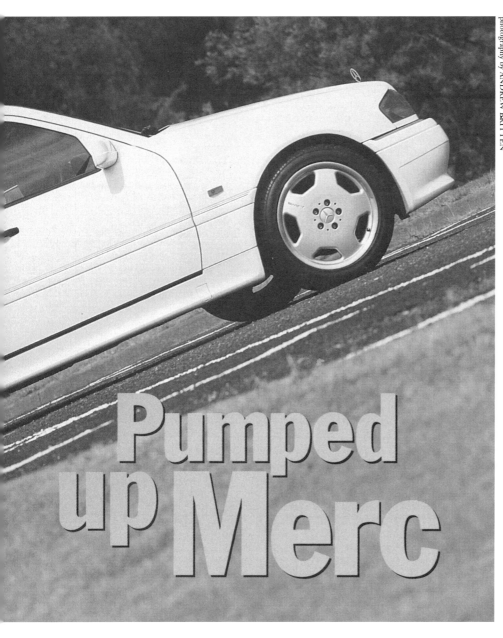

photography by ANDREW BRITTEN

Pumped up Merc

C-class model, from the $52,500 base-model C180 Esprit upwards.

As an image builder, it's a stunning, steroid-stacked solution. Our test C180 Classic in stark white drew admiring glances and appreciative comments from people who had previously been unmoved by the C-class aura.

Sitting squat and purposefully on its simply styled but impressive 17-inch AMG wheels, the AMG C-class has a totally integrated appearance that is rare in the body-kit business and comes only from complete co-operation between mainstream stylists and after-market artists at the pre-production stage.

This essential chemistry was certainly lacking in previous AMG, Lorinser and other German add-ons for the 190E, which on the Australian market today detract rather than add to re-sale value, whereas with their factory recognition and warranty, AMG C-class models are certain to retain their premium pricing.

Rather than a single option, the AMG kit is actually a body-building exercise in which you indulge as far as your wallet will allow.

The base kit costs $3636 plus about $1100 for fitting and painting to body colour. For that you get the deeper front and rear bumper sections, which incorporate front driving lamps, rocker-panel side-skirts, waist-line chrome strips, a polished metal scuff-plate covering the door sills, with AMG monogram and the all-essential boot badge. If you're adding it to an Elegance model it's slightly less, as the upper-crust C-class already has the chrome-inlaid side-protection strips.

A further option fitted was the twin AMG sports exhaust system, which delivers a muffled 'crackle' through its twin chromed exhaust extension, which by itself is an option on standard cars.

Then there's wheels and tyres. Let's face it, the standard 185/65x15-inch rubber on steel wheels would look like short pants on the AMG C-class, so you've got to bite the bullet.

A set of 15-inch AMG alloys with 205-section rubber as a changeover will add $2500, but once you've seen what a difference the glorious 17-inch AMG alloys and the Pirelli 225/45 ZR17 P-Zeros make to the total package, you'll probably fork out around $5000 for the up-market changeover or forever wish you had.

That takes care of the external optics, but with the AMG body-building exercise, it's only just the start of the transformation and the test car came additionally with a Sports Suspension package and an AMG Tuning Package for the four-valve 1.8-litre four cylinder engine.

The suspension mods are almost the same as those on 'Sport' versions of C180, C220 and C280 models and consist of lowered-height, re-set springs and modified damper settings. They cost $1100 fitted ($1300 for C280 models), but if you start off with an Esprit model as the base for your AMG C-class, then you already get the lower suspension setting (albeit without re-rated springs and dampers), so there's a saving to be had.

Finally there's the AMG tuning kit, which smacks somewhat of a desperation measure to overcome the inertia that challenges the standard 1.8-litre C180 to haul its 1350kg mass.

Consisting of an AMG inlet camshaft, engine-speed controlled camshaft adjuster (a feature rather like BMW's 'Vanos' system, which is standard on the larger C220 engine), re-worked intake manifold and mods to the

"...as an image builder, it's a stunning, steroid-stacked solution..."

Top looking body kit plus engine tuning add almost $17,000 to price of C180 and get you the all important AMG badge on the bootlid. Styling is subtle but aggressive and car is more suited to touring than High Street drags.

exhaust system, it lifts engine power from 90kW at 5500rpm to 103kW at 5850rpm. Torque, meanwhile, falls marginally from 170Nm at 4200 to 165 at 4500rpm. The tuning kit is only available on the 1.8-litre engine, bridging the gap to the C220's 110kW and adds a further $5800 fitted.

So let's total it up. As tested, with body kit, suspension kit, 17-inch wheel package and AMG Tuning Package, our five-speed manual C180 Class represented $76,136 plus on-road costs ($59,500 plus $16,636 for the AMG mods), which must set a new price benchmark for a 1.8-litre four cylinder engined-model. Mercedes-Benz is quick to point out that you don't have to go all the way down that path — it's just a suggestion. Consider a manual C180 Esprit (base price $52,500) with AMG body kit and 15-inch AMG wheel/tyre changeover package for around $59,236.

After a week with the test C180 AMG, I'm inclined to think that the latter is clearly the way to go, but probably in automatic, not manual form.

While our C180 White Knight looked stunning in its shining AMG amour, on the road it offered all the promise of Pavarotti, but performed more like Boy George.

With the AMG tuning package and manual gearbox, first impressions were disastrous. For starters, cold performance was plain dangerous, with virtually nothing available under 2000rpm for the first kilometre, so you had to disobey all the usual rules of mechanical empathy and rev the engine mercilessly until it got up to temperature. Even then progress for the first day or two in our hands was punctuated by hopeful tugs at the hand-brake release.

Driven like an average four cylinder Japanese car, using low to medium engine revs, the AMG Tuning Package just doesn't work for the manual C180 in Australian conditions and you are continually working to stay abreast of the 'commuter boxes' and Kenworths in the slow lane.

The problem is that the extra kilowatts have been gained at the top end and while Mercedes-Benz say the torque curve is flatter and more generous than for the standard car across the range, it doesn't feel that way in practice.

The other problem in manual form is that the ratios in the five-speed box are quite widely spread, with a noticeably large gap between first and second gears. Coupled to that, the gear change is one of the least pleasant on the market, being very 'clunky' until you master it, with a relatively long throw between cogs. The throttle on the test car was also quite 'sticky' and the engine had a 'flywheel' effect that meant the revs did not drop instantly the throttle was shut.

My belief is that the automatic version of the C180 would work much better with the AMG engine, as the torque converter would mask the lack of low-end pulling power, while still taking full advantage of the extra herbs at the top end.

The soon-acquired technique with the manual car is to work both the engine and the gearbox to the hilt and then the package starts to deliver. This meant winding the engine to at least 3500rpm in first gear for reasonable progress in order to surf through on the lower edge of the useful torque band and being prepared to use second (or even first) gear for every tight left or right hand turn. Do I sound paranoid about this?

Thankfully, there's a flip side. On the freeway or open road, the C180 AMG is a magnificent grand tourer, provided that you are prepared to revisit fourth or third gear for overtaking, or simply to stay ahead of interstate trucks on long uphill climbs.

The stiffer suspension compliments the already-superb C-class chassis, which is leagues ahead of anything else on the market with its blend of ride and handling, providing flatter cornering and better turn-in, while the fat 225-section Pirellis provide the adhesion missing from the basic C-class tyre and wheel package.

This is a chassis for the long way home, where its taut but compliant suspension, crisp, perfectly weighted and direct steering, fabulous headlights and reassuring ventilated disc brakes all round allow you to exploit the road to a degree only limited by the lack of suitable playing power. If ever a chassis outstripped its power-plant in potential, it's this one!

Inside, the test car was relatively standard, apart from a few filigrees of optional wood veneer on the dashboard and centre console area.

Like all C-class models, the seats are cloth-covered as standard and when first seated feel firm and rather 'dead'. This has doubtless cost Mercedes-Benz a few C-class sales to BMW and others, as my wife, like several other women who tried out the C180 AMG interior, found it austere and uncomfortable on first impressions — which in the case of potential buyers can be lasting ones.

Exactly why Mercedes-Benz has not offered a more luxurious seat for the C-class is a mystery to me, when full leather-clad lovelies are to be had from BMW for around $54,000 in the case of the 318i Signature Edition! If you want a more sporting interior, however, then you specify the 'Sport' model, with its more curvaceous seats and mock Kevlar dash and door trim.

With all its quirks and quite serious performance problems, I had expected the return of the test car to Mercedes-Benz be an easy parting but, after nearly 2000km at the wheel, I found it had grown on me more than I realised.

It was a car you always felt good in, whether driving or posturing and when not pressed for time, it was a delight to drive.

Forget about performance, you'll never find it in the C180, AMG kit or not. The magic of this car is its overall looks and competence, so dress it up, strut your stuff on the High Street and leave the road-burning to the Bimmers or C280s. In the AMG C-class you've got nothing to prove. **M**

QUICKCHECK

✓ Merc with muscles and extra style

✗ Cold engine hard work — gearbox unfriendly

FST·383
VICTORIA - GARDEN STATE

"... the AMG kit is literally a body-building exercise in which you indulge as far as your wallet will allow ..."

E=MerC²

Peter Robinson takes on the demon energy of Europe's most convincing muscle car saloon

Muscle car. An American term, of course, yet one never more appropriately bestowed than on the E50 AMG, the powerhouse iteration of the new Mercedes-Benz E-class.

Sledge-hammer muscle, the kind that occurs only when engineers squeeze a mighty 347bhp five-litre V8 into an engine bay that also lives with a puny 95bhp diesel. This is not double or even triple the power of the European-ubiquitous Merc taxi, but a ratio closer to four times greater. Huge muscle, guaranteed to breathe instant response, devastating acceleration and continent-crushing cruising speeds on a faithful Mercedes saloon. Were it not for the self-righteous electronic limitations applied to

the engine, the towering E50 would climb above 180mph. More importantly, it will disappear to 60mph in only 5.9sec. And it feels quicker.

Yet, the muscle car tag is an entirely inadequate way to describe a car so civilised, so refined in its ride comfort, so effortless in every facet of its behaviour. It is, in fact, just as brilliant playing the role of an opulent luxury saloon. Has any car maker devised a more compelling blend of energy, driver appeal and cultured finesse? Not to my knowledge.

The E50 AMG is the replacement for the E500 V8 and, like its predecessor, will only be built in left-hand drive. Unlike the E500, however, there are no plans at all to sell the car

over here. Instead, Mercedes buyers in the UK for whom the regular 220bhp E320 is deficient may, in three months, order the right-hand-drive-only 272bhp E36 AMG.

The engineers say its in-line six will be more sporting in character than the V8 and we know it has the same 155mph top speed and is a mere one second slower to 60mph. But, for all its obvious appeal, the E36 won't have the overpowering thrust of the E50, the consummate disdain of a saloon that never, ever seems to run out of power, nor the prowess to transfer it to the road.

The source of this frenetic energy comes from a Mercedes AMG modified quad-cam five-litre V8. Its induction and

exhaust systems have been fitted with twin pipes to reduce back pressure, and the cylinder heads receive larger valves, modified to improve breathing and efficiency.

In the E50, this storming engine develops 347bhp, up 21bhp over the old E500, and a huge 354lb ft of torque that is usefully constant from 3750rpm to 4250rpm. So horizontal is the torque curve, that 295lb ft is on tap at just 1800rpm.

Visually, the E50 doesn't look much like a muscle car. AMG says customers today want their high performance saloon to be even more discreet than the E500. So there are no subtly flared wheel arches. The most obvious change, compared with a normal Avant Garde E-class, ▶

Pure muscle applied with sophistication and finesse. The 347bhp E50 V8 is smooth beyond reproach, providing performance that never seems to relent

◆ is the fat 18in five-spoke alloy wheels and correspondingly wide rubber. Those who know will also notice a small chin apron, complete with beautifully integrated fog lights and cooling ducts. Barely distinguishable two-tone leather on the deeply dished sports seats, the new SL-style steering wheel and doors, and lashings of black bird's eye maple give the E50's interior its distinction.

There's one brief moment of disappointment when first you move off. Even the E50's throttle has that typically dead Mercedes feel over the first inch of movement. And that's it for any significant criticism. The engine, almost completely silent from inside the car at idle, slips its power so fluently through Mercedes' brilliant new five-speed automatic (there's no manual on offer) that changes can barely ever be felt.

Tickle the throttle past that dead zone and the engine bursts forth with real urge. Not vocally, though, at least not until the crankshaft is spinning beyond 5000rpm, when the woofle sound of a V8 in anger floats through to the cabin. There is instant torque, instant response, a seamless flow of energy. Boot the accelerator to the floor and the transmission slurs up to the next gear at

exactly the 6000rpm redline. This large-capacity V8 is every bit as smooth at the 6250rpm cut-out as it is at 1000rpm, or anywhere in between.

Next year's all-new 300bhp five-litre V8 will be cleaner and more economical, but I doubt the Mercedes engineers can possibly make it smoother, more refined, or more willing. This engine has evolved into one of The Greats.

The selector pattern carries a conventional Mercedes shift, except that '4' and 'D' lie on the same horizontal plane. 'D' gives entry to the very tall fifth gear, '4' locks it out and provides a more immediately sporting programme, delaying upshifts, picking up a lower gear and retaining it on downhill runs and in the twisty bits. Few automatics so quickly adapt to a driver's style.

Because there are five ratios, first can be low enough to maximise the lunge away from standstill. The forward thrust never seems to abate, yet because all this motion happens in so velvety a fashion, the impression of speed is completely unobtrusive. Relaxed, 120mph cruising is going to become the norm for E50 buyers in Germany.

Officially, the standing quarter mile takes just 14.2sec.

Kick down and the E50 surges from 35mph to 75mph in around 6.6sec. And Mercedes' acceleration figures are usually pretty conservative.

Where the E50 differs most from the E500 is in the harnessing of this enormous performance. In fact, the E50's capability puts it in a totally different class as an all-weather muscle car. Superb Bridgestone S-02 tyres, specially developed for the E50, give plenty of grip and, though the warning light for the traction control system flashes frequently on wet roads, the tail stays put and forward motion is never in doubt.

Philosophically, the chassis of the E50 also differs from the E500 because it is now possible, as on the M5, to turn off the skid control system. Not as easy as it seems, because today's complex electronics mean that the Merc's anti-lock brakes share the same electronics with the ASR skid control.

Even on its aggressive tyres, the E50 delivers staggering ride comfort combined with equally impressive body control. Avant Garde springs are used with firmer Bilstein dampers and anti-roll bars 1mm bigger in diameter. AMG says there's 15 per cent less roll than an E500, while the new rack-and-pinion steering is 11 per cent more

direct about the straight ahead.

Initially, because the E50 feels so comfortable thanks to impressive seats and a superb driving position, you can be lulled into thinking it lacks driver involvement. One quick avoidance, though, and the chassis reveals its true colours, displaying the agility, poise and grip of something like a Porsche 928. The communicative steering feeds back a high level of information, but in concert with a supple, absorbing ride and near neutral handling.

Purge the engine management system of the ASR and you can make the E50 dance any tune you desire, changing the car's attitude via the accelerator.

The two-piston front disc brakes come from the same supplier as those for the M5, the rears from the SL60. They have a long, spongy travel, but deliver massive stopping power.

No saloon I've driven displays the same feel and reality of total authority over roads and conditions. It has a force, a perhaps unique ability to transport three people in luxury at absurdly effortless speeds, while the driver indulges in his own private and utterly intoxicating world. No matter how talented the E36 may be, nothing can take the place of this giant among muscle cars. ●

Mercedes values of peerless build and pragmatic design combine with opulent cabin to deliver a fantastic cruiser

FACTFILE

MERCEDES-BENZ E50 AMG

HOW FAST?
0-60mph	5.9sec
Top speed	155mph
MPG: urban	17.1
56mph	31.4
75mph	26.9

All manufacturer's claimed figures

HOW MUCH?
£67,500 (est)
On sale in UK Never

HOW BIG?
Length	4795mm (188.7in)
Width	1799mm (70.8in)
Height	1411mm (55.5in)
Wheelbase	2833mm (111.5in)
Weight (claimed)	1675kg (3885lb)
Fuel tank	80 litres (17.6 gall)

ENGINE
Max power 347bhp
Max torque 354lb ft/3750-4250rpm
Specific output 70bhp/litre
Power to weight 207bhp/tonne
Installation longitudinal, front, rear-wheel drive
Capacity 4973cc, 8 cyls vee
Made of alloy head and block
Bore/stroke 97mm/85mm
Compression ratio 11.0:1
Valves 4 per cyl, dohc
Ignition and fuel Bosch HMS 6, electronic fuel injection

GEARBOX
Type 5-speed automatic
Ratios/mph per 1000rpm
1st 3.59/6.8 **2nd** 2.19/11.2 **3rd** 1.41/17.4
4th 1.00/24.6 **5th** 0.83/29.6
Final drive ratio 3.06

SUSPENSION
Front double wishbones, coil springs, anti-roll bar
Rear independent multi-link, coil springs, anti-roll bar

STEERING
Type power assisted rack and pinion
Lock to lock 3.2 turns

BRAKES
Front 334mm ventilated discs
Rear 300mm drums
Anti-lock standard

WHEELS AND TYRES
Size 8.0x18in (f), 9.0x18in (r)
Made of alloy
Tyres 235/40 ZR18 (f), 265/35 ZR 18 (r)
Bridgestone S-02

YOU CAN'T HAVE TOO MUCH OF A GOOD THING

This is the best hot Mercedes ever made. **PAUL HORRELL** took one home and liked it so much that he couldn't stop driving it. He did hundreds of miles non-stop, but even that wasn't enough

PHOTOGRAPHS BY PETER BURN

'*Properly quick cars all feel alive, dodging side-to-side along the little ruts that nibble the road surface*'

'The C36 feels like a proper sports car, hard and jiggly and sharp and full of kick'

SOMETIMES YOU JUST CAN'T STOP driving. It happened to me the other day. Got home, but couldn't cut the ignition and climb out. You know how it is: no idea why the urge takes hold, but it does. Could be your mood, the weather, the road. Or the position of the planets, state of your biorhythms or, for all I care, the vibes coming off your new-age crystal. But today I know exactly the reason. It's a calm, hot evening and I've got a hot car. A 280bhp Mercedes C-class, tuned up and tied down by AMG. Built for speed, built for distance. So here I am, three hours north of home, wafting up the A1, road-music cassettes blaring.

There is a peculiar tension, almost addictive, about cruising slowly in a very fast car, sticking to 80mph-odd on a motorway, using half the available speed, for hour upon hour. You're holding back, tight on the reins. You can't slacken off. Let your right ankle relax, and the slightest extra weight on the throttle sends the car steaming ahead. Your steering has to be spot-on, because properly quick cars all feel

alive, dodging and nudging side-to-side along the little ruts and tramlines that nibble the surface of any arterial road. The rear tyres (big 40-profile 17-inch jobs that amount to little more than a smear of rubber around the alloys' rims, rather than anything actually pneumatic) slap-slap against the concrete joints, and hum coarsely if the surface has any texture. The engine has a harsher bark than is usual for a Benz, reminding you that what it really wants is to be given a wide-open road and a wide-open throttle. But no. You're just restraining it with the rest of the traffic, making this shark swim with the minnows.

A big-engined S-class is just as mighty in acceleration and speed potential as this hot C-class, but 80mph in the C36 is a world away from the relaxing, silent, cruise-controlled waft of an S500. The C36 feels like a proper sports car, hard and jiggly and sharp and full of kick. It's edgy, ready to pounce, and I'm alert and working with it, my eyes scanning road-mirror-road-speedo, rhythmically in time with the tyre

thump and engine drone and the stereo's beat.

But no-one can keep temptation at bay for ever. After three hours of M1, M18 and A1(M), you crest a rise and view six lanes of divided carriageway, free of junctions and obstructions and any more than a sprinkling of vehicles. What would you do? Same as me. I turn down the music and unroll the pent-up flex in my ankle. Not brutally, just a steady push on the accelerator until it's clenched fast to the carpet.

Almost before the throttle is depressed at all, the harmonic straight-six note hardens, seeming to lift the star-topped silver bonnet a few inches upward. By the time the pedal has reached its full extent, the sound is rising rapidly in pitch, the rev-counter swinging madly upward as the four-speed automatic slurs smoothly but emphatically down to third. There's a real bark to the sound now, and the vehicles alongside are sucked backward, diminishing in the C36's mirrors. The acceleration grows more urgent as the rev-needle growls towards the 6400rpm red block. And now we're really flying, rushing

down the corridor between Armco and blur-ring Catseyes. It's a rush made tenfold more vivid by the slow tension of the preceding three hours. Yet still the tacho needle rotates mania-cally clockwise and my neck-hairs prickle.

Although it's perfectly safe, this type of thing is Plod-madness, licence-shredding stuff. So I back right off. The transmission nonchalantly shrugs up to top, letting the engine noise sub-side. All that's left is a gentle wind-rush and tyre-hum over the smooth bitumen. The speed falls away, but gently. The whole blast has lasted just a few seconds, but I've entirely con-sumed a small valley of the A1's topography.

Although the car's feel and power are so AMG-special, sitting in the cockpit the visual reminders are more or less exactly as per your ordinary C180 Sport. The gearknob has an embossed C36 logo, the steering wheel has a band of naff grey leather, the speedo reads to 170mph, and the upholstery is the optional leather, yes, but the seats are the usual sensible, supportive, hard chairs, and the controls and

Mock carbonfibre on dash mars otherwise first-class cabin. Engine extensively reworked to produce a Mercedes-reliable 280bhp out of 3.6 litres. It has four valves per cylinder and variable cam timing. C36's autobox is brilliant. It's smooth, and if you really want to hustle, you can use it like a manual

Optional body kit is subtle, enhances looks. C36 is staggeringly fast for an auto – top speed is governed to 155mph. Twin tailpipes hint that this is no ordinary C-class

switches have their accustomed firm precision. The interior design and furnishing is heavy-looking, heavy-feeling, heavy-duty and in places heavy-handed. The only attempt at flair is a series of decorative fillets of black plastic faux-carbonfibre. Even the most ardent supporter of cheap textured plastic would be forced to concede that these are no better than crap, nothing like as pretty or lustrous as the rare and costly real thing.

The car is rare and costly enough, though. It's built as an ordinary C-class, on the Mercedes line, and its engine starts life as a production unit. But AMG's re-working of the straight-six is comprehensive, as it would need to be to get a Mercedes-reliable 280bhp out of 3.6 litres. Helping it along, there are four valves per cylinder and variable camshaft timing. The last of which can claim partial responsibility for the billowing mid-range torque curve. You don't need big revs up before there's a lunge of torque to be had. AMG can also claim responsibility for a lowered, stiffened suspension, the wheels

and the optional body kit. The car is then sold as a complete Merc-warranted item at your local dealer for £40-odd grand.

Because of the wheels and dressed-up body, people do recognise this car as something special, which is why they ask about the price when I stop for fuel. These aren't the thoughts in my head, though. The glorious moors of Yorkshire and Northumberland are drawing me close and it's time to peel off the A1.

The C-class isn't a small car – if you drive it alongside the BMW M3 against which comparisons have inevitably been made, it feels a little large and slow to the tiller – but this AMG is a fabulously controllable and controlled one. I find the steering on most Mercedes saloons remote and unnervingly artificial, but on this AMG it's a confident, communicative mechanism that out-feels the M3's. All of which means that after only a short way I feel happy about pouring it into what bends there may be with quite some resolve.

It laps them up. The vast tyres would always

give stacks of grip on a smooth surface, but that's not what we're passing over. And yet the lumps on the road make little difference, which shows just how aristocratic the chassis is. It still hangs on. What's more, it still breaks loose so progressively that you can force it to the very edge without the least sweat. Imagine you get to a long, tight corner at ill-advisedly high speed. It'll understeer, pushing the front tyres out until you back away off the throttle, when it neatens itself up unflinchingly. Which might be a bit unexciting, but is after all a completely safe and reassuring characteristic for a situation in which you have, let's face it, been a bit of a twerp.

Get the entry speed right, though, and you soon realise that the heavens are smiling on you. The C36's balance of grip front-to-rear is as sweet as you like, and the steering wheel loads up, jiggles a little, then lightens in your hands so that you know just when the front tyres' purchase is running thin. Meanwhile, when you catch sight of the exit of the bend, you can mash the accelerator, get the car to squat a little as the

'After all these miles, it's still a wrench to turn the key anti-clockwise and walk away'

Sunset, but Horrell wants more. Ultra low-profile rubber coats lovely 17in alloys, and gives the car a jiggly but nicely composed ride along with prodigious grip and great handling

MERCEDES-BENZ C36 AMG

SPECIFICATION

Price	£38,250
Engine	3606cc 24-valve six, 280bhp at 5750rpm, 284lb ft at 4000rpm
Gearbox	Four-speed automatic
Suspension	Front: double wishbones, coil springs, anti-roll bar Rear: five links, coil springs, anti-roll bar
Tyres	Front: 225/45 ZR17 Rear: 245/40 ZR17
Length	4487mm

Width	1720mm
Wheelbase	2670mm
Weight	1560kg

PERFORMANCE

Top speed	155mph (limited)
0-60mph	6.5sec
In gears	First: 42mph Second: 72mph Third: 112mph
Fuel consumption:	Urban: 20.8mpg 56mph: 33.2mpg 75mph: 28.0mpg Test: 23.8mpg

huge rear tyres dig in to catapult you down the next straight. And if you've been early enough in your application of the throttle, after the squat will come a little sidestep from the rear as the tyres relinquish hold against the titanic torque. There's nothing scary here: it's a cakewalk to roll your hands on the wheel-rim a little so that the C36 drifts obediently and tidily straight again. No fuss, no mess.

In the wet, the powerslides can be quite lurid, but without malice. There's no snappiness or awkwardness. The amiability of the suspension must surely be down to the well honed complexity of Mercedes' new generation of chassis, which hangs the front wheels off double wishbones, and the rears from five separate links per side. All the better to look after control toe-in and camber angles while you've got other things to think about.

It's worth mentioning the transmission here. Too often, automatics can bring on a bit of raggedness when you're behaving in such a rowdy fashion. Halfway round a bend, when you floor the throttle they'll shift down with a thunk, sending the engine spinning towards its power peak and the back end of the car into a sphincter-tightening spasm. But the C36's is so well mannered that you can tug the selector backwards on the way into a corner and it'll shift down perfectly smoothly, so you won't need to be unsettled later. You use it like a manual, in other words. And if you leave it in D, it won't ever shift down from 3 to 2 unless you deliberately activate kickdown, so you're protected from any heart-stopping downshifts in the middle of wet corners.

But the rain is clear now, and I'm skimming along favourite roads in Northumberland. It looks like the Garden of Eden tonight, the heathered moorlands and lush patchwork dales all bathed in slanting golden-syrup light. I'm deep into the groove, making the engine sing up and down through the business end of its rev range, hearing it bark slightly whenever the tacho passes up past 3800rpm, the point at which it really goes to work. I'm slapping the transmission selector up and down through the gate, click-click, as the Benz dives towards each switchbacking bend as it loses speed to its ironfist brakes, then winding it through the arcs with a big, fat grin.

So the evening fades through pink to red and purple-black, but the driving goes on, concentration now contracting into a flare-pool from the headlamps. And I still can't bring myself to stop. Why is this car so captivating? Something to do with the completeness of a Merc and the complete madness of AMG; the dead hand of the three-pointed star and the liveliness of a real sporting car. It's a creative tension that means, after hundreds of non-stop recreational miles, it's still a wrench to turn the key anti-clockwise, climb out and walk away into the night. 🚗

FIRST DRIVE

- Exclusive AMG-tuned 'sportier' SL
- 6-litre, 375bhp V8
- On sale this autumn, cost £85,000 plus

SPORTY, BUT NO LIGHTWEIGHT

Sport. Evocative word that, particularly when you're in the business of selling cars. Mercedes-Benz has known all about the benefits and drawbacks of motorsport for almost 50 years, and for a long time many Mercedes road cars were based on racers. The legendary SL range (short for 'Sport Leicht') was launched in 1954, when the famous gullwing SL was winning sports cars races, including Le Mans.

In the 1990s, Mercedes is winning German Touring Car races, winning the Indy 500 and entering Formula One with Sauber. Trouble is, the Mercedes road cars we see in the showrooms today no longer seem to reflect the company's sporting success, and Mercedes Benz is rather more famous for big, heavy luxury saloons than sports cars. Though the SL concept has continued unbroken for thirty years, the current model, launched in 1989, is closer to Soft-top Luxury than Sports Light.

Now, to give this undeniably successful car an extra twist of lemon (5217 have already been sold in the UK), Mercedes has turned to their arch modifiers, AMG, to supply an engine, and the result is the new SL60, proposed as a 'true' sports car to convince the sceptics.

If only SL stood for Straight Line, then I could write that the SL60 is dazzlingly efficient at carrying out its brief. This former 5-litre V8 engine has been hollowed out to become a 6-litre (hence the SL60 name, but don't get mixed up with the SL600 — that's a 6-litre V12, you see?) AMG has wrung the neck of this new V8 unit to produce 375bhp, and when you let rip on a wide straight road you feel almost every cubic centimetre obeying the charge and rocketing you along. This is accompanied by a deep V8 grumble, which elevates with the revs to a powerful howl, the kind that would satisfy the most demanding of sports ears.

But just because I'm harping on about its straight line ability you shouldn't imagine for a moment that the car is poor around corners. 'SL' could well refer to the Stability Lesson that this Mercedes could give most cars in its class. All SL's sit absolutely four-square on the road, and the smaller engined versions in particular display quite superb agility and sure footedness despite their size and weight. The SL60 goes one step further, and AMG's own suspension modifications make the ride a little firmer and the cornering tighter. The legendary Mercedes build quality ensures the AMG car has zero rattles and no wibbly wobbly behaviour through potholes. In this respect, the car is a peach.

● *I think it would be safe to say that Mark enjoys his job*

● *Big tyres, bigger performance and the open road. No wonder he's smiling*

● *Three letters that signify this SL's special purpose*

And yet, despite this car's absolutely enormous appeal, I cannot put my hand on my heart and tell you that the SL60 fulfills Mercedes' SL sportscar role. The other models, especially the V12 version, are inescapably good cars, certainly amongst the most desirable in the world, but they are open cruisers. The V12's enormous torque makes it ideal for swishing along in a Grand Tourer style, and that, in the main, is what it's used for. Judging the SL60 as a true sportscar, however, it neither sets my heart alight nor gets my adrenalin pumpin'.

The main reason for this lack of emotion is the SL60's automatic gearbox. Attaching a six speed manual to the AMG engine would not only transform the car, it would change the sound it makes (more high revs please) and importantly it would change the driver's driving itself. The four speed automatic box that comes as standard on all the SL's is great, fabby, super dooper, I'm not complaining, OK? But it doesn't allow you to let your hair down and go wild. It reduces your progress to a nice lazy float — this may be at high speed, it may be at a crawl, but the SL60, like all the SL's, requires no more driver involvement at 85mph than at 35mph. You can't even order a manual box, because there's no demand for them. None at all. This isn't a problem. The SL60 is undoubtedly a truly great car and hugely desirable, but simply not quite my cup of tea. Maybe when I'm a little more refined, when my youthfulness has matured, when I'm blessed with more of Old Father Time's wisdom, even, maybe then an auto SL will be just the thing I'm after.

Right now, though, the SL60 seems like a hybrid of sportiness and casual luxury, and a waste of a good car as a result. A venerable colleague, blessed with more maturity and vision, came up with the real solution for Mercedes to convince the sceptics. Forget the ever more powerful engines, and strip out an SL to do a Club Sport version. Fit a manual gearbox. Dead right Brian, that car will evoke the halcyon days of Mercedes SL sportscars, and I'd want one of those. At an expected £85,000 to £90,000, I'll not be ordering an SL60 this year I'm afraid, but 15 people will. Both Mercedes Benz and I are confident of that.

Mark Walton

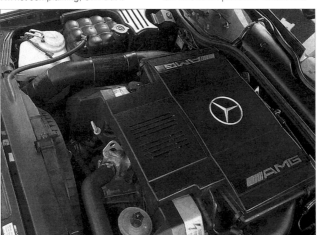

● *We're not worthy — SL60's 6-litre V8 has a useful 375bhp*

▲ **FOR** *Looks, grunt, quality*
▼ **AGAINST** *Heavy, no manual gearbox option*
● **VERDICT** *How about a Club Sport version?*

BMW M3 *meets*

AMG tweaks make the C36 shriek, but is the car a match for BMW's M3?

BY RICHARD HOMAN
PHOTOS BY JOHN KONKAL

COMPARISON
R&T
ROAD TEST

MERCEDES-BENZ C36

WOW. WOW IS plenty dramatic. But as a complete Road Test, let alone a Comparison Test, it strikes even me, the lonely writer hurtling headlong toward his deadline, as woefully inadequate. Wow is not only not a contender for the Ken Purdy Award for Excellence in Automotive Journalism, it's a one-way ticket out of the business. Just ask my editor.

But I remember the first time I saddled up a 1994 BMW M3 and spurred the throttle: The half-moon grin on my face was preceded by an exclamation that could not be mistaken for anything but praise. And this afternoon, Senior Editor Joe Rusz got back from an apparently spirited lunchtime workout in the new-to-the-U.S. Mercedes-Benz C36. His first time in it. I asked Joe what he thought of the car, and he was kind enough to write my lead for me: "Wow," he said.

I nodded. I knew what he meant, having driven the pilot European C36 a little more than a year ago in Germany (see "Autobahn Aristocrats" in our December 1993 issue). And readers of our August 1994 issue will remember our being wowed by the BMW M3 in a Road Test. Here were two top German carmakers, each seeing the other as primary competition, each bringing to the North American market a showcase performance car constructed from the best of its bread-and-butter automobiles (the M3 is based on the 325is Coupe, the C36 on the C280 sedan) and each casting a distinct image in our minds—"Mercedes-like" and "BMW-like" are certainly part of any enthusiast's vocabulary.

The U.S. introduction of the Mercedes-Benz C36 presented us with an ideal opportunity to put both cars under the harsh light of scrutiny and see which one, if either, blinked.

Our favorite performance laboratory for such scrutiny is the clinical research facility known as Willow Springs International Raceway, particularly the 1.3-mile asphalt snake known as the Streets of Willow. It was on this miniature road course that our two cars distinguished themselves (in general as well as from each other).

The BMW appeared to be having the most fun out at the track, but just barely. From its razor-sharp, variable-assist/variable-ratio rack-and-pinion steering and multilink suspension right down to its 40-series tires, the M3 chatted up a storm, keeping its driver in touch with every nuance of the road, responding to every steering input. The more nimble of the two cars, the BMW, was also the more exacting, with a penchant for oversteer. But the payoff for keeping tail dancing to a minimum was high. Any reasonable com-

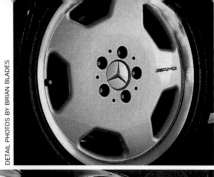

■ The styled 17-in. aluminum wheels, the leather-wrapped steering wheel and shift knob, the instrument cluster and, of course, the 268-bhp twincam inline-6 all bear the performance promise of the AMG logo. The Mercedes-Benz C36 never misses a beat as the E500 for buyers on a budget.

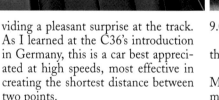

bination of steering, throttle and concentration went a long way toward turning in the most gratifying laps.

It's a bit harder to get into a rhythm in the Mercedes C36. The inputs aren't quite as keen as in the BMW; the steering is not as quick. The suspension isn't set up to be as taut as the BMW's, giving, instead, a nod to ride comfort. In its understeering nature, the C36 shows considerable bias toward its wider rear tires. In corners, it will tuck in reluctantly if you drop the throttle. But the fast way around in the C36 is to go deep into a corner, taking full advantage of the powerful brakes, repoint and then let the engine's immense low-end thrust fire you off toward the next transition. A different kind of driving than in the BMW M3, but just as effective, pro-

viding a pleasant surprise at the track. As I learned at the C36's introduction in Germany, this is a car best appreciated at high speeds, most effective in creating the shortest distance between two points.

Both cars appear to be getting the absolute best out of their respective inline-6 engines. There isn't a dull spot in either car's wide power band, and while the BMW may not have the operatic torque of the Mercedes, it balances the equation by playing its 5-speed manual gearbox (and lighter weight) to the Benz's 4-speed automatic. A pure driver's setup, the M3's pedal placement is ideal for heel-and-toe shifting. And while both cars can call up substantial power from anywhere in the rev range, the trip from 60 to 100 mph in the Mercedes is one of the best

9.0-second vacations we know of.

And you may ask yourself: How did they get here?

In a sense, both the C36 and the M3 are pioneer projects for their German parent companies. Mercedes has collaborated with famed tuner AMG to create the C36. For better than two decades, "Mercedes" and "AMG" have been coming off the lips of enthusiasts in the same breath, as though the companies were one and the same. In truth, however, AMG spent most of its time acting as a sort of personal trainer for M-B models, developing super-Benzes like the 300E-sedanbased "Hammer" (a 6.0-liter V-8, 365-bhp helping of Wow) and enlisting to help out with Mercedes' German Touring Car Championship efforts. The C36 is the first car acknowledged

as a joint effort by both M-B and AMG. As such, the yearly output of 1200 C36 models—including about 400 for the U.S.A.—will carry an AMG badge and be sold throughout the world by Mercedes-Benz dealers.

The journey from mild-mannered C-class to C36 begins at Mercedes' Bremen factory in northern Germany. At Bremen, the essence of a C280 sedan comes together along the C-class assembly line; however, the future C36 gets special treatment from the Mercedes workers, who fit a sturdier final drive, the larger vented front discs

of the SL600, the larger rears of the E420, stiffer front and rear anti-roll bars, shorter springs (to hunker the car down) and a quicker-ratio steering box. Before the C36-to-be leaves Bremen, the factory also mounts the 17-in. AMG wheels and damn-wide, low-profile Bridgestone Expedia S-01 tires (full-size spare included), and front fenders that have been modified on the inside to accommodate the broader rubber. Now the car, sans bumpers and skirts, is ready to head south to AMG.

It is at AMG's headquarters/work-

shops in Affalterbach, near Stuttgart, that the C36 meets its performance destiny. Special gas-pressure shocks are installed, and finishing bodywork—plastic rear bumper, side skirts and front bumper/apron—is attached. Besides adding to the C36's visual form, the front apron is also functional, incorporating a set of foglights and ducting air to the car's massive—bigger than a Ferrari 512TR's—front brakes, which, as mentioned, were spirited from the SL600 roadster.

The interior, swaddled in leather, is highlighted by electrically adjustable

sport seats (sporty, yes, but also kind to long-distance travelers), a Bose sound system, and an AMG instrument panel, two-tone steering wheel and shift knob to remind the lucky driver just how lucky he is. The faux carbon-fiber console trim of the European C36 gives way to the American expectations of a Mercedes—burled walnut—although the Schmevlar Kevlar is still used to set off the U.S. car's B-pillars.

None of this hard work would mean much if the engine wasn't a showcase piece. Not to worry. As soon as the car arrives at AMG's facility, Affalterbach's finest remove the drivetrain and begin the modifications. In the process, one dohc 24-valve inline-6 (2.8 liters, 194 bhp, 199 lb.-ft. of torque) comes out of the engine bay, and another, bored and stroked to 3.6 liters, is dropped in to take its place.

The AMG-altered six features a higher compression ratio and modifications to the cylinder head, block and engine-management computer. Taking it from the top, the engine gets these performance enhancers: a larger-diameter, variable-length intake manifold, enlarged cylinder-head ports, a new high-lift intake cam and revised variable intake-valve timing, and revised exhaust cam timing. The significant performance boost necessitates the use of forged-aluminum pistons, modified rods and a new crankshaft. Additional oil-spray jets are also installed in the engine block. At the purge end, a new low-noise, freer-flowing exhaust system sends emissions through two ceramic catalytic converters and out the dual, chrome-tipped pipes.

And at the end of the day, the C36's normally aspirated engine rings the bell at 268 bhp and a 280-lb.-ft. wallop of peak torque delivered at 4000 rpm. For a transmission, AMG scanned the three-pointed stars on the horizon and sourced the 4-speed automatic used in the V-8 E420 and E500 sedans. Driving absolutists, note: There is no manual gearbox anywhere on that horizon.

On the BMW side, the second-generation M3 is another kind of first. The Bavarian company's high-performance subsidiary, BMW Motorsport (newly baptized "BMW M"), not only is responsible for continuing to engineer (in some cases, build) the heat-seeking "M" cars, but also is in charge of the boutique business, BMW Individual. You say you want your 740i to come in Amethyst with a Forest Green leather interior, bird's-eye maple trim, a fax machine, color TV and a special mount for your golf clubs? No problem. BMW M can do that. M can also build an M5 Touring. Or provide a V-12 for McLaren's F1 supercar.

The M3 comes packed with individuality. At the leading edge is a revised, body-color front air dam that feeds air to the engine and front brakes. The aerodynamic side skirts, also done in body color, groove themselves pleasantly into one's memory, while the smallish side-view mirrors, which look suspect *and* limit the rearward view, do just the opposite. Inside the M3, leather-covered BMW M sport seats hold the driver and front-seat passenger firmly, while tasteful reminders of the blue/purple/red BMW M tricolor are planted in the seats, the shift knob, the stitching of the leather-covered steering wheel, and the gauges (recalibrated to reflect what this car is all about). If all this styling discretion goes against your enthusiast grain, you can substitute M3 cloth and suede upholstery (a no-cost option) and add a trunk-mounted spoiler (sorry, this one costs extra).

As is the case with the Mercedes C36, the core of the BMW's sublimely polished apple is its engine. When Munich decided to tailor a second-generation M3 specifically for the U.S., it was correctly confident that the 325is's dohc 24-valve inline-6—already plenty willing and able with 189 bhp and 181 lb.-ft. of torque—provided an excellent fabric to work with.

Enlarging the engine's displacement to 3.0 liters gives low- and midrange torque a shot in the arm, while a recalibration of the electronically controlled valve timing gives a booster shot to the upper-rpm range. Finish things off with a special large-diameter exhaust system, and the patient leaves the operating table healthier than ever, sounding better than ever and putting out 240 bhp and 225 lb.-ft. of torque.

PRICE

	BMW M3	Mercedes-Benz C36
Base price	$35,800	est $50,000
Price as tested	$38,407	est $55,815

Both cars include std equip. (dual airbags, ABS, leather int, air cond, AM/FM stereo/cassette; pwr windows, mirrors and door locks). **For M3:** pwr sunroof ($1120), cruise control ($455), luxury tax ($582), dest charge ($450). **For C36:** C1 Value Package (traction control, headlamp washer/wipers, heated front seats) $2835, retractable rear-seat headrests ($340), luxury tax ($2165), dest charge ($475).

GENERAL DATA

	BMW M3	Mercedes-Benz C36
Curb weight	**3145 lb**	3430 lb
Test weight	3295 lb	3585 lb
Weight dist, f/r, %	50/50	54/46
Wheelbase	106.3 in.	105.9 in.
Track, f/r	56.0 in./56.9 in.	58.9 in./58.2 in.
Length	**174.5 in.**	**177.4 in.**
Width	**67.3 in.**	**67.7 in.**
Height	**52.6 in.**	**55.6 in.**

ENGINE

	BMW M3	Mercedes-Benz C36
Type	dohc 24-valve **inline-6**	dohc 24-valve **inline-6**
Displacement	182 cu in./2990 cc	220 cu in./3606 cc
Bore x stroke	3.39 x 3.38 in./ 86.0 x 85.8 mm	3.58 x 3.64 in./ 91.0 x 92.4 mm
Compression ratio	10.5:1	10.5:1
Horsepower (SAE)	**240 bhp @ 6000 rpm**	**268 bhp @ 5750 rpm**
Torque	**225 lb-ft @ 4250 rpm**	**280 lb-ft @ 4000 rpm**
Maximum engine speed:	6800 rpm in 1st and 2nd, 6500 rpm in 3rd and 4th	6400 rpm
Fuel injection	dual Bosch HFM-Motronic	modified Bosch HFM-Motronic
Fuel	prem unleaded, 91 pump oct	prem unleaded, 91 pump oct

CHASSIS & BODY

	BMW M3	Mercedes-Benz C36
Layout	**front engine/rear drive**	**front engine/rear drive**
Body/frame	unit steel	unit steel
Brakes, f/r	**12.4-in. vented discs/12.3-in. vented discs;** vacuum assist, ABS	**12.6-in. vented discs/10.9-in. vented discs;** vacuum assist, ABS
Wheels	cast alloy, **17 x 7½J**	cast alloy; **17 x 7½J f, 17 x 8½J r**
Tires	Michelin Pilot SX MXX3, **235/40ZR-17**	Bridgestone Expedia S-01; **225/45ZR-17 f, 245/40ZR-17 r**
Steering	**rack & pinion,** power assist	**recirculating ball,** power assist
Turns, lock to lock	3.0	3.1
Turning circle	38.0 ft	35.2 ft
Suspension, f/r	**MacPherson struts, double-pivot lower arms,** coil springs, tube shocks, anti-roll bar/**multilink,** coil springs, tube shocks, anti-roll bar	**upper & lower control arms,** coil springs, tube shocks, anti-roll bar/ **5-link,** coil springs, tube shocks, anti-roll bar

DRIVETRAIN

		BMW M3		Mercedes-Benz C36			
Transmission		**5-speed manual**		4-speed automatic			
Gear	Ratio	Overall ratio	(Rpm) Mph	Ratio	Overall ratio	(Rpm) Mph	
1st, :1	4.20	13.23	(6800) 36	3.87	11.11	(6100) 36	
2nd, :1	2.49	7.84	(6800) 60	2.25	6.46	(6400) 66	
3rd, :1	1.66	5.23	(6500) 86	1.44	4.13	(6400) 103	
4th, :1	1.24	3.91	(6500) 115	1.00	2.87	est (6400) 148	
5th, :1	1.00	3.15	est (6230) 137*				
Final drive ratio			3.15:1	2.87:1			
Engine rpm @ 60 mph in top gear			2725	2625			

*Electronically limited.

ACCOMMODATIONS

	BMW M3	Mercedes-Benz C36
Seating capacity	**4**	5
Head room, f/r	38.0 in./34.0 in.	36.5 in./35.5 in.
Seat width, f/r	2 x 19.0 in./52.5 in.	2 x 16.5 in./50.5 in.
Front-seat leg room	43.5 in.	45.5 in.
Luggage space	9.2 cu ft	11.6 cu ft

FUEL ECONOMY

	BMW M3	Mercedes-Benz C36
Normal driving	24.5 mpg	25.0 mpg
EPA city/highway	19/27 mpg	18/22 mpg
Fuel capacity	17.2 gal.	16.4 gal.

INTERIOR NOISE

	BMW M3	Mercedes-Benz C36
Idle in neutral	40 dBA	44 dBA
Maximum, 1st gear	72 dBA	73 dBA
Constant 70 mph	69 dBA	72 dBA

HANDLING

	BMW M3	Mercedes-Benz C36
Lateral accel (200-ft skidpad)	0.90g	0.86g
Balance	mild understeer	moderate understeer
Speed thru 700-ft slalom	62.6 mph	62.2 mph
Balance	mild understeer	mild understeer

ACCELERATION

	BMW M3	Mercedes-Benz C36
Time to speed	Seconds	Seconds
0–30 mph	1.9	2.3
0–40 mph	3.0	3.3
0–50 mph	4.1	4.6
0–60 mph	5.4	6.0
0–70 mph	7.2	7.7
0–80 mph	9.1	9.9
0–90 mph	11.4	12.2
0–100 mph	14.1	15.1
Time to distance		
0–100 ft	2.9	3.1
0–500 ft	7.7	8.0
0–1320 ft (¼ mi)	14.1 @ 99.5 mph	14.5 @ 98.5 mph

BRAKING

	BMW M3	Mercedes-Benz C36
Minimum stopping distance		
From 60 mph	122 ft	120 ft
From 80 mph	212 ft	210 ft
Control	excellent	excellent
Pedal effort for 0.5g stop	14 lb	12 lb
Fade, effort after six 0.5g stops from 60 mph	16 lb	17 lb
Brake feel	excellent	excellent
Overall brake rating	excellent	excellent

Subjective ratings consist of excellent, very good, good, average, poor; na means information is not available.

■ Take a look at two of the world's finest work stations: the BMW M3's interior—straight-faced, spare and brilliantly efficient—and its 240-bhp engine, the first 6-cylinder M3 ever.

=M3

DETAIL PHOTOS BY BRIAN BLADES

BMW M employs a ZF 5-speed manual transmission to relay this power to the M3's rear wheels, through a 25-percent limited-slip differential.

Having the spirited balance of the 325is platform to build on is a blessing in that the 3-Series already has one of the sportiest suspension setups available in the under-$30,000 league. BMW M wisely chose to eschew any unnecessary gestures, opting instead to simply lower the car and add heft to the heroics already present in the BMW suspension.

As on the M-B C36, more car means bigger brakes, and the M3 delivers with thicker vented rotors front and rear. Those brakes are tucked neatly inside 17-in. BMW Motorsport (BMW M) wheels. And those wheels, in turn, are surrounded by supercar-low-profile 235/40ZR-17 Michelins.

Mercedes refuses to allow that the C36 spells competition for the BMW M3, and its four doors, automatic transmission and $50,000 price tag (versus two doors, a 5-speed manual and relatively painless $35,800 for the M3) would tend to bear this out. BMW may not have gotten M-B's "We come in peace" message, however. Munich showed a 4-door M3 at last year's Paris auto show, and an automatic transmission is also on the way (as is a convertible).

Strictly speaking, however, this isn't really a Comparison Test—A versus B—it's a Distinction Test. True, both cars are tops in quality and appointments, both feature hotted-up twin-cam inline-6s and game suspensions. (And both enjoy full manufacturer's warranties, no fine print.) But what they really are is the best of Benz and

BMW taken to performance extremes. The M3 feels light, sharp—a match for anything you're likely to meet on the road, priced to never grow moss on the showroom floor. Frankly, it's the best $36,000 an enthusiast can possibly spend on a BMW, and he'll still feel like he's getting a bargain. The Mercedes-Benz C36, on the completely other hand, establishes its credentials for opulence, quietness, bank-vault solidity and comfort, and then adds gobs of performance, courtesy of AMG. Its price puts the C36 in a more exclusive category, but it's also the smartest $50K that you can drop on a Mercedes today.

We Americans have a word for it. A short word that makes a decent lead for a Road Test and, for these two German thoroughbreds, a decent conclusion: Wow. ⊙

MERCEDES-BENZ E50 AMG

Faro, Portugal—

The Mercedes-Benz 500E/E500 will go down in history as the perfect stealth sedan. It was blindingly fast, easy to control, and so well camouflaged that only connoisseurs could tell it from lesser sister models. Its replacement, the somewhat clumsily badged E50 AMG, is an even more complete piece, but its looks are less understated, and its bigger body is a tighter fit on narrow roads. Trouble is, the E50 will not be imported to the United States for the time being. Mario Spitzner, the chief product manager, explains: "Although North America is a key market for this car, we just couldn't homologate the E50 in time. The current engine is going to be replaced before long by a brand-new V-8. There will again be an AMG derivative of this powerplant, and it will definitely be offered in the States."

The Hammer is back— but it won't come to the States before 1998.

BY GEORG KACHER

While America waits, we put this superfast five-seater Mercedes to the roads of Portugal's picturesque Algarve coast. And after two and a half days and close to 500 miles, I was extremely reluctant to give back the key. Better equipped yet a couple of grand less expensive than the late E500, the 347-bhp (DIN) E-class is a seriously fast grand tourer that combines addictive driving pleasure with a high level of comfort and safety.

PHOTOGRAPHY BY RICHARD NEWTON

It's especially addictive to pilot the wide, low-riding E50 with the traction control switched off. By pushing the ASR button in the center console, one can modulate the throttle to control the car at its limit, thus unimpeded by the drive-by-wire interface. The brake-activated portion of the traction control remains on duty, but it disengages above 50 mph to protect the pads.

Even with ASR sleeping the sleep of the just, the expertly tuned springs and dampers, the stiffer anti-sway bars, and the broad-shouldered Bridgestones provide incredible roadholding. Although the AMG engineers claim that the steering of the E50 is two percent quicker than that of the E500, the new car's extra weight, girth, and length relay the impression that it is about ten percent slower. The switch from recirculating-ball to rack-and-pinion steering has improved on-center feel, but the turn-in is now fractionally less spontaneous, and

the steering also becomes a little artificial as you wind on more lock.

Although the E500 was modified by Porsche in Zuffenhausen, the E50 is shipped from Mercedes-Benz in Sindelfingen to the AMG shop in Affalterbach and then back to Sindelfingen. Mercedes is in charge of flaring the fenders to accommodate the eighteen-inch wheels, but most of the mechanical tuning work is carried out by AMG. The most labor-intensive item is the engine, which consists of more than 600 individual parts. Among the main differences between the 347-bhp (DIN) E50 engine and the 322-bhp (DIN) version from which it was derived are a recalibrated engine-management system, larger-diameter intake valves and manifolds, hotter camshaft profiles, stiffer valve springs, a higher 11.0:1 compression ratio, a dual-ram breathing apparatus, and a more voluminous free-flow exhaust system. As a result of these changes, the peak power output increased by 25 bhp, and the engine develops maximum torque at 3750 rpm instead of 3900 rpm.

The E50 can accelerate from 0 to 62 mph in 6.2 seconds and reaches an electronically limited top speed of 156 mph. According to AMG, it is thus 0.5 second quicker off the mark than the E500. According to the original Mercedes press kit, however, the 500E (as it was initially called) could do the same job in an even more impressive 6.1 seconds. It's either a case of post-production geriatrics or AMG's stopwatch being on steroids. Fortunately, there is no argument about the fuel consumption, which averages 19.6 mpg on the European cycle, an 8.4 percent improvement over the E500. Predictably, the car ignored this environmentally friendly target under hard testing. Our E50

returned 10.2 mpg, indicating a tight driving range of just over 200 miles.

The most convincing single feature of the E50 is its totally redesigned braking system. The deceleration of early 500Es never matched the brilliance of their acceleration, but the new model stops with vigor and surprising stamina. Producing up to 1.2 g, the four discs give a riveting performance that is virtually immune to pressure. Although the rear brakes stem from the SL600, the ones up front have been developed from scratch. A fixed-caliper twin-piston setup was chosen to reduce the brake-fluid temperature, thereby cutting fade to a bare minimum. Also new are the so-called floating discs. Providing a 26 percent larger swept area, they consist of a cast iron rotor mated to a light aluminum chamber via twelve steel pins. This race-proven technology not only copes remarkably well with the high thermic stress, it also virtually eliminates shudder, undue noise, and excessive wear.

The good, the fad, and the ugly: The beautiful black bird's-eye maple in the E50's doors and dash is set off by an unappealing concession to Swabian fad. A deluxe interior nonetheless.

The other big advantage the E50 enjoys over the E500 is the truly astonishing ride comfort. At low speeds in particular, the new double-wishbone front suspension reacts much more smoothly to expansion joints, potholes, and patchwork tarmac than the defunct spring/strut layout. Despite the low-profile tires (265/35ZR-18 in the rear), the bratwurst-sized anti-roll bars, and the stout springs, the top-of-the-line E-class rides with amazing compliance. However, the gas-pressure shock absorbers permit too much horizontal travel and don't always tie the body down in time for the next corner. Although maintaining decent directional stability is often a problem for sporty cars shod with XXL tires, the E50 tracks like a bullet, and it won't

tramline under braking unless it gets caught in deep longitudinal grooves.

The 347-bhp engine is mated to a newly developed five-speed automatic transmission with a sport-mode selector. Between 3000 and 5000 rpm, the gearbox doesn't always know whether to change down one gear or two, and on certain road profiles it also loves slipping from fourth into fifth and back. Having said that, one cannot but praise the transmission for its quick action, smooth up- and downshifts, and sense for holding a given gear when required. Despite the trick electronics, it makes sense to lock out fifth on country roads and to slip into third for any serious switchbacks. Atypical for Mercedes, the throttle response is immediate, and the pedal travel is commendably short.

The matte monoblock AMG wheels are a nice design, but the reworked front and rear bumpers are a little loud and the contoured sill extensions are downright tacky. It must be said, though, that these aerodynamic modifications help reduce axle lift by ten percent, and they are also said to be responsible for keeping the drag figure at a low 0.28. Inside, the E50 typifies modern Swabian baroque. The black bird's-eye

maple looks quite tasteful, but the contrasting leather (gray, silver, blue, or green) on the seats, the door panels, and the steering wheel doesn't. As one would expect from a car costing $100,000, the standard-equipment list was compiled in paradise. It includes every conceivable extra plus a handful of offbeat goodies like three remote-control rear headrests; side air bags up front; wipers activated by rain sensors; gas-discharge headlamps; memory seats, mirrors, and steering wheel; and a particularly sensitive anti-theft device that even objects to the car being towed.

In about two years, the E50 AMG will face stiff competition from the upcoming V-8–engined BMW M5 and the brand-new 330-bhp Audi S8. For the time being, however, the son of the legendary Hammer offers an unbeatable blend of speed and safety. You cannot currently buy it in the States, but Mercedes-Benz of North America wants to sell it here when the C36 is discontinued, so we are likely to see it in 1997 as a 1998 model. Americans might also be offered the next-generation model —badged E55—which will boast an even more powerful 375-plus-bhp, 5.5-liter engine and an uprated chassis equipped

with the clever electronic stability program (ESP) and advanced active damping system (ADS). If there is ever going to be an Überhammer, this will be it. ⬤

MERCEDES-BENZ E50 AMG
Front-engine, rear-wheel-drive sedan
5-passenger, 4-door steel body
Base price (in Germany) $98,900/price as tested
  (in Germany) $103,360

POWERTRAIN:
32-valve DOHC V-8, 303 cu in (4973 cc)
Power DIN 347 bhp @ 5750 rpm
Torque DIN 347 lb-ft @ 3750 rpm
5-speed automatic transmission

CHASSIS:
Independent front and rear suspension
Variable-power-assisted rack-and-pinion steering
Vented front and rear disc brakes
Anti-lock system
235/40ZR-18 front, 265/35ZR-18 rear Bridgestone
  Expedia S-02 tires

MEASUREMENTS:
Wheelbase 111.5 in
Length x width x height 188.7 x 70.8 x 55.5 in
Curb weight 3850 lb

PERFORMANCE (manufacturer's data):
0–62 mph in 6.2 sec
Top speed (electronically limited) 156 mph
European-cycle fuel economy 19.6 mpg

COMPETITORS:
Audi S8 4.2
Jaguar XJR
Maserati Quattroporte

firststeer

Tel. 071-738

100'S
OF VINYLS
TO CHOOSE FROM

N312 WVV

Muscle Merc

Just over a year ago I was thundering round the Nurburgring in a Mercedes E500 in hot pursuit of a BMW M5 and a Jaguar XJR. The Merc might not have been a match for the Beemer or Jag in terms of outright speed or handling, but its wide-bodied touring car styling and unbeatable Autobahn stability were mighty impressive.

Now, sadly, the E500 is no more (as, indeed, is the M5). But Mercedes, with the help of tuning firm and racing car builder AMG, has come up with a suitable replacement – actually two replacements. For Germany there's the E50 with five litres and 347bhp of V8 power and, for us Britishers, the E36.

Mercedes says it's not worth the cost of converting V8 E-Classes to right-hand drive; the market is too small. We don't get the V8 E420 either.

But you needn't worry about being under-endowed. Despite having just six cylinders and 3,606cc, the engine does sterling service. There's 272bhp at 5,500rpm and 284lb ft of torque at 4,250rpm. Even coupled to the standard four-speed automatic gearbox (there's no manual option), it turned in an impressive performance at a rain-soaked Millbrook test track.

With the ASR traction control on, it stomped to 60mph in 6.6 seconds and passed the 100mph mark in 16.1 seconds. Like all its high performance models, Mercedes has limited the E36 to 155mph but on the tyre-scrubbing high speed bowl we fell a bit short at 152.1mph. Given a straight enough,

long enough stretch of road, I'm quite sure the E36 would bounce merrily off its limiter. It didn't feel as solid at high speed as the E500, though.

Straight line performance, then, is unquestionably impressive, but the way the car gets there is a little less so. The problem lies with the pedals and the auto gearbox. The accelerator travel is ludicrously long and its action is stiff. You have to push beyond what seems to be the end of the pedal's reach to operate the kickdown switch so that the gearbox won't change up until maximum revs. The same method is needed for speedy overtaking to ensure the gearbox drops down a gear or two.

And when you're not in a hurry the pedal action makes driving smoothly very tricky. Too gently on the accelerator and you sit still while the torque converter winds up. Too hard and you lurch off with the traction control light flashing. The gearchanges aren't exactly seamless going up, even under part throttle, and should you trigger the kickdown, the change comes in with a jolt. The brakes, though powerful, take a firm push and grab just before you stop, which means another jolt.

It's not the most refined Mercedes, but if it's refinement you want you don't buy a car that lets out an almighty 'vwoaaar!' when you plant the pedal. Or a car that runs on 18-inch alloy wheels with ultra low-profile Dunlop tyres, that has lowered, stiffened suspension and a deep spoiler.

Despite the body mods, the E36 is still understated compared to the old DTM-styled E500 – too understated.

At £53,400 the E36 is £16,600 more than the E320 Avantgarde on which it's based. Park the two side by side (which we did) and it's not at all obvious where the money has gone.

Standard equipment is the same, too; you get ABS, double airbags, traction control, remote locking/immobiliser, power steering and an electric roof.

The grey and black interior is smart, well designed and up to the usual standard, but the flat, hard seats don't match the car's sporty nature. They don't support you when cornering – a trick the E36 does rather well. Whilst it can't match a 5-Series, the AMG does have well-sorted steering (though an oversized wheel) and the stiff suspension keeps it fairly flat in bends.

When the grip eventually runs out, the nose runs wide. Persevere with the power and you might get a twitch from the rear before the yellow ASR traction control light flashes and the car gets back on track. But the no-funmeisters haven't been allowed to have it all their own way. Unlike most Mercs, the ASR can be switched off – almost. A certain amount of wheelspin is allowed (enough for power oversteer out of a corner) before the system tells you to behave. So you can have fun without much risk of turning your E36 into a 60 grand hedge trimmer.

There's also little risk of finding another E36 in the company car park as Mercedes is only bringing in ten a month. It's just a shame it doesn't look more exclusive □

Story: Nik Berg
Photography: Paul Debois

FACT FILE	
Model	four-door super saloon
Engine	3.6-litre, six cyl, 24v
Power	272bhp @ 5,500rpm
Torque	284lb ft @ 4,250rpm
Transmission	four-speed auto/rear drive
Suspension	f: dbl wishbones r: multi-link
Brakes	discs, ABS
Wheels, Tyres	8Jx18, 235/40ZR18
0-60mph (secs)	6.6
0-100mph (secs)	16.1
30-50mph (secs)	2.4
50-70mph (secs)	3.2
Top speed (mph)	152.1
Braking 70-0mph (m)	54.2
Euromix mpg	26.3
Price (as tested)	£53,500 (£60,554)
Rivals	Jaguar XJR, Audi A8

PHOTOGRAPHS BY TIM ANDREW

DIFFERENT CLASS

THEY ARE BOTH SILVER, THEY ARE both Mercs and they both share a 3.6-litre six-cylinder AMG-tuned engine of about 280bhp. They are both fast. But they are not the same. The small one is the C36, Mercedes' BMW M3-chasing baby saloon, while the bigger car is the hot new version of the E-class, which replaces the highly specialised – and very expensive – left-hand-drive E500. The E500 has been replaced by the E50 in Germany (see *CAR*, April) but there was no time for AMG to convert it to right-hand drive before its motor gets a revamp in late '98. We *will* be getting that car, but

AMG's E36 is, on paper, largely similar to its C36. **RICHARD BREMNER** bids to separate these luxury hot-rods, and finds bigger to be substantially better

for now we must make do with the E36.

Not that you find yourself having to make do when you drive the E36, stop-gap special or not. This is one capable car, combining the roles of svelte grand tourer and, should the need arise, bounding, growling sports saloon. What does arise, after a short drive in this car, is not the *need* to go faster, but the desire, because it is just so damn good at it. Bang the transmission lever back into third, sink the accelerator and hear the honeyed hum of that straight-six spilling power to those fat rear wheels. Not that there's anything boisterous in its behaviour. Instead, a 284lb ft wave of torque al-

Don't get
hoodwinked
into thinking
these engines
are the same.
C (rear) is
tuned for
280bhp, eight
more than E

In both cars, auto-shift is a mismatch with gutsy, revvy motor. Grey-trimmed wheel in C (above) is a mismatch with anything bar a pair of grey slip-ons. Wet grip (far right) big on both cars

lows the E36 to gather speed with an authority suggesting that its mission is to travel at an absolute minimum of 80mph. All the time.

Of course, you can enjoy that same sensation for rather less than the £53,500 the E36 costs by ordering yourself a £42,050 C36 instead. As we've mentioned, it has the same tuned engine from AMG, and has also had its suspension lowered, its brakes upgraded and its wheel-arches filled with big wheels and corpulent rubber. So the recipe is the same. But the pot carrying it is not.

Clearly the bigger pot, the E-class pot, is roomier and has a more voluminous boot. You are not surprised to find an engine of 3.6 litres beneath its bonnet. It is, after all, a big car. By contrast, much of the appeal of the Mondeo-dimensioned C36 is that a 3.6-litre straight-six is not necessarily what you'd expect to find behind the grille. Three point six litres in this car is promisingly excessive.

But there's more to the story than this. Compare the weights of these two cars, and you discover that the E weighs but 80kg more than the C. That's about the weight of a passenger. Which is why Mercedes quotes the same 0-62mph time of 6.7 seconds for these cars. Near as damn it, they do the same job in the go department, despite the fact that there are slight differences in engine tune, caused by their necessarily different exhaust runs. The C36 musters 280bhp, the E36 272bhp, while both generate identical torque – 284lb ft – but at differing peaks, the smaller car over a span from 4000-4750rpm, the larger at 4250rpm.

In the end, the differences are piffling. Of more significance, and completely unexpected, is that it's the bigger car that feels the livelier. Why? Because it has a more responsive throttle. It must be something at the pedal end of the linkage, or the routing of the cable, because at the throttle-body end of the proceedings the linkages appear the same.

'While the E issues cultured, mellifluous tones, the C36 sounds harder-edged, raspier and ruder'

The E displays greater enthusiasm for cornering, too. Rack and pinion steering gear is the reason: this apparatus is more direct and more precise than Mercedes' traditional recirculating-ball system, with which the C is equipped. Even in the first mile, you notice that the E36 will scythe into bends with greater conviction than older examples of the breed. Including the C36.

Despite its compact dimensions, the smaller car just doesn't feel as wieldy as its big brother. The problem is largely down to the steering, which feels weighty but unconnected through its initial movement – although, once swivelled, the wheel provides greater precision than might have been expected. Another surprise is that the cars don't sound the same. While the E36 issues cultured, mellifluous tones, the C36 sounds harder-edged, raspier and ruder. What both have in common is power, and plenty of it, especially once the crank's spinning at 3500rpm or more, when the tachometer needle takes off with electrifying zeal.

But getting the best of it can be hard work because you're hampered by the auto box. Automatic this transmission is not. At first you will have been encouraged by the presence of a little button on the shift console marked 'S' and 'E'. 'Aha,' you will think, snicking the button into 'S', 'a sports gearshift management strategy – how very appropriate in so sporting a bolide.' But no. 'S', it turns out, is for standard, not sport, and 'E', as you might expect, is for economy, in which mode the box singlemindedly attempts to slip into top at the slightest opportunity. In 'S', the box can be roused from its torpor with a firm kicking from your right foot, but you still get the distinct impression that this transmission would rather be sludging about in a Stuttgart taxi. The answer is either to wait for next year's five-speed auto – sadly, for the C36 only – or palm the shiftlever about yourself.

E (left) wears its bodykit better than C. It's a more refined package all-round

The results of such armwork will be very satisfying, whichever Merc you're aboard. You get the most wonderful, rangey performance in third, terrific sprinting ability out of turns, and sufficient engine braking to make bounding between corners an extra-smooth, extra-satisfying sensation. To rocket out of really tight turns, you need to slip down another gear and get second, a policy that on wet roads will give the traction-control system you get as standard on the E36 some work to do.

The C36, as befits its slightly louder demeanour, comes with no such device, allowing you the odd tail-slide. If you want such excess in the E36, you can cut out the system with a stab of the ASR button. Great entertainment is guaranteed, although you shouldn't leave with the idea that these cars don't hang on in the rain because they do.

They're at their best in long sweepers, where they feel wonderfully settled, steer with satisfying accuracy and change direction with little of the unseemly body flop that lesser big cars would display. Again, it's the E36 that is most satisfying, mainly because it is the more fluent of the two.

The E scores over the C in other areas, too: its brakes feel firmer underfoot and are easier to modulate as a result, while its suspension swallows bumps with greater resolve and in greater silence.

Neither car rides with the pillowy imperturbability of a limo, not least because of those extra-low profile tyres. The wheels do much to announce that these are the sporting Mercedes saloons. But there are other, more minor (one hesitates to use the word subtle) artefacts to telegraph the message.

There is, for instance, a nasty piece of mock Kevlar plastered on the B-pillar of the E36, but that doesn't look half as crass as the mock Kevlar dominating the C's cabin. Decor like this leaves very little scope for the vulgarians who occasionally get hold of Mercs and dress them in the worst possible

SPECIFICATIONS

Model name	C36 AMG	E36 AMG
Price	£42,050	£53,500
Engine	3606cc 24V six	
Bore/stroke (mm)	91.0/92.4	
Compression (to one)	10.5	
Power (DIN/rpm)	280bhp/5750	272bhp/5500
Torque (DIN/rpm)	284lb ft/4000	284lb ft/4250
Specific output	78bhp per litre	75bhp per litre
Power-to-weight ratio	179bhp per tonne	166bhp per tonne
Transmission	Four-speed automatic, rwd	
Front suspension	Independent, double wishbones coil springs, anti-roll bar	
Rear suspension	Multi-link, coil springs, anti-roll bar	
Brakes	Discs, ventilated	
Tyres (front)	225/45 ZR17	235/40 ZR18
(rear)	245/40 ZR17	235/40 ZR18
Length/width/wheelbase	4487/1720/2690mm	4890/1799/2833mm
Weight	1560kg	1640kg
Maximum speed	155mph	155mph
0-62mph	6.7sec	6.7sec
Fuel consumption, mpg	25.7	26.1

'It's hard to shrug off the idea that the C36 AMG is a car aimed at well-to-do boys of width'

taste, so there's disappointment in store for them. They won't have to change the C's steering wheel, either, whose rim is part-covered in a sleeve of grey leather to contrast with the black. It's about as attractive as a pair of grey shoes. The E's cabin is more subdued and all the better for it, though not every owner will go for wood trim that looks like it spent half a day in a charcoal brazier before being varnished. But at least the steering wheel is subtle.

So is the E36's bodykit. You could almost call it tasteful, and that's a bit of a novelty for an AMG-tinselled Mercedes. Still, you spot a vestige of the past below the front bumper, where the chin spoiler is besmirched by a (tiny, fortuitously) AMG badge that must have cost at least five pfennigs to make.

Being older, the C36's sportswear is rather less successful, its sill extensions looking like the add-ons they are, even if the bumpers are reasonably attractive. And the little rubber eyebrows that cap the wheel-arches aren't unappealing, either. But it's hard to shrug off the idea that this is a car aimed at well-to-do boys of width.

The E36 is the better car, and not merely because it provides more room. It is, quite simply, a slightly more satisfying driver's car, concedes little in go to its smaller sibling, and is more refined to boot. But, there is the small matter of the £11,450 extra it costs over the C36, and the fact that for another £1495 (a mere nothing at this level) you can have a BMW M5 that is a second quicker to 60mph. Not much, you may say, but it is in percentage terms. And the C36, incidentally, costs £8000 more than the quicker BMW M3 that is very shortly to be replaced by a yet faster, and only slightly more expensive, version. This car does not represent value for money. But there is something very compelling about the combination of those sterling Mercedes qualities and the performance of a hot-rod. Especially at 6500rpm in third.

AMazingly Grunty

AMG Mercs haven't exactly been thick on the ground here in the UK. Tuned, fettled and largely assembled by the Mercedes-owned firm of AMG, these added-status Mercs first trickled into dealers in small numbers a couple of years ago.

Then you could choose between the C36, based on the C-Class, or the E36, a modified E-Class. As those numbers suggest, Mercedes didn't befuddle customers with a range of engines; both were ably powered by an AMG-tuned 276bhp 3.6-litre six-cylinder unit.

Not any more, for although the choice remains equally straightforward, both the C43 and E55 AMGs now flaunt brawny V8s of 4.3 and 5.5 litres respectively. Both engines are based on Mercedes' new 24-valve 279bhp E430 motor, although with AMG's atten-

tions both produce significantly more torque and horsepower than standard.

To elaborate slightly, the C43 is officially the first C-Class with a V8, and it replaces the C36, while the E55 technically replaces the E50. But the E50 wasn't sold in the UK so it could reasonably be argued that the E55

is an all-new model. Got that? Good.

So how do they go? Well, in the words of one senior official, AMG wanted to make the C43 'a real sports car' and in almost every respect they've succeeded. With a new double-fluted, enlarged intake system, long duration composite camshafts, new valve assem-

blies, new oil cooling and a new exhaust system with freer-flowing ceramic catalysts the C43 makes 306bhp. And while some cars have a torque curve resembling a Douglas Fir the C36's looks more like Ayers Rock with 302lb ft of torque spread all the way from 3,250 to 5,000rpm.

So in performance terms it's certainly 'a real sports car'. Given a sufficiently hefty right foot 0-62mph takes as little as 6.5 seconds while top speed remains limited at 155mph. Accompanying this is the subdued but beautifully mellow bellow of the V8's twin exhausts.

The chassis lives up to the sports car tag too. Starting with Mercedes' Sports suspension package the C43 has stiffer anti-roll bars and springs and special gas-filled dampers. Run on low-profile tyres and connected to the ESP handling control system, the result is a car that has a firm but decent ride and is

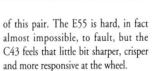

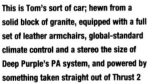

This is Tom's sort of car; hewn from a solid block of granite, equipped with a full set of leather armchairs, global-standard climate control and a stereo the size of Deep Purple's PA system, and powered by something taken straight out of Thrust 2

very unlikely to lose grip on a dry road unless there's a either a talented stunt driver or a complete idiot at the wheel.

Taut steering helps the C43's surprising manoeuvrability and gives the driver a real at-one feeling on a twisting road, as do the superbly supportive sports seats and just-so driving position.

Where the C43 falls short of being a 'real sports car' is in the transmission. Many would argue, and I'm one of them, that the words 'auto' and 'sports car' go together like Pernod and Worcester Sauce. The C43's E-Class five-speed transmission has been adapted by AMG for a sportier driving style, but many times, on a test drive dominated by an endless succession of hairpin bends, the transmission-induced delay between pedal and power was irritating. Exacerbating this was the ESP which, despite an on/off switch, never fully relinquishes its duties and

still further confuses the transmission's brain, so further diminishing a true 'sports car' driving experience. Shame.

Before stepping into the mighty E55 I'd imagined it to be a larger, heavier, more muscular animal than the C43, but being pretty similar to drive. I was wrong. It is larger both inside and out, it's heavier by 140kgs and yes, it's more powerful – 354bhp and a mountain of low-rev torque see to that. But the E55 is very different on the road.

For a start the beefy engine and exhaust is all but inaudible from inside the climate-controlled cabin. The ride, even on poor roads, remains excellent and despite low-profile tyres it borders on the magical on a smooth surface.

Although there's still bundles of grip, tireless brakes and decadent performance – it's nearly a second quicker than its little brother from 0-62mph – the smaller C43 emerges as the sportier

of this pair. The E55 is hard, in fact almost impossible, to fault, but the C43 feels that little bit sharper, crisper and more responsive at the wheel.

But where the E55 really shines is out on the open road. It's a 'bahnstormer par excellence. The E55 has the continent-crossing prowess of a light aircraft. It will rumble from Calais to Cannes in less time than it takes others to crawl from Putney to Piccadilly, and with a lot less fuss and a mansion more comfort. What's more, with a phone fitted it has no less than 95 switches and buttons to keep one amused.

But though both new AMGs are eminently proficient, exclusive and every bit as well-built and reliable as a standard Merc, they face powerful competition from Audi, BMW and Jaguar. In the end, your choice will very probably boil down to which badge you prefer, where your personal

loyalties lie and of course whether you want to change gear. Or possibly whether you have a lot of stuff to carry, for, uniquely, both these AMGs will also be available in estate form. Ideal for the over-luggaged lottery-winner □

Story: Tom Stewart
Photography: Ian Dawson

FAC43 FILE	
Model	four-door saloon, five-door estate
Engine	4,266cc, V8, 24v
Performance	0-62 6.5secs, 155mph max
Price	approx £45,000
On sale in UK	Feb '98
Rivals	Audi S4, BMW M3, Jag XJ8 4.0

FACT FILE55	
Model	four-door saloon, five-door estate
Engine	5,439cc, V8, 24v
Performance	0-62 5.7secs, 155mph max
Price	approx £65,000
On sale in UK	April '98
Rivals	Audi S8, Jag XJR, Daimler Super V8

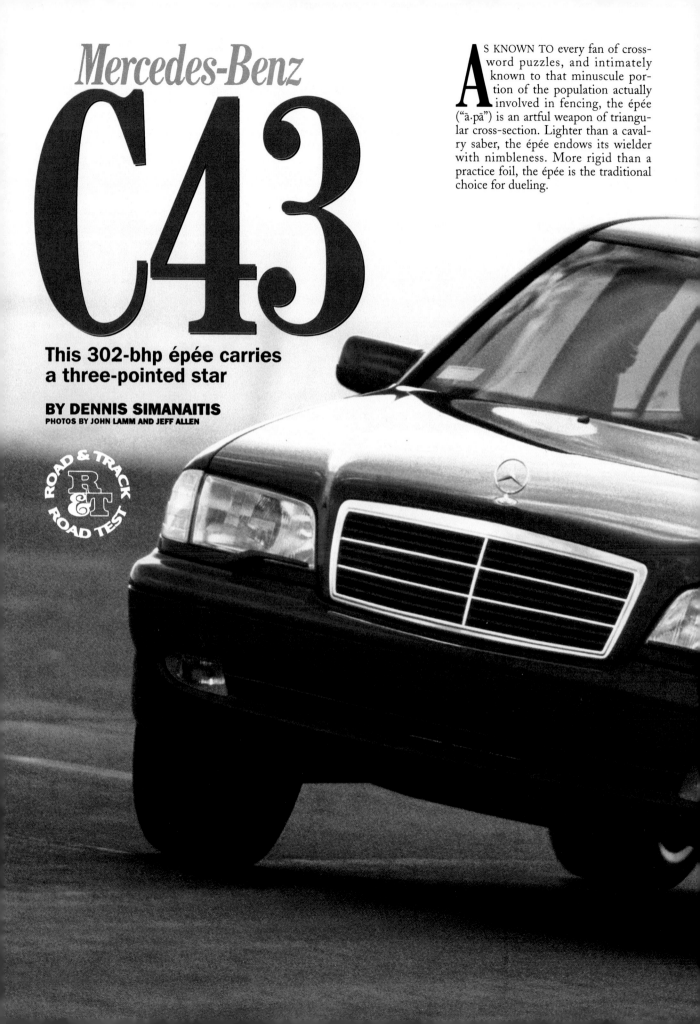

Mercedes-Benz

C43

This 302-bhp épée carries a three-pointed star

BY DENNIS SIMANAITIS
PHOTOS BY JOHN LAMM AND JEFF ALLEN

ROAD & TRACK
ROAD TEST

A S KNOWN TO every fan of crossword puzzles, and intimately known to that minuscule portion of the population actually involved in fencing, the épée ("ā·pā") is an artful weapon of triangular cross-section. Lighter than a cavalry saber, the épée endows its wielder with nimbleness. More rigid than a practice foil, the épée is the traditional choice for dueling.

With this in mind, think of the newly introduced C43 as a 302-bhp épée carrying the Mercedes-Benz three-pointed star.

I'm not exactly into fencing, you understand. But I appreciate its blend of grace, agility and strength. And I recognize a proper automotive analogy when I drive it.

The idea of such a factory hot rod is straightforward and particularly appealing to enthusiasts: Take an elegant sedan, have a talented tuner stuff in the largest V-8 that'll fit, and upgrade hardware appropriately. In this case, the elegant sedan is the Mercedes-Benz C-Class. The talented tuner is AMG, with whom Mercedes-Benz had earlier established joint ventures. And the V-8 is Stuttgart's new-generation all-aluminum powerplant, first seen over here in the larger E430 and appearing this fall in the CLK430 coupe and ML430 sport utility.

The C43 ups the power ante on the C36, an earlier Mercedes/AMG delight. Check out our February 1995 test and you'll learn the C36 was powered by the Mercedes 268-bhp inline-6 and bore an as-tested price of $55,815. Our 1998 C43 has 2 more cylinders, coincidentally the same number of valves (24), 34 more horsepower—and costs $55,880.

In standard form, the 4.3-liter V-8 produces 275 bhp and 295 lb.-ft. of torque. But a trip to AMG's Affalterbach facility affords this powerplant its modified intake hardware, high-pressure lubrication (via oil jets beneath the pistons), stronger valve springs and new, lighter camshafts. These last are of modular fabrication, their more aggressive cam lobes forged individually and then affixed to the camshaft. Retained is the V-8's twin-spark-plug/3-valve configuration.

Efficacy of these modifications is in the C43's enhanced specifications. Power rises to 302 bhp at 5,850 rpm and torque expands to 302 lb.-ft. across a broad range from 3,250 to 5,000 rpm. The car's adaptive-shifting 5-speed automatic, the only gearbox offered, is a high-torque-capacity unit shared with the Merce-des 5.0

liter V-8s and 6.0-liter V-12s.

I surely didn't miss any manual gearbox, as the C43 combination is so extremely well matched and so in tune with the car's character. Barely audible at cruise, the AMG exhaust gives a proper V-8 blat on mild acceleration, the engine's mechanical purrs and whirs becoming evident when pushed. Shifts are torque-controlled marvels, but with an enthusiast-gratifying sense of urgency.

Summon this sense of urgency from a standing start and you'll see 60 mph in as little as 5.9 seconds. Pursue matters—conditions permitting this, of course—and you'll cover a quarter mile in 14.4 sec. at 98.5 mph. And, if there's an *Autobahn* around (lucky you!), the C43 is capable of continuing on up to an electronically limited and politically correct 155 mph.

Reflecting its German heritage, the C43 will be stable at whatever speed you choose. What's more, I found it to be a remarkably quiet place at elevated velocity, albeit somewhat less than its stated top speed. Exploiting Arizona's 75-mph Interstate limit—I confess, maybe "exploiting" isn't precisely the word—I could carry on normal conversation with my passenger or enjoy the standard Bose AM/FM/cassette system, even with the sunroof opened.

Alas, I wasn't able to enjoy the Wagner, Rasputina or Amédée Breaux I had brought along, as our particular test car was not fitted with the 6-disc CD player, optionally teamed with a choice of integrated mobile ($1,495) or portable ($1,895) cell phone. More's the pity, as I for one would gladly swap the standard 10-way power, high-bolstered, heated sport seats for a standard CD slot.

Another noteworthy aspect of the C43 is its handling and ride; the latter all the more exemplary when you consider the car's modifications in the interest of high performance. The coil springs that AMG specifies for the C-Class double-A-arm/5-link layout are 24 percent stiffer up front and 12 per-

■ The AMG logo implies an enhancement of V-8 power to 302 bhp and a 302-lb.-ft. torque curve that's really a torque straight, from 3,250 to 5,000 rpm. The three-pointed-star logo implies that all this performance is combined with bank-vault durability. Only 500 C43s will come to the U.S. each year.

THE COMPETITION

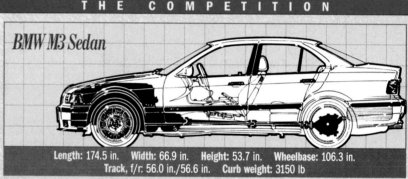

BMW M3 Sedan

Length: 174.5 in. Width: 66.9 in. Height: 53.7 in. Wheelbase: 106.3 in.
Track, f/r: 56.0 in./56.6 in. Curb weight: 3150 lb

■ The fencing foil of our trio, the M3 is the lightest, smallest, quickest, best handling, least expensive—and the only one available with a manual gearbox. In fact, one might argue that it's actually a half-notch over from these other two. On the other hand, the 3 Series 4-door is roomy and comfortable too, giving little away to the C43 in this regard. Some find its styling a bit dated; others appreciate this most traditional of high-performance sedans from the Bavarians who made the concept a viable one. *(Tested: 5/97)*

Current list price	$40,270
Engine	dohc 3.2-liter inline-6
Horsepower	240 bhp @ 6000 rpm
Torque	236 lb-ft @ 3800 rpm
Transmission	5-speed manual
0–60 mph	5.6 sec
Braking, 60–0 mph	114 ft
Lateral accel (200-ft skidpad)	0.91g
EPA city/highway	20/28 mpg

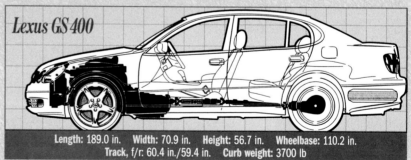

Lexus GS 400

Length: 189.0 in. Width: 70.9 in. Height: 56.7 in. Wheelbase: 110.2 in.
Track, f/r: 60.4 in./59.4 in. Curb weight: 3700 lb

■ The saber of our trio, the GS 400 is the largest and heaviest. In fact, it bridges a gap in past comparisons, competing admirably against larger models from Munich and Stuttgart. The GS 400 is the most controversial as well. Some find its styling avant-garde; others term it ungainly. Its interior is equally unorthodox, even to the pushbutton-progressive option of its 5-speed automatic. There's no mistaking its high-performance intent, however: 300 bhp and scathing acceleration attest to it clearly. *(Tested: 10/97)*

Current list price	$44,800
Engine	dohc 4.0-liter V-8
Horsepower	300 bhp @ 6000 rpm
Torque	310 lb-ft @ 4400 rpm
Transmission	5-speed automatic
0–60 mph	6.1 sec
Braking, 60–0 mph	122 ft
Lateral accel (200-ft skidpad)	0.83g
EPA city/highway	17/23 mpg

1998 Mercedes-Benz C43

IMPORTER

Mercedes-Benz of North America, Inc.
One Mercedes Drive
Montvale, N.J. 07645-0350

PRICE

List price	**$52,750**
Price as tested	**$55,880**

Price as tested includes std equip. (dual airbags, side airbags, ASR, ESP, AM/FM stereo/cassette, air cond, 10-way adj heated seats; pwr windows, heated mirrors, remote locking; retract. headrests, sunroof), Xenon headlights ($960), headlight washers ($340), luxury tax ($1235), dest charge ($595).

0–60 mph	**5.9 sec**
0–¼ mi	**14.4 sec**
Top speed	**est 155 mph***
Skidpad	**0.84g**
Slalom	**62.7 mph**
Brake rating	**excellent**

TEST CONDITIONS

Temperature	72° F
Wind	moderate
Humidity	24%
Elevation	1010 ft

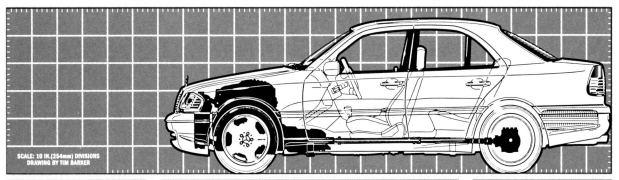

SCALE: 10 IN.(254mm) DIVISIONS
DRAWING BY TIM BARKER

ENGINE

Type	aluminum block and heads, **V-8**
Valvetrain	sohc 3 valve/cyl
Displacement	260 cu in./4266 cc
Bore x stroke	3.54 x 3.30 in./ 89.9 x 84.0 mm
Compression ratio	11.0:1

Horsepower

(SAE)	**302 bhp @ 5850 rpm**
Bhp/liter	70.8
Torque	**302 lb-ft @ 3250–5000 rpm**
Maximum engine speed	6000 rpm
Fuel injection	Motronic ME 2.0 elect. sequential port
Fuel	prem unleaded, 91 pump oct

CHASSIS & BODY

Layout	**front engine/rear drive**
Body/frame	unit steel

Brakes

Front	**13.2-in. vented discs**
Rear	**11.8-in. vented discs**
Assist type	vacuum; ABS
Total swept area	583 sq in.
Swept area/ton	345 sq in.
Wheels	AMG alloy; **17 x 7½ f, 17 x 8½ r**
Tires	Michelin Pilot SX MXX3; **225/45ZR-17 f, 245/40ZR-17 r**
Steering	**recirculating ball,** vari power assist
Overall ratio	15.4:1
Turns, lock to lock	3.0
Turning circle	35.2 ft

Suspension

Front	**upper and lower A-arms,** coil springs, tube shocks, anti-roll bar
Rear	**5-link,** coil springs, tube shocks, anti-roll bar

DRIVETRAIN

Transmission	**5-speed automatic**

Gear	Ratio	Overall ratio	(Rpm)	Mph
1st	3.59:1	11.02:1	(6100)	37
2nd	2.19:1	6.72:1	(6100)	61
3rd	1.41:1	4.33:1	(6100)	94
4th	1.00:1	3.07:1	(6100)	133
5th	0.83:1	2.55:1	est (5680)	155*

Final drive ratio	3.07:1
Engine rpm @ 60 mph in 5th	2200

*Electronically limited.

GENERAL DATA

Curb weight	**3380 lb**
Test weight	3560 lb
Weight dist (with driver), f/r, %	57/43
Wheelbase	105.9 in.
Track, f/r	62.6 in./58.4 in.
Length	**177.4 in.**
Width	**67.7 in.**
Height	**56.1 in.**
Ground clearance	6.5 in.
Trunk space	16.5 + 6.7 cu ft

MAINTENANCE

Oil/filter change	variable (see text)
Tuneup	100,000 mi
Basic warranty	48 mo/50,000 mi

ACCOMMODATIONS

Seating capacity	**5**
Head room, f/r	38.0 in./36.0 in.
Seat width, f/r	2 x 19.5 in./54.0 in.
Front-seat leg room	46.0 in.
Rear-seat knee room	20.0 in.
Seatback adjustment	80 deg
Seat travel	11.5 in.

INTERIOR NOISE

Idle in neutral	46 dBA
Maximum in 1st gear	76 dBA
Constant 50 mph	68 dBA
70 mph	71 dBA

INSTRUMENTATION

160-mph speedometer, 7000-rpm tach, coolant temp, fuel level

ACCELERATION

Time to speed	Seconds
0–30 mph	2.3
0–40 mph	3.3
0–50 mph	4.5
0–60 mph	5.9
0–70 mph	7.6
0–80 mph	9.7
0–90 mph	12.1
0–100 mph	14.9

Time to distance	
0–100 ft	3.1
0–500 ft	7.9
0–1320 ft (¼ mi): 14.4 sec @ 98.5 mph	

FUEL ECONOMY

Normal driving	est 21.0 mpg
EPA city/highway	17/22 mpg
Cruise range	est 323 miles
Fuel capacity	16.4 gal.

BRAKING

Minimum stopping distance

From 60 mph	123 ft
From 80 mph	219 ft
Control	excellent
Pedal effort for 0.5g stop	na
Fade, effort after six 0.5g stops from 60 mph	na
Brake feel	very good
Overall brake rating	excellent

HANDLING

Lateral accel (200-ft skidpad)	0.84g
Balance	heavy understeer
Speed thru 700-ft slalom	62.7 mph
Balance	moderate understeer
Lateral seat support	excellent

Test Notes...

■ Through the slalom, the C43 drifts very easily but never feels as if it's a steering-wheel crank or a throttle blip away from being back under complete control.

■ Around the skidpad, the C43's big V-8 creates heavy understeer at steady throttle, but lift off the throttle, and chassis dynamics easily rotate the car.

■ Despite the C43's power and acceleration skills, at idle, it's relatively quiet at 46 dBA. Only under full throttle does the otherwise M-B silent C43 really growl.

Subjective ratings consist of excellent, very good, good, average, poor; na means information is not available.

cent stiffer in the rear, compared with those on the C36; the latter, already a sporty package. Shock absorber calibrations are stiffer as well, with 20 percent more rebound control in front and 8 percent greater rebound damping in the rear.

Add to this ultra-low-profile Michelin Pilot SX MXX3 tires: 225/45ZR-17s in front, 245/40ZR-17s at the rear.

In an earlier age—eons ago in tire technology, like maybe 1993—such a suspension would have handled like crazy, but jiggled you to death on anything rougher than a billiard table. Today, the C43 has a subtle snubbed feel, on any surface, with nary a discomfort.

Amazing.

And, in truth, shock absorbers of innovative character deserve part of the credit. Now that you finally understand what "progressive" shock absorbers do, forget it. For these owe their ride-enhancing control to *digressive* operation. That is, they react to high-frequency disturbances, tar strips, for instance, with peak-enveloping softness. Yet, when confronted by low-frequency changes—whether road- or vehicle-dynamics-induced—their response stiffens to give a firm stance and eliminate any potential float.

Confidence in this handling gets a mixed enhancement of ASR traction control integrated in the standard-equipment ESP Electronic Stability Program. I say "mixed," as I'm still uncertain whether these devices simply give the average driver a higher-speed accident when he finally overcooks it. On the other hand, I can report that ESP worked in exemplary fashion when I encountered El Niño-inspired rain/hail/snow as I gained elevation along Arizona's Mogollon Rim.

And, if I'm feeling all that snooty about it, I can click ESP off. However, this dashboard switch affects only the throttle aspects of ASR/ESP; brake interventions still occur in the interest of directional stability.

In our slalom, we recorded a speed of 62.7 mph in weaving from cone to cone; and I suspect our Road Test Editor, Kim Reynolds, wouldn't have minded ESP on or off. Around the skidpad, our 0.84g was influenced by the C43 knowing better than we did which way it wanted to point.

There's still that icy road down from Strawberry, Arizona, however.

FSS, Mercedes' Flexible Service System, is another standard-equipment gizmo that shows promise. An oil-change-interval analyzer, it's unique in that it gets information from a dielectric sensor that identifies the amount and type of contaminants in the oilpan. This and other monitored criteria dictate oil-change intervals from 10,000 to 20,000 miles, depending on use and contaminant levels.

As you might gather, I found the C43 to be what I term a "feel-good" car. For as long as I owned (for many, leased) the C43, I'd derive pleasure from its handsome set of black-on-white gauges, their AMG logo reminding me that this is no ordinary Mercedes. Yet, of course, it *is* a Mercedes, with all this implies about sturdiness, durability and resale value. And, with only a little self-consciousness, I'd derive pleasure as well from knowing to say "Ah Em Gay," for AMG.

The C43 enters that most rarefied of atmospheres, the hypersedan segment populated by the likes of the BMW M3 Sedan and Lexus GS 400, to name two cars of similar size and performance. And it does so in most rarefied numbers: Mercedes plans to produce only 6,000 C43s over three years; only 500 a year will be allotted to our market.

And once more that fencing analogy comes to mind. In a direct comparison, I suspect the M3 would feel—and indeed is—lighter; it's the fencer's foil. And without stretching our analogy too far, the GS 400 would seem to be the saber, larger and heavier, though no less purposeful.

The C43 is the épée, the one with the three-pointed star, and isn't there a traditional duel of quite another sort shaping up here? ⬡

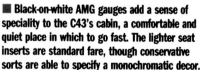

■ Black-on-white AMG gauges add a sense of speciality to the C43's cabin, a comfortable and quiet place in which to go fast. The lighter seat inserts are standard fare, though conservative sorts are able to specify a monochromatic decor.

MERCEDES-BENZ
C43 AMG

Herrsching, Germany—

Exit C36, enter C43. The new Mercedes AMG model is several thousand dollars more expensive, but it also has a lot more to offer—like a V-8 instead of a straight-six, a displacement of 4.3 liters instead of 3.6 liters, 302 bhp instead of 276, and an extra helping of midrange torque. The C43, which arrives Stateside this spring, is also even more generously equipped than the car it replaces. It has a new five-speed automatic transmission, the advanced ESP electronic stability program, and orthopedic electrically operated leather-trimmed sport seats.

Externally, the C43 is differentiated from lesser C-class models by its AMG monoblock alloy wheels and an AMG body kit featuring redesigned bumpers and sills. Inside, there's carbon fiber trim (U.S. models will have burled walnut), off-white bespoke AMG instruments, and a leather-wrapped sport steering wheel. It's a pleasant and purposeful driving environment that is more in sync with dynamic businessmen than with amateur racers.

To raise the power output of the twin-spark V-8 from 275 bhp (as in the E430) to 302 bhp, the engineers fitted hotter camshafts, a switchable intake plenum, larger-diameter inlet tracts, and a rerouted free-flow exhaust. The brawny and surprisingly vocal V-8 is mated to a five-speed automatic transmission that offers a choice of driving modes (economy, sport, and winter) as well as an adaptive shift pattern. The AMG suspension is notably tauter, lowering the ride height by an inch, and—together with the seventeen-inch wheels—also widening the track. The beefed-up brakes employ bigger vented two-piece discs.

The C43 does indeed decelerate with impressive determination and stamina. The recalibrated steering, however, is too heavy, too slow, and too Porsche 928–like to be truly inspiring. The dialogue between driver, engine, and transmission leaves something to be desired, too. Throttle lag is a problem; the engine takes a little too long to reinstate the torque flow when you step back on the gas. This fault is exacerbated by excessive throttle pedal travel, a slow kickdown action, and what appears to be a rather soft torque converter setup. Another factor that comes between you and unrestricted driving pleasure is the ESP. Although the throttle-control function of the electronic watchdog can be deactivated, the braking function remains active at all times, automatically applying the brakes to stop wheelspin.

The C43's natural territory, therefore, isn't a slow, tight corner. It prefers fast sweepers, challenging autobahn sections, and substandard surfaces that barely affect the supple, nicely balanced ride. The smooth-running (but thirsty) engine produces torque by the bagful, and the impressive urge continues throughout the 60-to-125-mph bracket because the transmission is so well geared. At all speeds and in all conditions, the Mercedes oozes competence, quality, and that trademark blend of comfort and safety. This is a wonderfully refined long-distance cruiser, a perfectly acceptable four-seater, and the number-one choice for performance-oriented customers who must have an automatic transmission. But the hefty premium charged for the AMG badge does stretch the friendship. —Georg Kacher

THE NUMBERS

On sale: spring 1998
Price: base (estimated) $55,000/as tested (estimated) $57,000
Engine: 32-valve DOHC V-8, 260 cu in (4266 cc)
Power SAE net 302 bhp @ 5850 rpm
Torque SAE net 303 lb-ft @ 3250 rpm

Mercedes-Benz
C43

MODEL TESTED C43 AMG **ON-ROAD PRICE** £47,640
TOP SPEED 156mph **0-60MPH** 6.4sec
30-70MPH 5.4sec **60-0MPH** 2.5sec **MPG** 21.1
FOR Performance, body control, discreet styling, V8 engine note
AGAINST Lofty price, high-speed tyre noise, firm low-speed ride

STAN PAPIOR

Buyers of compact super-saloons could be forgiven for feeling somewhat starved of choice recently. The genre-defining combination of supercar performance clothed in a prestigious four-seater body has hitherto been the preserve of just one car: the BMW M3.

But unrivalled success for the Munich manufacturer's iconic Q-car has spurred its rivals back into action. Although different in interpretation and execution, the Mercedes-Benz C43 AMG and Audi S4 have taken the fight to BMW. And as the saying goes, you've never had it so good. But while Audi struggles with production gremlins on the S4 (deliveries finally begin at the end of this month), Mercedes gets to take the first shot at the M3.

On sale now, the C43 costs an eye-watering £47,640, some £9220 more than the M3 coupe. Yet this has not prevented a typical Mercedes waiting list from developing, in this case six months long.

In return for your generosity and patience, Mercedes rewards with a potent and discreet package. The five-year-old C-class is clothed in a menacing AMG body kit. It won't have heads turning at every street corner, but those in the know will recognise it. Small side skirts, bigger front and rear bumpers, twin chromed tail pipes and 17in alloy wheels create the unique AMG signature. Inside, the AMG treatment extends to orange on white instruments and two-tone black and white leather for the seats and steering wheel. The seats themselves are unique to the C43 and feature a wealth of adjustable bolsters.

Changes out of sight are significantly more dramatic. Mercedes has broken with class tradition and abandoned six cylinders for a huge V8. In doing so, it's achieved a first for the genre. Out goes the

3.6-litre straight six that powered the previous C36 and in comes an AMG-tuned version of the new 4266cc V8 that powers the E430.

Thanks to AMG's efforts, the all-alloy 24-valve V8 now produces 306bhp at 5850rpm and 302lb ft of torque between 3250rpm and 5000rpm. That's 27bhp and 7lb ft up on standard E-class tune. It is sufficient to comfortably eclipse the 280bhp C36, although it's still 15bhp short of the M3 itself. As is usual even with AMG-tuned Mercs, the C43 is available only with Mercedes' own five-speed automatic gearbox. Yet that doesn't appear to stand in the way of rivetting performance figures.

We tested a left-hand-drive,

German-registered example in a group test in March. That car reached 60mph in 5.8sec and hit a top speed of 158mph. However, this right-hand-drive car struggled universally to match those times. The sprint to 60mph took 6.4sec (0.6sec slower than before and 1.1sec slower than an M3). To 100mph it fared no better: 15.2sec versus 14.1sec originally and 12.2sec for the six-speed manual M3. Flat out, it hit 156mph on the banking, 2mph slower than both the left-hand-drive model and the BMW. It doesn't matter where you look; this particular C43 doesn't match the car we tested previously on any count, even though the 30-70mph sprint is still mighty at 5.4sec.

Turn off the ESP traction control and the C43 is enormously adjustable

Mercedes claims there are no differences between UK and Continental C43s, and its own figures suggest the C43 reaches 60mph in 6.5sec. We can only conclude that the German test car was an exceptional example of the breed. But the records will remember this car to be a fraction slower than the previous C36.

Despite the raw figures, our car never felt short changed out on the road. The combination of a broad spread of torque and a supremely smooth adaptive automatic transmission means the Benz specialises in effortless muscle, not peaky top end power. As a result, the engine is even more usable than an M3's. But that's not to say the C43 lacks top end power. When

Cramped cabin not to everyone's taste, but boot is decent shape and size

required, the auto 'box seamlessly drops two or even three ratios in quick succession, allowing the driver to steal the last 500rpm before the 6200rpm red line, in the process launching the Mercedes past slower-moving traffic.

The performance is made all the more special by the C43's deliciously cultured V8 growl, which, though ever present, is sufficiently muted at cruising speeds to ensure that it is never intrusive. Only excessive road noise from the wide, low-profile tyres spoil the C43's otherwise excellent long-distance cruising ability. A maximum of 435 miles is possible between fills, based on our impressive touring route figure of 31.9mpg. Similarly, the 21.1mpg overall ◆

ENGINE

Layout 8 cyls in a vee, 4266cc
Max power 306bhp at 5850rpm
Max torque 302lb ft at 3250-5000rpm
Specific output 72bhp per litre
Power to weight 204bhp per tonne
Torque to weight 201lb ft per tonne
Installation Front, longitudinal, rear-wheel drive
Construction Aluminium alloy head/block
Bore/stroke 89.9/84.0mm
Valve gear 3 valves per cyl, sohc per bank
Compression ratio 10.0:1
Ignition and fuel Microprocessor-controlled engine management, HFM injection

GEARBOX

Type Five-speed automatic by Mercedes-Benz
Ratios/mph per 1000rpm
1st 3.59/6.7 **2nd** 2.19/10.9 **3rd** 1.41/17.0
4th 1.00/24.0 **5th** 0.83/28.8
Final drive ratio 3.07:1

MAXIMUM SPEEDS

5th 156mph/5420rpm **4th** 149/6200rpm
3rd 105/6200 **2nd** 68/6200 **1st** 42/6200

ACCELERATION FROM REST

True mph	sec	speedo mph
30	2.7	30
40	3.8	40
50	5.0	50
60	6.4	60
70	8.1	70
80	10.3	80
90	12.6	90
100	15.2	100

Standing qtr mile 14.9sec/99mph
Standing km 26.2sec/126mph
30-70mph through gears 5.4sec

ACCELERATION IN K'DOWN

mph	sec	gear
10-30	1.9	1st
20-40	2.0	1st
30-50	2.3	1st/2nd
40-60	2.6	1st/2nd
50-70	3.1	2nd/3rd
60-80	3.9	2nd/3rd
70-90	4.5	3rd
80-100	4.9	3rd

STEERING

Type Recirculating ball, power assisted
Turns lock to lock 3.4

CONTROLS IN DETAIL

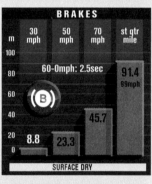

1 Climate control is standard although poor-sounding CD player is £185 option 2 Slick-shifting five-speed automatic offers choice of sport or winter modes 3 Supremely supportive seats have pneumatic adjustment which soon loses novelty value 4 Chunky wheel irritates some drivers intensely 5 Carbon fibre trim part of AMG treatment, as is two-tone leather 6 Traditional foot-operated parking brake released by hand

SUSPENSION

Front Double wishbones, coil springs over dampers, anti-roll bar
Rear Multi-link axle, coil springs over dampers, anti-roll bar

WHEELS & TYRES

Wheel size 7.5Jx17in (f), 8.5Jx17in (r)
Made of Cast alloy
Tyres 225/45 ZR17 (f), 245/40 ZR17 (r)

BRAKES

Front 334mm ventilated discs
Rear 300mm ventilated discs
Anti-lock Standard

BRAKES

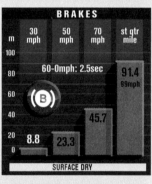

	30 mph	50 mph	70 mph	st qtr mile
	8.8	23.3	45.7	91.4 99mph

60-0mph: 2.5sec

SURFACE DRY

GEARING

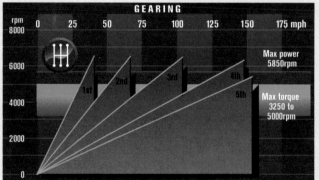

Max power 5850rpm
Max torque 3250 to 5000rpm

FUEL CONSUMPTION

TEST RESULTS

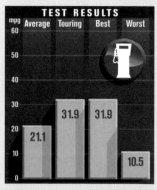

Average	Touring	Best	Worst
21.1	31.9	31.9	10.5

GOVERNMENT CLAIMS

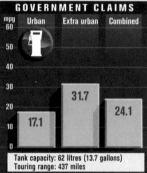

Urban	Extra urban	Combined
17.1	31.7	24.1

Tank capacity: 62 litres (13.7 gallons)
Touring range: 437 miles

NOISE

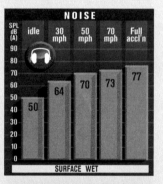

idle	30 mph	50 mph	70 mph	Full accl'n
50	64	70	73	77

SURFACE WET

LAYOUT

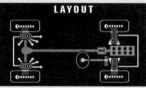

Body 4dr saloon **Front/rear tracks** 1509/1483mm **Turning circle** 10.7m **Min/max front leg room** 930/1140mm **Min/max rear leg room** 570/810mm **Front head room** 990mm **Rear head room** 910mm **Interior width front/rear** 1430/1420mm **Min/max boot width** 880/1520mm **Boot length** 1000mm **Boot height** 450mm **VDA boot volume** 430 litres/dm³ **Kerb weight** 1500kg **Weight distribution f/r** 56/44 per cent **Max payload** 400kg

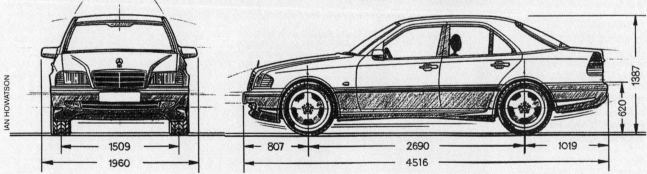

IAN HOWATSON

1509
1960

807   2690   1019
4516

1387
620

Uprated suspension gives tight body control with a firm but still comfortable ride. Tyre roar is excessive, though

Elsewhere, it is firm yet never uncomfortable and simply rides better the harder it is driven.

The rest of the C43 lives up to the usual high standards of a Mercedes-Benz. Peerless build quality, lots of badge prestige and high residual values are offset by that faintly ridiculous price. Naturally, exclusivity is guaranteed; just 240 C43s will be sold this year in Britain. But the £9000 price premium over the M3 and an £11,000 premium over the Audi S4 is still difficult to swallow. Particularly when the M3 is faster and more agile, and the S4 offers four-wheel drive and almost as much power.

♦ figure is an encouraging result considering the engine capacity and number of cylinders. It places the C43 between the S4 (19.6mpg) and M3 (23.6mpg) in real terms.

If anything, the Mercedes stops even more impressively than it goes. Huge ventilated discs (334mm at the front and 300mm at the rear) provide exceptional fade-free stopping power, although the brake pedal's lack of initial bite makes low-speed braking difficult to moderate smoothly. Despite this, there is no doubting the system's efficiency; 60-0mph took just 2.5sec, matching a Ferrari 550 Maranello. Mercedes' novel Brake Assist system contributes further to the result on the road, activating maximum braking power before the pedal even reaches full travel if it detects the driver is in an emergency braking scenario.

AMG-tweaked V8 good for 306bhp

Side skirts, 17in alloys and badges are subtle pointers to C43's potential

However, the C43 must offer more than decent straight-line performance and outstanding brakes in order to mount a credible challenge to the M3. In most areas it does just that, especially in the dry. On a dry day it can be driven confidently at speed thanks to outstanding body control and well-judged damping. High levels of adhesion help further, due mainly to the large Michelin MXXV tyres (225/45 at the front and 245/40 at the rear).

Although the recirculating ball steering lacks the crispness of an M3's rack and pinion

helm, the C43 is friendly and even adjustable when the ESP traction control is turned off via a switch on the dashboard. But only the brave or the talented should consider such actions in the wet. The C43's combination of over 300lb ft with rear-wheel drive demands respect, and the flashing amber warning light signalling the electronic intervention of ESP is often welcome.

The C43 even maintains a decent ride quality. Any harshness expected as a result of the superb body control only makes itself felt at low speeds.

But to view the C43 in such an objective fashion is to miss the point somewhat. Highly similar on paper to its rivals, the C43 plays a subtly different tune. With effortless, laid-back V8 character and discreet styling, the Mercedes pulls heart strings that the average M3 driver will only partially understand. Or even wish to, for that matter. But for those looking for the traditional super-saloon blend of power, performance and prestige without shouting it out to all around, the C43 is intoxicatingly effective.

WHAT IT COSTS

On-road price		£47,640
Total as tested		£48,476
Cost per mile		101.7p
EQUIPMENT		
(**bold** = options fitted to test car)		
Automatic transmission		●
Cruise control		●
Anti-lock brakes/Brake Assist		●/●
Airbag driver/passenger/side		●/●/●
RDS radio/CD player		●/£185
Climate control		●
Leather upholstery		●
Metallic paint		£651
Electric/heated front seats		●/●
● standard – not available		
INSURANCE		
Group		20
Typical quote		£1215
WARRANTY		
1 year/unlimited miles, 1 year anti-corrosion, 12 months free recovery		
SERVICING		
Interim 6000 miles, 1.5 hours, £7.49		
Major 12,000 miles, 2.5 hours, £24.50		
Max service cost £781		

C43 is the thinking man's M3 ★★★★

Grip is impressive in dry thanks to wide, low-profile rubber, but steering lacks crispness

CLK-GTR = Mac F1 x 2

Apparently, it makes the McLaren F1 look boring, but then again it costs twice as much. Welcome to the world's least logical road car

TOLD MY WIFE I WAS GOING to drive the Mercedes-Benz CLK-GTR the other day. 'Oh really, what's that?' she asked.

'Oh, you know: 200mph road-going Le Mans racer that costs £1.1 million,' I said.

'That'll be nice then,' she said. Nothing. Not a flicker.

'And then I'm going to fly the Space Shuttle,' I added.

'Lovely.'

That's the problem with your million-pound supercars. Like light

at the far end of the spectrum, they're so extreme they're invisible to the human eye. Compare it with a mere £150,000 supercar – you might not be able to afford one, but it is at least possible to *aspire* to a Ferrari. But a McLaren F1? Even if I could afford it I couldn't afford it.

And they don't get any more extreme than the 612bhp V12 CLK-GTR. This is now the most expensive production car in the world – 'production' meaning they'll build 25 (or AMG will,

although as of January, Mercedes will own AMG); 'expensive' meaning DM2,650,000 plus taxes. That's £1.1 million in the UK – more or less two McLarens.

In fact, four customers – 21 of the 25 cars are already spoken for, and one has been delivered – turned up for CLK-GTR test-drives in McLaren F1s. 'McLaren drivers get out and say the F1 is boring in comparison,' said an AMG staff member, smiling. Quite fast then. And two customer test-drives have

already ended up written off in the barrier, he added. I see. As far as omens go, this is a magpie opening and closing umbrellas inside a ladder factory.

The GTR really does make you gasp when you see it, it's so low, wide and brutish. It's like a regular CLK that's been stretched at the corners, like a tarpaulin, all the way down to the tarmac. It's simply a Le Mans car with numberplates.

But there's something else – get close, and the detailing is beautiful,

The super-sensitive throttle unleashes 612bhp. You don't need a very long straight to hit 200mph. All you can do is hang on…

the paint, the panel fit, the amazing 23-spoke 18-inch wheels. This car is clearly not thrown together to scrape through homologation.

Based on the 1997 V12 racer, rather than this year's 5.0-litre turbo V8 competition car, these GTRs are cars Mercedes didn't have to build. The FIA World Sports Car homologation rules require one road version of any race car, priced at no more than a million dollars. Like the Porsche 911 GT1 and Nissan R390 road cars, the official Mercedes road car came and went a few months ago, but the response from rich collectors around the world was serious enough to prompt AMG into building more, and doing it properly this time. Now it is assembling 25 cars by hand, and fitting standard

Mercedes air-con, central locking, CD player, ABS, anti-skid, two airbags and a stupendously German chequered seat fabric. All inside a carbonfibre racing car that still has its underfloor airjacks.

There was a second bad omen at AMG's official launch at Hockenheim. First journalist out in the car was Paul Frère, distinguished writer, former F1 and sports-car racer, and driver of every supercar built since the 12th century. Hands so safe they could deliver babies. Half a lap in and those same hands put a GTR into the tyre wall.

'The throttle is very sensitive,' he said later. No kidding.

And now it's my turn.

Fifteen black-uniformed AMG team members surround the car like

East German border guards as I twist and corkscrew my legs through the bug's-wing doors and in below the steering wheel. It's tight: the slot you have to fit your legs down is so long and narrow, in two days I never actually saw the pedals.

Inside, it's warm and dark and claustrophobic. And noisy. The engine, just a muffled whirr from the outside, is idling quickly and urgently behind me. I look out through the door and see a face, crouching down to give instructions.

'Ze gearchange iss vith der paddle behind ze steering wheel: right changes up, left changes down. But iss manual, so you must press ze clutch all the way to der floor. And ze throttle is very sensitive, so be careful, ya?'

He looks so serious I can't bring myself to nod. 'What's the top speed of this thing?' is the only pertinent thing I can think of to say.

'Electronically limited. To 320km/h.'

And with that, the face was replaced by a pair of well creased black trousers, and the carbonfibre door was closed down with a brisk clump.

I'm lying on the floor, in seats so narrow I can't fit my fingers between me and the bolsters. The windscreen rises up from the nose, all the way to my forehead. There are no sunvisors (no room), no rear-view mirror (no rear view) and no gearlever.

So, press the heavy clutch, grip the steering wheel, and feel the metal paddles tight behind. Press the

Air-con, central locking, CD player, airbags, chequered fabrics... don't be fooled, this is less like a road car than anything ever built

right one and hear a precise aerospace click, followed by a mechanical *clunck* behind. We're now in first. Nudge the throttle, cringe at the violent burst of sound (no flywheel at all) and with a judder, a jump, a flash of revs as I dip the clutch and let go again, I kangaroo down the Hockenheim pit-lane, learner style.

When I get out onto the first straight and press the throttle, all hell breaks loose. In second, the acceleration is a fuming, boiling, rampant, warlike lunge: the engine turns savage and bellows into the cabin, my neck snaps back till my head hits the bulkhead behind, and the next corner fast-forwards into the windscreen. Every single hair on my entire body stands on end and my eyes stare like golf balls.

Fortunately, the International Touring Car-derived brakes are gargantuan and the steering is full of feel. Unlike the McLaren F1, the GTR has power steering, and it's better for it – so quick, light and positive, yet sensitive enough to feed back every bump and camber in the tarmac, every minuscule change in grip. It fills you with confidence, not in your ability, or in the car's willingness to stay on the road (which, I suspect, it probably won't for long), but because you know you'd feel it the moment it started to slide, front or rear. In that respect, the car is closer to an Elise than a big supercar. In every other respect, it's nothing like anything.

This engine is remarkably smooth, considering it's race-derived, considering it's bolted to the tub you're sitting in, and considering all that noise. But its sheer strength makes it dangerous in every gear, every situation. It'll pull from dawdle to total destruction in an instant, even in fifth or sixth; third disgorges enough torque, and the revs are long enough to 7000rpm to catapult from one corner to the next so fast your brain's in a state of mild shock when you get there. You leap between corners without any build-up or preparation, and arrive 40 or 50mph faster than you expected. It is without doubt the most ludicrous road car I've ever driven.

But it's not really a road car. Ignore the central locking and airbags – that hair-trigger throttle, hard bobbing ride, jerky on/off easy-to-stall clutch and zip visibility make it all but unusable on the road. It is fascinating, and so exciting, so extreme; but (I hate to admit this) the GTR belongs in the subterranean garage of a rich collector, or on a privately hired race track. Rush-hour traffic and NCP car parks? Forget it.

So far, one Mercedes CLK-GTR is on its way to the UK. A country that is simply too small.
MARK WALTON

MERCEDES CLK-GTR ★★★★★	
(or ★ depending on your view)	
Price:	£1,100,000
Engine:	6898cc 48V, V12, 612bhp, 571lb ft
Performance:	200mph, 3.8sec 0-62, 13.1mpg
On sale in UK:	Now

TOM SALT

Styling is discreet to the point of anonymity; only the chrome badge gives the game away

There are high-powered cars, there are over-powered cars and there is the Mercedes C55 AMG. Any level-headed person would have thought that shoe-horning a 4.3-litre V8 into a Mercedes C-class would be more than enough to satisfy the most hardened adrenalin addicts. Apparently not. Somewhere out there exists a small band of power junkies for whom the regular C43's 306bhp and 302lb ft of torque is simply not enough. They crave something more, something absolute, something so powerful that it's impossible ever to look back.

This is the type of hit which only the C55 AMG can provide. Drive one and you will never look at a C-class in the same light again. Trust me, I've been there and it's not easy coming back.

Thankfully the C55 is not something you can buy over the counter from any Mercedes dealership. Securing one requires patience, guile and a bank balance with at least one and preferably two commas in it. First you have to put yourself on the waiting list for a new C43 AMG at a cost of £47,640; then, when it arrives around six months later, send it straight back to AMG with a further cheque for £24,760. In return they will upgrade the 4.3-litre engine to the same 5.4-litre lump that powers the monstrous E55. Apart from a new rear axle with a higher final drive, a specially made exhaust and a recalibrated speedometer to cope with the higher unlimited speeds of the C55, that is the sum total of your investment. Doesn't sound like great value for money, does it?

Sitting on the damp tarmac of Millbrook proving ground, this is the thought which keeps running through my head: £72,400 for a C-class – who are they kidding? I've seen meaner looking C180s driving around town. Dressed up with their tarty aftermarket skirts, blacked-out windows, drainpipe exhausts and 747 wings, they could outpose a C55 any day. The fact that the stereo is more powerful than the engine doesn't seem to bother the brain-dead occupants. The C55 has no time for these visual fripperies. Apart from the discreet sill extensions, twin AMG tail-pipes and simple chrome badge, there is little to give the game away. Even the pumped-up 18-inch alloys with ultra-low profile tyres are a £4885 option. Admittedly the metallic black finish of the paintwork gives it a foreboding presence that hints at the evil

within, but it's hardly a Lamborghini Diablo.

The driver's door opens and shuts with that familiar Mercedes thud and your eyes take in the same hard architectural shapes that greet a thousand Stuttgart taxi drivers every morning. Not for this car the soft touch and rich perfumes of hand-stitched leather and polished wood. The cream-coloured dials and mock carbon fibre trim give a clue to its greater purpose, but the ambience is still one of dark, austere functionality.

The contrasting blue-on-black leather seats bring a welcome splash of colour into the cabin, but even these are built for speed rather than comfort. The cushions are schoolbench hard and the side bolsters clasp you with a little more force than is strictly necessary. You can adjust their

Dark and functional cabin's multi-adjustable sports seats keep you firmly in your place

C MONSTER

SUPERCAR TEST **MERCEDES-BENZ C55** AMG's outrageous saloon is too expensive, too powerful and too good for Hugo Andreae to resist

grip as well as the lumbar and underthigh support by means of four electronically inflated cushions, but either way you're not going far from their all-enveloping grasp. Place your hands on the chunky four-spoke steering wheel and your fingers automatically lock into the 10 to two position. A small series of grooves on the underside and a raised hump to hook your thumb around make it uncomfortable to hold it any other way. In short the cabin is designed not to please the eye or the touch but to focus your attention on the business of driving and hold it there whether you like it or not.

Slot the bladeless infra-red key into the dash-mounted ignition and a small series of electronic whirrs and buzzes indicate that you have privileged access to what lies in front of the bulkhead. Two

clicks to the right and a series of dash-mounted warning lights flash orange to indicate that all is well. Brightest of all is a large triangular hazard sign that illuminates in the centre of the speedometer. Remember it well. You'll be seeing it again later. One more turn and the

starter motor jumps into life with a fast, insistent whine. Not even the resistance of eight high-compression cylinders slows its pace, and before the crankshaft has completed a full revolution the 5.4-litre V8 is spinning under its own momentum. For a moment the

revs swing up to 1500rpm before settling back down to 700rpm. If a big-capacity V8 brings to mind a lazy off-beat idle that rocks the car from side to side with its uneven rhythm, think again. This engine sounds urgent, smooth, and impatient; like an edgy ◆

Five-speed automatic is no hindrance to performance. Traction control is kept busy.

◆ racehorse waiting for the stalls to open.

Work the slim automatic gear lever through its crooked gate until it locks into Drive and keep your left foot planted on the brakes. Even at idle this engine develops more torque than a hard-charging Ferrari F355. Take a deep breath, check once more that the mile straight is clear, then push your right foot through the heavy Mercedes throttle spring while simultaneously lifting your left foot off the brake. Almost before you've registered the

Massive torque of 5.4-litre V8 makes C55 a handful in the wet; wheelspin at 90mph

C55 uses the same 5.4-litre engine as E55, although power drops from 354 to 347bhp

shove in your back, that orange traction control light is winking at you again. Try as it might the electronic brain is unable to match the power of the engine to the grip of the tyres, and the rear wheels continue to spin away some of the excess. Not that this seems to slow the C55's progress. It breaks 30mph in 2.3sec (C43 2.7sec), hammers past 60mph in 5.2sec (C43 6.4sec) with the traction control light still blinking and shows no sign of slowing down as it blasts through the 100mph barrier in 12.4sec (C43 15.2sec). What it would manage on a dry, still day will remain the subject of hushed speculations over a pint or six. So for that matter will the top speed. Road test editor Stephen Sutcliffe volunteers to take it onto Millbrook's banked high-speed circuit to verify the owner's claim that the normal 155mph limiter has been removed, but returns five minutes later looking several shades paler. The C55 breezed past 155mph alright and was still pulling like a train when the computer logged 170mph, but a combination of rear-end lift, a damp surface and the circuit's notorious bump flicked the tail out into momentary oversteer. Not the kind of experience that's conducive to a steady heartbeat. Sutcliffe wisely decides to call it a day.

Suffice it to say that if you can find a long enough straight and a driver with few enough brain cells, it may well reach the high 170s before finally running out of puff.

Impressive stuff, but these dry facts and figures still can't convey what it feels like to drive a C55 on the road. After all, to go by these indications alone the C55 is no quicker than a BMW M3, let alone a Porsche 911. That's why you have to go somewhere with fast, open roads punctuated with bumps, curves, straights

and the occasional burst of traffic. Roads where torque, throttle reaction, comfort and vision play as much a part as absolute power. Roads like the ones we found near Chatteris, Cambridgeshire. Typified by their long raised straights, rippled tarmac, humpback bridges and sudden 90-degree corners, they demand the utmost respect from car and driver. Choose a wrong gear and you'll feel like you've hit the rewind button; misjudge a hump and it'll knock you metres off course; underestimate the severity of a bend and you'll end up in one of the watery dykes that run alongside.

This is where the C55 comes into its own. With 376lb ft of torque at a lazy 3000rpm and what feels like 90 per cent of that all the way from idle to 6000rpm, there is no such thing as the wrong gear. If the five-speed automatic gearbox chooses not to kickdown from third you suffice with what amounts by any normal standards to brutal acceleration. If on the other hand it does kickdown you'd better be prepared for the consequences. The first sign that anything unusual is about to happen is a brief let-up in the rate of acceleration as the torque convertor absorbs the slack between third gear disengaging and second gear slotting into place. Just enough time for you to tighten your grip on the wheel and prepare for the coming onslaught. If the road surface is anything less than perfect the tyres will instantly be ripped from the road in a banshee shriek of rubber against tarmac. If it's wet the same thing happens in third and even fourth. Find a good surface, however, and the C55 flings you down the ♦

Optional 18-inch alloys bring 255/35 tyres but even these can't tame C55's traction deficit

◀ road with the force of an aircraft carrier's steam catapult. It's as if the weight of the car and inertia of the drivetrain don't exist. It's just you, an almighty V8 and four wheels. Hit the throttle at a steady 40mph and the next thing you know you are doing 120mph. The increments in between barely have time to register on your brain. This is the magic which only colossal torque and a quick-shifting automatic gearbox can perform. There are other cars which can match the C55's torque-to-weight ratio of 235lb ft per tonne, but none which can do it so effortlessly.

A Bentley turbo seems cumbersome by comparison, a Dodge Viper crude and a Lamborghini Diablo just plain hard work. And none of these icons will shred rubber with quite such contemptuous ease. The C55's traction control switch is best seen as a money-saving device rather than a safety feature. Switch it off and your tyres will barely survive the month, leave it on and you might stretch it to six.

Then again, running costs are not a big factor when you have spent £80,000 on a car. That said, fuel consumption was better than expected. We averaged just under 20mpg with a best of 27mpg over the touring route. More problematic is the undersized 62-litre fuel tank which is easily drained in around 250 miles of hard motoring.

The fact that AMG hasn't done anything to upgrade the C43's suspension and brakes says more about the competence of the C43's chassis than any lack of development on the C55. The recorded braking distances are higher than for the C43 because of the damp tarmac, but they still feel powerful and fade-free. Once or twice I found myself wishing

for a little more stopping power at the end of a long East Anglian straight, but I suspect this was as much to do with the comparative lack of rubber and the extra speed we were carrying as any failing of the brakes. Even the optional front 245/35 ZR18 tyres are relatively modest given the enormity of the C55's performance.

Despite the low-profile tyres and undeniably stiff suspension set-up, the C55 was still able to deliver an acceptably compliant ride over the area's badly rutted roads. Around town the narrow-shouldered

tyres crash clumsily over potholes and road repairs, but once above 50mph they ignore the minutiae of the surface and focus on the bigger picture. Really lumpy roads can set up a mild bobbing sensation, not dissimilar to the previous generation Porsche 993, but harshness never enters the picture. The occasional creak from the leather rear seats is the only reminder of the huge stresses and strains that the standard C-class shell is having to cope with.

Even the steering feels surprisingly light with a lazy 3.4 turns between locks and a

nicely judged balance between feedback and over sensitivity. It's no Lotus Elise, but given this car's high-speed cruising potential it makes sense to have a built-in sneeze factor. You can still feel the cambers and bumps attempting to knock the front wheels off course, but a gentle correction is all that's required to keep the car on course rather than a wrestling match.

I doubt whether ultimately you'll be able to go around corners much quicker than in an M3 or even a C43 for that matter. The back end feels a little too skittish over mid-corner bumps, particularly with the threat of all that torque hanging over you like the sword of Damocles. It's easy enough to provoke an unintentional slide without having to go looking for it, particularly when drenched by the sort of downpour which engulfed us shortly after arriving in East Anglia.

In this light it's hard to justify spending such a copious amount of cash on what amounts to no more than a C43 with an extra 41bhp, but in no way does this give an accurate reflection of the truth.

Optional Xenon lights cast an eerie blue hue. Twin oval tail-pipes shared with C43 AMG

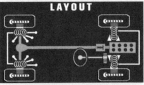

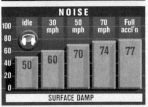

ENGINE	
Layout	8 cyls in a vee, 5439cc
Max power	347bhp at 5500rpm
Max torque	376lb ft at 3000-4300rpm
Specific output	64bhp per litre
Power to weight	217bhp per tonne
Torque to weight	235lb ft per tonne
Installation	Longitudinal, front, rear-wheel drive
Construction	Aluminium alloy head, cast iron block
Bore/stroke	97.0/92.0mm
Valve gear	4 valves per cyl, dohc
Compression ratio	10.5:1
Ignition and fuel	Bosch HMS 7.0 sequential multi-point fuel injection

GEARBOX	
Type	5-speed automatic
Ratios/mph per 1000rpm	
1st 3.59/7.4 **2nd** 2.19/12.1 **3rd** 1.41/18.7	
4th 1.00/26.4 **5th** 0.83/31.8	
Final drive ratio 2.82	

BRAKES	
Front	334mm ventilated discs
Rear	300mm ventilated discs
Anti-lock	Standard with brake assist

STEERING	
Type	Recirculating ball, power assisted
Turns lock to lock	3.4

SUSPENSION	
Front	Double wishbones, coil springs, gas-filled dampers, anti-roll bar
Rear	Multi-link, coil springs, gas filled dampers, anti-roll bar

WHEELS & TYRES	
Wheel size	7.5x18in (17-inch standard)
Made of	Cast alloy
Tyres	245/35 ZR18 (f), 255/35 ZR18 (r)

MAXIMUM SPEEDS
5th gear 170+mph **4th** 164/6200rpm
3rd 116/6200 **2nd** 75/6200 **1st** 45/6200

ACCELERATION FROM REST

True mph	sec	speedo mph
30	2.3	31
40	3.1	41
50	4.1	51
60	5.2	62
70	6.7	72
80	8.4	82
90	10.2	93
100	12.4	103
110	15.2	114
120	18.8	124
130	23.3	134
140	29.0	145
150	39.9	155

Standing quarter mile 13.8/105mph
Standing kilometre 24.5/132mph
30-70mph through gears 4.4sec

ACCELERATION IN KICKDOWN

mph	sec
20-40	1.6
30-50	1.8
40-60	2.1
50-70	2.6
60-80	3.2
70-90	3.5
80-100	4.0
90-110	5.0
100-120	6.4
110-130	8.1
120-140	10.2
130-150	16.6

BRAKING
From 30/50/70/105mph in neutral
9.6/25.0/49.4/113.1 metres (damp)
60-0mph 2.6sec (damp)

WHAT IT COSTS
On-the-road price	£72,397
Total as tested	£81,317
Cost per mile	n/a

EQUIPMENT
(**bold** = options fitted to test car)

Metallic paint	£651
Alarm with immobiliser	●
Leather sports seats with electric adj	●
Airbag driver/passenger/side	●/●/●
Anti-lock brakes	●
RDS stereo/CD changer	£750/£718
Climate control	●
Headlamp wash/wipe	●
Alloy wheels/18-inch AMG option	●/£4886
Remote central locking	●
Elec windows/mirrors/sunroof	●/●/£1255
Xenon headlamps	£710

● standard – not available
Insurance group 20

WARRANTY
1 year/unlimited mileage, 1 year free recovery, 1 year anti-corrosion

LAYOUT

NOISE

	idle	30 mph	50 mph	70 mph	Full accl'n
	50	60	70	74	77

SURFACE DAMP

BRAKES
30 mph	50 mph	70 mph	st qtr mile
	60-0mph: 2.6sec		113.1 105mph
9.6	25.0	49.4	

SURFACE DAMP

FUEL ECONOMY
GOVERNMENT CLAIMS

mpg	Urban	Extra urban	Combined
	16.5	33.2	24.1

Tank capacity: 62 litres (13.7 gallons)
Touring range: 370 miles

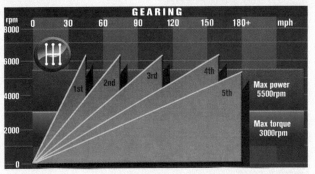

GEARING

BP All Autocar road tests are conducted using BP Unleaded Fuel or BP Greener Diesel with additives to help keep engines cleaner

VITAL STATISTICS

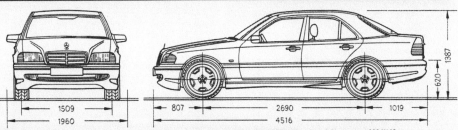

Body 4dr saloon **Cd** 0.32 **Front/rear tracks** 1509/1483mm **Turning circle** 10.7m **Min/max front leg room** 930/1140mm
Max front head room 990mm **Interior width front/rear** 1430/1420mm **Min/max boot width** 880/1520mm **Boot height** 450mm
Boot length 1000mm **VDA boot volume** 430 litres **Kerb weight** 1598kg **Weight distribution f/r** 53/47 per cent

THE AUTOCAR VERDICT
Overpowered, overpriced and utterly addictive mega Merc ★★★★

Figures are mighty impressive but real appeal of awesome C55 defies logic

Wheel is contoured to fit hands

The C55 has a draw that transcends logic and appeals to deeper, darker emotions. To drive one is to indulge in an excess of power that only despots and tyrants can empathise with.

It can leave you feeling giddy for days, and when you finally come to your senses all you can think of is when you can get your next fix. It is for this reason that I want one, need one, must have one. For those of you untainted by the experience, I can only offer this humble advice. Just say no.

Mercedes-Benz
E55

Torque is *not* cheap.

BY BARRY WINFIELD

German engineers mining for torque deposits near Affalterbach must have hit a mother lode. At least, that's what it feels like from behind the AMG-monogrammed steering wheel of this E55. Somewhere between here and the three-pointed gun sight at the leading edge of the hood is housed 391 pound-feet of torque, available from 3000 rpm onward.

This is the kind of urge that prompts you to adjust your head-rest—and those of the passengers—because a careless thrust at the throttle pedal will, in most circumstances, produce a lunge that snaps back heads faster than a space-shuttle launch.

Press the ESP button located on the console, disabling the stability-control system (lighting a prominent yellow triangle in the dash), and you can expect wheelspin if you mash the throttle from rest. That's with the five-speed automatic transmission that is standard equipment, folks. Brake-torque the E55 for a second before you go, and you'll light up the 35-series rear tires in a serious fashion.

But if you balance your launch in a mature manner, you can expect propulsion of a decidedly quick nature: 0 to 60 mph in 4.9 seconds and a quarter-mile sprint in 13.5 seconds at 105 mph. To get that sort of thrust from a big luxury car like this, did AMG turn the E55 into a hot rod of the brutal, kidney-crushing variety?

Well, yes and no. Fast it is. Rude it ain't. In fact, so suave is this E-class muscle car that its real potential will not be recognized by many passengers. You could pick up your boss at the airline terminal and transport him to his hotel at quarter-throttle, and he'd swear it was a luxury ride under him. That's because the quiet 5.4-liter V-8 wuffles along with hydraulic smoothness and slurs gearshifts in a seamless sequence. Even at low revs, there's enough torque to waft up hills without losing speed or digging for another gear.

And only if the roads are bad will your VIP sense the tensioned suspension (35 percent higher-rate springs, Bilstein shocks, beefier stabilizer bars) and high-pressure, low-profile doughnuts under him. As for the drivers around you, they'll just recognize another E-class Benz with the Sport package they're accustomed to seeing on E430s. Unless they close up tight on the car's tail, that is, and read the chrome letters that proclaim the

car to be an E55 by AMG.

Yes, the latest "Hammer" from Mercedes and its in-house speed wizards is a Q-ship. According to Mike Jackson, the recently appointed boss of Mercedes-Benz of North America, the Germans are currently into inconspicuous consumption, and they want their cars—particularly the tuner-prepped rocket ships—to be unobtrusive. But that's not what Jackson wanted for his mid-size giant killer in our market, and the E55 you see here is the resulting compromise. It uses an existing AMG-derived Sport package, but it's allowed a subdued boast from its tail-mounted insignia, along with subtle AMG badging on the steering wheel and gauge cluster.

It's not a car that needs superfluous decoration, that's for sure. At a suggested price of $71,717 (cheaper by 15 or so grand than its predecessor, the Porsche-assembled E500), every one of the 2000 examples earmarked for the U.S. over the next four years will be snapped up. Heck, most of the first shipment will likely be absorbed by dealer principals before the public even gets a shot.

Which is a pity, because this is an extraordinary vehicle, versatile beyond our wildest expectations, and as rewarding as the best drivers' cars around. To have achieved this at a lower price than that of the preceding E500 is commendable, accomplished by keeping as much of the original E-class car intact. Unlike the E500, the E55 is essentially a fully assembled and trimmed vehicle off Mercedes-Benz's Sindelfingen line before it is sent off to the AMG skunkworks in Affalterbach for its stroked and breathed-upon engine, its heavy-duty V-12–derived transmission, its uprated suspension and brakes, and its

big wheels and tires. Because of that, the essence of the E-class car has been preserved, but with dynamic parameters that have been extended in every way. The primary differences are manifested as a more jiggly ride with much tauter roll control, a throttle that gets into the power without the Benz-signature long and progressive pedal travel, and acceleration—anytime—that is in another league. Oh, yeah, and an engine note that changes from a polite V-8 burble to a hard-edged snarl when the pedal's down and the tach is reaching for six grand.

Surprisingly, the steering-assist mechanism is identical to that of the E430, and it remains light at most speeds. So light that the mechanism in a BMW 328i feels leaden in comparison. But it directs the E55 with such accuracy and fluency that more weight at the rim doesn't seem necessary. In fact, when you add the car's tenacious grip (0.88 g on the skidpad) and tightly tied-down body motions to the razor-sharp helm, the E55 can take on almost anything in the corners. But be warned, the driver will likely need some recalibration; the car's abundantly stiff structure and good isolation lead one to underestimate corner entry speeds. On the introductory ride-and-drive in Napa, California, a couple of drivers from other publications went off the road, and we

143

suspect that those incidents were partly due to the deceptive ease with which this car gathers speed.

What shouldn't go unnoticed in the E55 (and this is particularly seductive) is the push in the back you get when you pin the throttle. The torque is so prodigious (41 pound-feet more than a Corvette's), and the torque curve so flat, that the E55 pulls hard all the way through each gear, producing a concerted thrust like that of a 757 on a takeoff run. It just keeps on coming.

Aerodynamic drag beyond triple-digit speeds does little to blunt its charge, and our E55 was still accelerating when it hit an electronic limiter at 158 mph. Hard enough to suggest a real top speed somewhere around 180 mph. Still, 158 ought to be enough for most people, and at that speed the E55 tracks as straight as a die.

At more reasonable rates of travel, the E55 assumes its more civilized persona, providing a smooth, quiet ride that will take its occupants on interstate travel with

little discomfort. This is perhaps the car's most noteworthy aspect. When not being flogged hard, it behaves more like a limo than a supercar. In fact, the transmission's computer reads driver inputs and adjusts its activities accordingly.

The compromises you accept for this broad operating bandwidth are few. A suspension designed for high speeds and massive cornering potential can't be expected to traverse broken surfaces without transmitting some impact shock and movement

into the car. On the other end of the scale, the factory-issue seats (available in all-black leather or in two-tone combinations of black and blue and black and silver) are firm and supportive enough for a cross-continent tour, but they lack the wrap-around support of dedicated sport seats. We also found the leather-wrapped wheel (also available in solid or two-tone hues) to have a rather obstructive arrangement of spokes and thumb pads, leaving too little rim available for those of us with large hands. Understand, please, that this is deliberate picking of the smallest nits.

For most people's needs, the mix of sporting and luxury attributes is right on the money. As the two companies involved in the E55's genesis have drawn closer (AMG is being acquired by Daimler-Chrysler), so the levels of sophistication have increased. Thus, the E55 retains all the elaborate technical aspects of the V-8–powered E-class cars: the stability- and traction-control systems; the twin-plug cylinder heads; the variable-volume intake tract; the oil-quality monitor—in short, all the assets of a factory-backed product.

Indeed, this close integration of a leading-edge manufacturer and its specialist engineering consulting service is really what defines the new E55 and its nearly perfect blend of pedigree and power. Remember, 1998 saw Mercedes and AMG bring home two world-championship motorsports trophies as well as launch the E55. It looks like a winning streak to us. ●

C/D TEST RESULTS

ACCELERATION
	Seconds
Zero to 00 mph	1.9
40 mph	2.7
50 mph	3.8
60 mph	4.9
70 mph	6.3
80 mph	8.1
90 mph	10.0
100 mph	12.1
110 mph	14.7
120 mph	18.1
130 mph	22.4
140 mph	27.4
Street start, 5–60 mph	5.1
Top-gear acceleration, 30–50 mph	3.0
50–70 mph	3.4
Standing ¼-mile	13.5 sec @ 105 mph
Top speed (governor limited)	158 mph

BRAKING
70–0 mph @ impending lockup	156 ft
Fade	**none** light moderate heavy

HANDLING
Roadholding, 300-ft-dia skidpad	0.88 g
Understeer	minimal **moderate** excessive

FUEL ECONOMY
EPA city driving	16 mpg
EPA highway driving	23 mpg
C/D-observed fuel economy	**18 mpg**

INTERIOR SOUND LEVEL
Idle	45 dBA
Full-throttle acceleration	75 dBA
70-mph cruising	69 dBA
70-mph coasting	69 dBA

MERCEDES-BENZ E55 AMG
Vehicle type: front-engine, rear-wheel-drive, 5-passenger, 4-door sedan

Price as tested: $73,302

Price and option breakdown: base Mercedes-Benz E55 AMG (includes $595 freight and $2022 luxury tax), $71,717; six-disc CD changer and cellular telephone, $1495; luxury tax on options, $90

Major standard accessories: power steering, windows, seats, locks, and sunroof; A/C; cruise control; tilting and telescoping steering wheel; rear defroster

Sound system: AM/FM-stereo radio/cassette/CD changer, 10 speakers

ENGINE
Type	V-8, aluminum block and heads
Bore x stroke	3.82 x 3.62 in, 97.0 x 92.0mm
Displacement	332 cu in, 5439cc
Compression ratio	10.5:1
Engine-control system	Bosch ME2.0 with port fuel injection
Emissions controls	3-way catalytic converter, feedback air-fuel-ratio control
Valve gear	chain-driven single overhead cams, 3 valves per cylinder, hydraulic lifters
Power (SAE net)	349 bhp @ 5500 rpm
Torque (SAE net)	391 lb-ft @ 3000 rpm
Redline	6000 rpm

DRIVETRAIN
Transmission .... 5-speed automatic with lockup torque converter
Final-drive ratio .... 2.82:1, electronic limited slip

Gear	Ratio	Mph/1000 rpm	Max. test speed
I	3.59	7.3	43 mph (6000 rpm)
II	2.19	11.9	71 mph (6000 rpm)
III	1.41	18.5	111 mph (6000 rpm)
IV	1.00	26.0	155 mph (6000 rpm)
V	0.83	31.4	158 mph (4950 rpm)

DIMENSIONS AND CAPACITIES
Wheelbase	111.5 in
Track, F/R	60.2/59.9 in
Length	189.4 in
Width	70.8 in
Height	56.7 in
Curb weight	3765 lb
Weight distribution, F/R	52.6/47.4%
Fuel capacity	21.1 gal
Oil capacity	8.0 qt
Water capacity	11.8 qt

CHASSIS/BODY
Type	unit construction
Body material	welded steel stampings

INTERIOR
SAE volume, front seat	51 cu ft
rear seat	44 cu ft
luggage space	15 cu ft
Front seats	bucket
Seat adjustments	fore and aft, seatback angle, front height, head height
Restraint systems, front	manual 3-point belts; driver and passenger front, side, and head airbags
rear	manual 3-point belts
General comfort	poor fair **good** excellent
Fore-and-aft support	poor fair good **excellent**
Lateral support	poor **fair** good excellent

SUSPENSION
F: .... ind, unequal-length control arms, coil springs, anti-roll bar
R: .... ind; 3 lateral links, 1 diagonal link, and 1 toe-control link per side; coil springs; anti-roll bar

STEERING
Type	rack-and-pinion, power-assisted
Turns lock-to-lock	3.1
Turning circle curb-to-curb	37.1 ft

BRAKES
F:	13.2 x 1.3-in vented disc
R:	11.8 x 0.9-in vented disc
Power assist	hydraulic with anti-lock control

WHEELS AND TIRES
Wheel size	F: 8.0 x 18 in, R: 9.0 x 18 in
Wheel type	cast aluminum
Tires	Michelin Pilot Sport; F: 245/40ZR-18, R: 275/35ZR-18
Test inflation pressures, F/R	36/36 psi

CURRENT BASE PRICE* dollars x 1000

| LEXUS GS400 | BMW 540i | JAGUAR XJR | MERCEDES-BENZ E55 |
0 16 32 48 64 80

ACCELERATION seconds
■ 0–60 mph ■ 1/4-mile

| MERCEDES-BENZ E55 | JAGUAR XJR | BMW 540i | LEXUS GS400 |
0 3 6 9 12 15

BRAKING 70–0 mph, feet
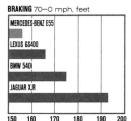
| MERCEDES-BENZ E55 | LEXUS GS400 | BMW 540i | JAGUAR XJR |
150 160 170 180 190 200

ROADHOLDING 300-foot skidpad, g
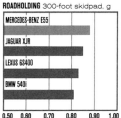
| MERCEDES-BENZ E55 | JAGUAR XJR | LEXUS GS400 | BMW 540i |
0.50 0.60 0.70 0.80 0.90 1.00

EPA CITY FUEL ECONOMY mpg
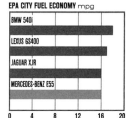
| BMW 540i | LEXUS GS400 | JAGUAR XJR | MERCEDES-BENZ E55 |
0 4 8 12 16 20

* Base price includes freight, any performance options, and all applicable luxury and gas-guzzler taxes.

The speedometer of the S55 AMG we're driving reads to a recklessly optimistic 320mph. Say that again. Three hundred and twenty miles an hour. Yes, miles, not 320 kilometres per hour. By any road car standards 320km/h is fast – 198.75mph to be precise – but 320mph is beyond the preposterous.

You see, it's possible, using the right combination for the various buttons built into the steering wheel, to switch from an imperial to metric display. On other S-class saloons we've driven the graduations change to take advantage of the new scale. On this S55, a small km/h display swaps over to mph, but the progression of numbers remains unchanged, which means even the mighty 155mph S55 uses barely half the speedo

WHAM BAMG

DRIVE MERCEDES AMG S55 A 180mph, 360bhp S-class might sound like excess, but AMG's S55 leaves the excellence of Merc's luxury saloon untouched, reports Peter Robinson

range – unless you ask AMG to remove the electronic restriction, as many customers do, when tyres become the limiting factor. The Dunlop Sport 2000s fitted to our car are legal to 270km/h (168mph), but even that's not quick enough for hottest S-class. Find a long enough stretch of autobahn and

the engineers from AMG, who developed the package, claim the S55 will finally run out of power somewhere between 175mph and 180mph.

We have two days on German autobahns with the S55, time enough to explore the serious half of the mph speedo and to decide if the extra £24,750 over

the already quick S500 can be justified. AMG knows the demand for this £100k limo is going to be small, but says there are enough potential buyers who want to add a more sporting character to the refinement of the new S-class to warrant adding a hot rod S-class to a line-up that already includes an SL55, SL73 and even G55.

These customers either don't want to wait for the 362bhp V12 S600 – though it's only months away – or understand that the V8 is going to be lighter (by 90kg, using the CL coupe as a guide) and, with less weight over the front wheels, will probably have better balanced handling. AMG's marketing people also understand that their customers aspire to even greater individuality than the choices offered by Mercedes options list.

The engine comes straight from the E55, AMG's conversion of the Mercedes sohc V8 that stretches both bore and

stroke to take the capacity from the S500's 4966cc to 5439cc and power to 360bhp, a 54bhp increase. Torque climbs from 339lb ft at 2700-4200rpm to a prodigious 391lb ft across a high plateau from 3150rpm to 4500rpm. AMG's work includes giving the engine a stronger bottom end, forged aluminium pistons and new camshafts.

To improve breathing, the three-valves-per-cylinder V8 uses a new twin-stream intake system, and a bigger exhaust pipe diameter to reduce back-pressure. While passing all noise pollution requirements, this endows the S55 with an exhaust note almost Italian in its high-edged melody. AMG has tweaked the engine management system without raising maximum rpm beyond 6000. Don't be disappointed; this engine produces more adrenalin than most drivers can regularly employ.

Controlling this power are

Steering is ultra-light in town, yet firms up to provide near-perfect weighting at high speed. Car feels rock-solid

Sophisticated air suspension of standard S-class easily copes with S55's extra performance

Test car wears subtle body-coloured skirts, AMG wheels and beefier tyres

345mm ventilated four-piston, front and 315mm ventilated two-piston rear disc brakes, previewing the system for the CL600 and S600. Tyres grow to 245/45 R18 front and 275/40

R18 rears on five-spoke AMG wheels. And the suspension? Forget the normal go-faster treatment of firmer springs and dampers, and bigger diameter anti-roll bars. AMG says the

S-class's air suspension and adaptive damping effortlessly cope with the extra power and speed of the S55.

We collected our test car from Mercedes' headquarters in Stuttgart. If you know what to look for, then the S55 stands out from other S-class models. Especially when, like ours, they come with the optional AMG body kit (AMG prefers the term "styling package") that adds deeper, body-coloured front, side and rear skirts. Otherwise, it's left to those special wheels and the rear badging. This is a ▶

It seems incredible that a luxury limousine can rocket forward so eagerly; S55 sprints from 0-60mph in 5.5sec

TOM SALT

S55 has plenty of grip; set adaptive damping to Sport for more control

◀ convincing shape, cleverly disguising its sheer size with subtle tapering at both ends and beautifully sculptured form to the body sides.

Not so good is the interior, at least of the test car. Someone has decided to give this S55 an overdose of chestnut finish. The light coloured, excessively shiny wood is liberally applied. Even to half of the steering wheel, Jaguar-style. We'd do without, thank you, and save the near-£7500 price tag. AMG says most of its customers love the wood treatment, so what do we know? The point is, AMG offers a staggering choice to personalise the interior.

Of course, the S55 is a drawing room on wheels. Roomy and brilliantly comfortable up front, the driving position can easily be tailored to suit via various electric motors that move the seat. Those in the back will find more space than they could reasonably expect. There's even an optional cooler built in behind the fold-down centre armrest, so it pokes into boot space.

Apart from the 320km/h and

Switchable speed limiter on cruise control stalk is designed to avoid fines

mph speedometer the interior is pure S-class. You know this is an opulent limousine, but it doesn't prepare you for the S55's brutally civilised performance.

The friendly manners start with a smoother throttle action as you move away. AMG says there's no difference in software between E55 and S55, so maybe it's the bigger car's extra 240kg of mass. Whatever, the S55 lacks the fierce initial movement of the E55, so it's easier and more fluent to drive through heavy traffic. The impression of immense bottom-end torque remains, it's just sweeter and more flowing as it blasts away.

Despite the S55's hefty 1875kg weight, the 5.4-litre V8 provides the performance of a supercar rather than a heavyweight limousine. It just doesn't seem possible that a car so big and so heavy can rocket forward as instantly and eagerly as the S55. But it can, of course, and it induces a contiguously ◀

Brilliant adaptive five-speed auto seems to anticipate the driver's mood; willing to kick down to fourth at 145mph

INSIDE MERCEDES' MUSCLE CAR DIVISION

Technicians build V8s at a rate of 2.5 a day

AMG, the muscle car division of Mercedes-Benz, has been fully integrated into the parent company. On 1 January Mercedes-Benz took control of 51 per cent of the company Hans-Werner Aufrecht, a former Mercedes engineer, founded in 1967, and it became Mercedes AMG.

Mario Spitzner rejoins AMG from Mercedes

The C43, E55 – and soon the CLK55 and ML55 – will be included on every Mercedes dealer's price list. This year about 3500 of each saloon and 1000 of the hot coupe will be produced. Niche models, like the S55 SL55, SL73, G55 and C55, must be ordered through AMG.

Mario Spitzner first worked for AMG in the early '90s before joining Mercedes in 1992. Now he's back at AMG as marketing boss.

"We don't just have sales responsibility but some R&D freedom," says Spitzner. "We're able to certify models as Mercedes AMG and they don't need to be okayed by Mercedes-Benz because our endurance testing applies the same internal standards."

The Mercedes "Designo" individuality programme is run by AMG and amounts to about 15,000 cars a year. Most customers choose different leather colours, specific paint treatments and wood.

Spitner says AMG is now a crucial part of the model development process at Mercedes and claims it's involved

The E55 arrives minus engine, wheels and trim

from the very beginning of each new model.

Next year, when Mercedes finally slots the V6 engine into the SLK, AMG will present a tweaked version of the SLK. No doubt it will be the fastest and most satisfying SLK yet.

C43 now on official Merc price list

S55 has impeccable manners and delivers astonishing power with ease

◀ broad grin in any enthusiastic driver. Try zero to 60mph in an always repeatable 5.5sec. Even more dramatic is the mid-range torque which hands down so much effortless oomph at virtually any speed, the transmission blurring each downshift. If the driver is brave enough to maintain full throttle it slides through each upshift at 6100rpm, delivering a seamless and linear flow of refined power. Which means fourth slips into fifth at just over 170mph.

We're cruising in near silence in fifth, speedo needle happily resting at 100mph, rev counter reading just 2950rpm, air con gently maintaining the desired 21deg C, the Bose sound system delivering crisply sonorous sound. Prod the accelerator – not to the floor, but enough to let the engine's electronic brain know you're serious. Instantly, the auto has picked up not fourth, as you might expect, but harmoniously dropped down to third to extract the ultimate acceleration, changing up to fourth at 120mph. Any car that will kick down on part-throttle to fourth at an indicated 145mph warrants the tag super-responsive. Mercedes' switchable speed limiter, that works via the cruise control stalk, and is intended to help avoid speeding fines, works up to 150mph.

So tall is the S55's gearing, that at 150mph the engine is running at a mere 4400rpm, and there is still plenty of urge left. Mercedes' brilliantly adaptive five-speed auto seems to anticipate the driver's mood. It doesn't try to sneak into D when you're approaching a bend or setting up for a fast sweeper. It quickly adjusts to individual driving styles, and only rarely does its intelligence let it down. Any jerky changes come as a real surprise.

Dynamically, the S55 has two huge advantages over the E55.

AMG offers a staggering choice to personalise the plush and roomy interior; shiny chestnut trim priced at £7500

The first is an almost complete lack of tyre roar. The bigger car's Dunlops are notably quieter than the whining Bridgestones fitted to the E55.

Then there's the ride. The S55 feels as if it travels on a cushion of air, which is exactly what it does. It floats, delivering a supple ride that the pleasantly tautly sprung E55 can't hope to rival. Sometimes, however, when both front wheels hit a large pothole at low speeds, the air suspension stumbles and a sharp reaction is passed through to the cabin. Everywhere else, the suspension smoothes out the ride without impairing handling.

The rack-and-pinion steering, too, is light to the point of being weightless at parking speeds. Yet it imperceptibly firms up, so that the weighting is close to perfect at high speeds or when cornering. The S55 feels rock solid, and its straight line stability means you can cover ground quickly and effortlessly.

This car is too big and bulky to be called agile, yet switch the adaptive damping over to Sport and you notice an immediate improvement in body control. The firmer setting means the S55 turns in more obediently and without the excess lean of the default setting. Instead of

scrubbing off speed by indulging in an excess of understeer, the S55 is near neutral, flat and controllable, with plenty of grip – at least on the dry roads we experienced.

Just before the limit of adhesion, the weight obviously shifting on to the outside tyres, the electronic guardian angel slows you down. Yes, you can turn it off and indulge in power oversteer, but that's not the S55's natural driving manner.

Under hard braking, too, you're aware that this is a weighty flagship, yet pedal pressures are low and the discs easy to modulate. When really pressed, this car's stopping power remains impeccable, brake dust and pad smells notwithstanding.

Don't dismiss the S55 as a rich man's toy. It's far too competent and enjoyable for that. You could drive it for years and feel utterly detached from the outside world. Or you can use its amazing performance to stir the emotions like a proper Q-car.

Obviously the forthcoming S600 has been designed to play another role, leaving room enough to justify the S55. And that extravagant speedometer. ◎

FACTFILE

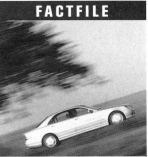

MERCEDES-BENZ S55

HOW MUCH?	
Price	£98,790
On sale	Now

HOW FAST?	
0-62mph	6.0sec
Top speed (limited)	155mph

HOW THIRSTY?	
Urban	14.3mpg
Extra urban	29.7mpg
Combined	21.1mpg

HOW BIG?	
Length	5158mm
Width	1855mm
Height	1444mm
Wheelbase	3085mm
Weight	1875kg
Fuel tank	88 litres

ENGINE	
Layout	8 cyls in vee, 5439cc
Max power	360bhp at 5500rpm
Max torque	391lb ft at 3150-4500rpm
Specific output	66bhp per litre
Power to weight	192bhp per tonne
Installation	Longitudinal, front, rear-wheel drive
Made of	Alloy heads and block
Bore/stroke	97.0/92.0mm
Compression ratio	10.5:1
Valve gear	3 per cyl, sohc
Ignition and fuel	Electronic fuel injection

GEARBOX	
Type	5-speed automatic
Ratios/mph per 1000rpm	
1st 3.59/7.8	2nd 2.19/12.8
3rd 1.41/19.9	4th 1.00/28.1
5th 0.83/33.8	
Final drive	2.82

SUSPENSION	
Front	Four-link axle, adaptive damping, anti-roll bar
Rear	Multi-link, adaptive damping, anti-roll bar

STEERING	
Type	Rack and pinion, power assisted
Lock to lock	3.0 turns

BRAKES	
Front	345mm ventilated drilled discs
Rear	315mm ventilated drilled discs

WHEELS AND TYRES	
Size	8.5Jx18 (f), 9.5Jx18 (r)
Made of	Alloy
Tyres	Dunlop Sport 2000 245/45 R18 (f), 275/40 R18 (r)

VERDICT	

A remarkably homogeneous Mercedes super-saloon capable of absurdly effortless high performance.

Surgeon generals

**Audi's clinical S6 and Mercedes'
stitch-and-sew E55 AMG demonstrate two
different ways to handle power implants**
Story by Georg Kacher
Photography by Tom Salt

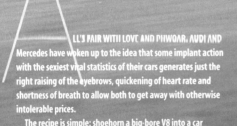

ALL'S FAIR WITH LOVE AND PHWOAR. AUDI AND Mercedes have woken up to the idea that some implant action with the sexiest vital statistics of their cars generates just the right raising of the eyebrows, quickening of heart rate and shortness of breath to allow both to get away with otherwise intolerable prices.

The recipe is simple: shoehorn a big-bore V8 into a car normally powered by a humble four, five or six-cylinder unit and uprate the chassis, brakes and steering. That's it. Instant bhp bimbo. You know who you are, second-generation S6 and E55 (son of 500E).

The latest Audi and Benz are amazingly close in concept, competence and character. The S6 features the fourth variation of the recently modified Audi V8. The 4.2-litre unit, which now sports five valves per cylinder, delivers 300bhp in the A6 4.2, 310bhp in the A8 4.2, 340bhp in the S6 and 360bhp in the S8. Since the displacement and the compression ratio are absolutely identical in all four cases, the difference in power and torque is above all a matter of chip tuning. Different black boxes and a choice of two and three-stage intake manifolds permit varying rev limits, twist-action peaks and accelerator-to-engine characteristics. The power output figures are thus not so much the result of intensive dyno testing, but of intensive round table talks dominated by the marketing department. In the case of the S6, both the intended and the actual performance is spot-on.

Mercedes installs the 5.5-litre V8 in no fewer than eight different AMG models. Any difference in power output is due to marginal modifications to the exhaust system. In the recently facelifted E-class, the twin-cam eight-ender develops 354bhp at 5500rpm. Unlike Audi, which offers a choice of six-speed manual and five-speed automatic for the S6, the E55 AMG is only available with a five-speed self-shifter. And while the S6 boasts permanent four-wheel drive, its rival drives the rear wheels only. The AMG price list does contain a 4-Matic

conversion, but since the price is only quoted on request we are presumably talking big money here. This does not mean that the off-the-peg E55 is a bargain. Quite the contrary: at a likely £65,000, it is roughly £10,000 more expensive than an Audi S6 tiptronic. But then the Merc is also better equipped, featuring power-operated, heated two-tone leather seats with memory, a decent sound system, fat 18in wheels and a multi-functional steering wheel. These and other items cost extra at the Audi dealer, which brings the actual price difference down to less than £6500.

While the first-generation S6 and the 500E were quite subtle variations of the respective base models, the new S6 and the E55 AMG leave the onlooker in no doubt about their true mission. The S6 sports flared wheel arches, lowered suspension, extra-wide 17in wheels, twin chrome tailpipes, prominent badges, a bespoke grille and a pair of polished door-mirror housings that can be spotted a mile off. The E55 is fitted with monoblock AMG wheels (8J 235/40ZR18 at the front, 9J 265/35ZR18 at the back), and a comprehensive AMG styling kit consisting of body-colour rubbing strips, sill extensions, front spoiler and rear apron. Not loud enough? Then how about even wider three-piece rims or a tall, bootlid-mounted tail rudder with integrated brake light...

Inside, these two crackerjacks provide a go-faster atmosphere that is quite different in execution and taste. Normally, the Audi A6 would win the living-room-on-wheels contest hands down, but our S6 simply was not up to the usual high standard. It was fitted with Recaro seats trimmed in a combination of grey Alcantara and black leather. The chairs look fine, but they are thinly upholstered, not sufficiently adjustable and, despite a pull-out element, desperately short of thigh support. People of average height and up will be better off with the standard leather-trimmed seats available at no extra cost. The other debatable S6 cabin feature is the omnipresent fake carbonfibre trim. The designers hate the

AUDI S6
Price:
£55,000 approx
Engine:
4172cc 40V V8
Power and torque:
340bhp at 7000rpm
310lb ft at 3400rpm
Transmission:
Six-speed manual
four-wheel drive
Suspension, front:
Four-link,
coil springs,
anti-roll bar
Suspension, rear:
Double wishbones,
coil springs, anti-roll bar
Weight:
1735kg
Performance:
156mph
5.7sec 0-62mph
Fuel consumption:
20mpg

stuff, which looks like laminated pieces of a turn-of-the-century morning gown, but chairman Paefgen thinks it's really spiffy and it reportedly took a while to convince him that polished wood must be offered as a no-extra-cost alternative. It is the classier choice by a long shot.

The cabin of the facelifted E-class looks and feels like a downsized S-class. Strong points include the multi-functional steering wheel, the voice-activated carphone, and the comfortable heated seats which have inflatable back cushions and can be had with integrated ventilation.

Sat-nav works equally well in both cars: the large colour display is easily legible, the controls are logically laid out, and you don't need to be a Harvard graduate to understand the basic functions. One advantage the Mercedes has is passenger space, offering far more leg and headroom, front and back.

The Audi V8 has five valves per cylinder and a displacement of 4.2 litres. It produces 340bhp at 7000rpm and 310lb ft at 3400rpm. Mercedes' V8 has only three valves per cylinder but a displacement of 5.5 litres. It churns out 354bhp at a more relaxed 5500rpm and a massive 390lb ft at 3000rpm. Weight difference is marginal (1735 v 1710kg in favour of the Merc), and so is the difference in performance. The six-speed S6 and the E55 will both do 0-62mph in 5.7sec. But when you compare apples with apples, the S6 auto loses exactly one second from standstill to 62. Both cars can reach an identical, artificially limited top speed of 156mph. While Audi claims an average fuel consumption of 20mpg for the manual S6, Mercedes lists the E55 at 23mpg. Our own figures support this data. The car from A6 returned 19mpg: its competitor checked out of the pumps at 17mpg. The size of the fuel tanks does not differ much (82 v 80 litres in favour of the Audi), but the AMG-prepared Benz has a notably bigger boot (500 litres) than its challenger (434 litres). Those who need even more space can of course always opt for the roomier Avant/T-model estate.

When these cars were developed, ride comfort obviously was not high on the priority list. The low-profile Michelins of the Mercedes offer hardly any compliance at all and the uprated chassis is not particularly spine-friendly either. Stiffer springs, fatter anti-roll bars, tauter shock absorbers and the lowered suspension help to improve handling and roadholding, but they are at daggers drawn with potholes and transverse ridges to name only the worst of the Merc's enemies. Sadly, the S6 does not fare much better. Its 17in tyres are a little less uncompromising, and the dampers will occasionally have mercy with the occupants, but the lowered ride height, the shortened springs and the stiffer suspension mountings still permit too many vertical body movements. Both cars display a disappointing degree of harshness in the chassis department, where the new M5 remains the undisputed leader of the pack. Even the Jaguar XJR is a more pleasant long-distance travel companion.

Confirmation that the E55 really is a sports car in disguise comes first of all from your eardrums, which are bound to register the sonorous exhaust note, the unbridled intake roar, the barely muffled high-rev thunder, the noisy suspension and the virtually unfiltered tyre hum. Initially, these acoustic attacks are a little irritating, but after a day at the wheel you no longer mind it. Unlike lesser E-class models, the flagship has shed all filters, and in the process refinement was replaced with a very intense, in-you-face sensation of sheer speed. But what the E55 lacks in manners, it will return in ability and, more important still, in driver appeal.

The S6 is, by comparison, a velvet-glove super saloon. Relatively quiet, relatively refined and relatively detached, its prime ambition is to cover ground in a fast, fuss-free style. On a rainy day, the Audi is very possibly a twinkle quicker from Oberhausen to Unterhausen, but it is not as entertaining as the E55. Composure is its prime forté, even though the standard ESP cuts in way too early, taking away torque prematurely like a novice guardian angel. Quattro is an

unquestionable bonus on snow-covered blacktop, and occasionally a must on gradients. But the 50:50 torque split is too passive and too safety-conscious, and although wheel spin will theoretically trigger a more entertaining 20:70 front to rear torque distribution, it takes a surface as slippery as liquid soap to induce it. We have said it before and we say it again: what Audi needs is an evolution of the quattro principle, a more dynamic reinterpretation, like the Haldex clutch introduced in the TT and S3. As it stands, the S6 does not make full use of its genetic talent. Sure, it's well-balanced, its directional stability is faultless and traction and grip are sensational. But to qualify as a top-ranking driver's car, it needs a more clear-cut handling bias.

The Mercedes scores 10 out of 10 in the entertainment sweepstakes. It has lovely steering: not overly quick or overly light, it provides feel, feedback and fluidity. In addition, the E55 musters a tighter turning circle than the Audi. The steering of the S6 is well balanced, well geared and well damped, but more often than you might think the driven front wheels will interfere ever so slightly and blur the positive picture. Probably through motor racing, AMG has learned how to tune ESP right to its physical limit. As a result, the E55 refrains from interfering with driver inputs until it is absolutely imperative to do so. It even permits a touch of oversteer before showing the red card. If you want to see the whole road through the side window, switch off ESP and brace yourself for a degree of tail-happiness that is best experienced on a circuit.

In the brakes department, both cars do exceptionally well. The Mercedes needs a little more pedal pressure, but its anchors have enormous stamina and its two-piece compound discs are virtually immune to recurrent high-speed deceleration manoeuvres. The brake pedal of the S6 is lighter and easier to modulate, and it too has the kind of stopping power only thoroughbred sports cars can rival.

The Audi is clearly the more modern contender. It looks terrific both in notchback and Avant guise, and is very well equipped. The suspension is supple, at least to a degree. Its subframes, which are now made of aluminium instead of steel, do reduce the unsprung weight. There is a certain

welcome elasticity to every move this car makes. It feels lighter than it actually is, uses its mechanical muscles well, and is nimbler through the twisties than the Benz. But at the same time, the S6 is more nervous and less settled than the ground-hugging E55. At the limit of adhesion, you often wonder what comes next. Understeer? Oversteer? Four-wheel drift? ESP interference? The Audi also displays a little more body roll and a little more nose-heaviness than is ideal. And then there is the engine, which depends on high revolutions to deliver the goods. Nine out of 10 V8s are relaxed growlers that fetch the torque from the basement. The 4.2-litre V8 from Ingolstadt, however, unfolds in a more progressive and linear fashion: horsepower and revs rely on each other.

The Mercedes looks a little outmoded, even in facelifted form. It wears its AMG treatment like hair gel. And most of the engine tuning was done in the shop, not by tweaking the chips. Predictably, it wins the drivetrain contest by virtue of 5.5 v 4.2 litres, 391 v 310lb ft and 354 v 340bhp. The three-valver offers notably more grunt at lower revs, and responds promptly to throttle orders. It also is a more relaxed high-speed cruiser. Predictably, the five-speed automatic is better suited for slicing this loaf of torque than the Audi's rubbery six-speed manual. In terms of roadholding, the E55 AMG is synonymous with conventional, old-fashioned fun. Its cornering attitude is always clear-cut, its straightline stability impeccable (with the exception of some tramlining under braking on crater-pocked roads), and the feedback relayed by the controls is unambiguous. Yes, it is noisy. No, it does not ride very well. But it's an honest car, and it complements the driver.

The S6 is the right choice for those who live in the snow belt and for those who are more interested in absolute speed than in how to master it. The Audi is more affordable to buy but more expensive to run. It is an extremely competent but strangely soulless car – cool and distant, like the characters in the marque's current commercials. The E55 has its flaws, no doubt. But it is clearly the sportier sports saloon of the two, it is marginally faster, it represents a bigger challenge and offers a bigger reward. If the key to driving pleasure is driver involvement, the AMG badge is the one to go for.

MERCEDES E55 AMG

Price:
£60,540

Engine:
5439cc 24V V8

Power and torque:
354bhp at 5500rpm
390lb ft at 3000rpm

Transmission:
Five-speed automatic,
rear-wheel drive

Suspension, front:
Double wishbones,
coil springs, anti-roll bar

Suspension, rear:
Multi-link,
coil springs,
anti-roll bar

Weight:
1710kg

Performance:
156mph,
5.7sec 0-62mph

Fuel consumption:
23mpg

Quick Silver

A racing car toned down for road use, the Mercedes-Benz CLK-GTR is mighty rapid. And then some. **by Mark Gillies**

Hockenheim, Germany—

There's fast, like a Chevrolet Corvette or a Porsche 911, and then there's amazingly, almost scarily, fast. As in a select group of street cars, among them the Ferrari F50, the McLaren F1, and the Jaguar XJ220. The latest addition to this group is the 612-bhp Mercedes-Benz CLK-GTR, which will run 199 mph and costs 2.6 million deutsche marks (or about—gulp—$1.4 million).

Looking a bit like a CLK coupe that has been squashed and stretched and outfitted with a massive rear wing, wide, wide, wide wheel arches, and a ground-scraping front spoiler, the GTR has its roots in the Mercedes GT racing program that began in 1997. The car won the FIA GT championship that year and, with a V-8 engine in place of the original V-12, won the title again in 1998. Originally, the regulations called for the racing cars to spawn a series of street cars, but the FIA, motorsport's governing body, changed its mind on that. Nevertheless, Mercedes and its AMG spe-

cial build/tuning arm pressed on with making and selling twenty-five street-legal GTRs. Currently, number sixteen is being built and all twenty-five are spoken for.

For a lot of money, you do get a lot of car. There's a 6898-cc, 48-valve, DOHC V-12 engine with 612 bhp (DIN) and 572 pound-feet of torque mated to a six-speed sequential transmission that's actuated by groovy Formula 1–style paddles (right for up, left for down). The eighteen-inch wheels are shod with gumball 345/35 rear and

PHOTOGRAPHY BY RICHARD NEWTON

295/35 front tires. Traction control, ABS, a brake booster, and a CD changer are among the sops to usability. The chassis is a carbon fiber monocoque to which the engine and transmission are directly attached.

The V-12 engine is based loosely on the block from the old S600, except that AMG threw out all the internals, fitted dry-sump lubrication, and added variable valve timing that enables the unit to produce more than 440 pound-feet of torque from 2000 to 7000 rpm. Maximum torque of 572 pound-feet is delivered at 5250 rpm. The gearbox uses X-trac dog-ring internals with hydraulic actuation. In keeping with its race-car breeding, the car has a four-wheel double-wishbone suspension with pushrods and rockers actuating horizontally mounted coil spring/damper units that have separate reservoirs. The anti-roll bars are adjustable and the dampers can be altered for either jounce or rebound, should you care to fiddle around. Monstrous vented disc brakes are fitted, with AP Racing six-piston alloy calipers at the front and four-piston devices at the rear. The rack-and-pinion steering is power assisted.

As one might imagine for an outlay of more than a million bucks, the workmanship is quite exquisite, if not perhaps as beautiful as the McLaren F1's. The GTR is, however, hardly an everyday car, because it needs two people to remove the rear bodywork. It's assumed that aspiring and existing owners aren't going to be peering into the engine compartment—one has men to do that.

Actually getting into the GTR requires a certain amount of nimbleness and a vertically challenged body. Indeed, the only reason I'm at Hockenheim, charged with the onerous task of driving this beast, is because European editor Georg Kacher couldn't manage to contort his six-foot-eight-inch frame into the driver's seat. It must be tight in there, because Herr Kacher would do anything but surgically remove body parts to drive highly exotic and—more important to him—incredibly fast cars. Anyway, for the broader of girth, AMG thoughtfully provides a removable steering wheel to aid ingress and egress. Getting into the GTR is still a bit of a struggle, as you slide across a wide sill and down into a supportive bucket seat. The driving position is racy: straight arms and legs, with your butt close to the road and the sculpted front fenders at eye level.

The cabin is quite civilized. Wool, leather, and alcantara blend elegantly with carbon fiber trim. There's air conditioning, a decent stereo, and some space in the sills for nicely crafted bespoke luggage. The simple instrument panel, center console, and steering wheel all look like a Mercedes-Benz's rather than some wild semi-racing car's, although the little silver button for reverse looks strange. Of course, in lots of ways, this is about as far removed from a Mercedes street car as you can get. It feels incredibly wide because you and your passenger sit close together in the center,

AMG AND HWA

Factory-approved fast Mercs for road and racecourse.

On January 1, 1999, DaimlerChrysler obtained a majority interest in AMG, Mercedes-Benz's high-performance satellite founded thirty-two years ago by Hans Werner Aufrecht. It was agreed that DC would increase its stake from 51 to 75.1 percent in January 2001. In 2009, the remaining 24.9 percent is due to change hands. The complex integration process is supervised by the new chairman, Wolfgang Bernhard, and by Domingos Piedade, who had already acted as managing director under Aufrecht.

In 1998, AMG employed 400 assembly-line workers and about 200 R&D specialists. The company built more than 6000 cars; bestselling models were the E55 (2900 units) and the C43

(2700 units). Revenues reached a record high of $194 million.

New activities include the coachbuilding and special vehicles branch, which is looking after mega-rich repeat customers like the Sultan of Brunei; the so-called AMG Manufaktur division, which specializes in extensively revised interiors and exteriors; and the *designo* program, which offers more elaborate paint jobs and trim. In the long run, Mercedes wants AMG to prepare a sporty version of each volume car line, along with a distinctive styling kit (wheels, skirts, aprons) that would also be available in combination with lesser engines. At present, the company in Affalterbach near Stuttgart is offering the following models: C43 and C55, E55 and E60, S55, SL55 and SL73, CLK55 (coupe and convertible), G55, and ML55.

In the near future, AMG plans to use superchargers as a means of creating even more power and torque. According to an insider, the new C-class and the face-lifted SLK will be the first models available with an artificially aspirated 3.2-liter V-6 good for about 325 bhp and 332 pound-feet of torque. In a second step, we should see a 5.0-liter V-8 Kompressor, which is

expected to deliver 450 bhp and 458 pound-feet of torque.

Even further down the road, there will be a massive, 6.0-liter V-10 for the S-, CL-, and SL-series, a brawny 5.0-liter V-8 turbo-diesel, and a new type of clutchless paddle-shift transmission. HWA is DaimlerChrysler's new force in sports car racing. Named after its owner and founder Hans Werner Aufrecht, HWA has a five-year contract with DC—but after the debacle of the very first race at Le Mans, this freshly forged partnership is now in limbo. It is not clear whether the three-pointed star will ever return to endurance racing, be it at the North American Le Mans series or at next year's Le Mans. It is also doubtful whether the proposed German sedan-car championship, which is destined to repeat the success of the popular DTM series, will actually take off as planned next spring. Should it, HWA is expected to enter a 4.0-liter V-8–engined next-generation C-class that is currently being prepared. Although the F1 activities with McLaren are safe through 2003, the DC board is due to make a final decision on the arrangement with HWA before the end of the 1999 race season.   —Georg Kacher

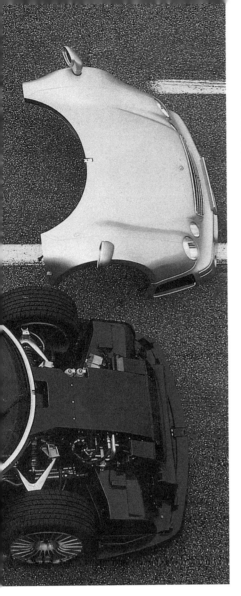

flanked by those super-wide sills. Despite pretty good fender-mounted mirrors, I have about as much an idea as to what's going on behind or how long the tail is as I do about international diplomacy. It's a good thing Mercedes decided to fit its Parktronic parking aid to this car—the carbon fiber bodywork is kind of expensive to fix after a parking scrape.

One of your men closes the scissors-type door and then you turn the key, depress the clutch, click the right-hand paddle back to select first gear, and attempt to ease the heavy racing clutch in without stalling. The car chunters away, you give it some more gas, and the GTR gathers pace. Dip the clutch, snick the right paddle back, and you're into second.

When you roll away from rest, it's apparent this is a racing car modified—nicely modified—for road use. The engine is loud and the gear whine omnipresent, and the car wants to follow the road's contour. Out on the track, that impression is enhanced because this car is *super* fast and does everything with a racer's edge. The V-12 engine is to die for. The engine note, a mixture of exhaust, induction, and (more subdued) whirring metal, wells in volume and barks gutturally as the revs rise, filling the cockpit and assailing your eardrums.

From low down in the rev range there's massive power, which peaks at 6800 rpm and is cut off electronically at 7200 revs. Mercedes claims 0-to-62-mph acceleration

in 3.8 seconds and 0 to 124 mph in 9.9 seconds, which is about four seconds faster than a Ferrari 550 Maranello makes it to 120 mph and on a par with the McLaren F1. Corners become exercises in delicacy as you try to feed all that power and torque to rear tires that are barely restrained by the traction control system. When you pluck up the courage to mash the throttle pedal in a straight line, the next braking area looms with alarming, other-worldly rapidity.

Braking, grip, and handling are also other-worldly. Like any car that's great to drive, the steering and brakes and chassis all work so well together that it is difficult to separate the different functions. You brake and the GTR slows from outrageous speeds outrageously quickly, then you apply the sublimely direct and sensitive steering and the car nuzzles into the apex. Then you unwind lock and the car sets and goes. But there's little room for error. Brake too late, turn in too late, and the car misses the apex, even wants to run off the road. Get it right by neutralizing the GTR's attitude with throttle on turn-in, then balance the car through the corner before rocketing away down the next straightaway, and you'll feel an adrenaline rush few other road-car drivers will ever experience.

The handling is pretty well balanced, but it pays to recall that there's a lot of machinery behind you and that once it starts becoming wayward, a firm hand is needed, quickly. Rotate the car too hard into a bend

A BLESSING IN DISGUISE Three CLRs flip, but the drivers escape unhurt.

Yes, we have seen it before—racing cars that lift off, become airborne, and flip over. Joachim Winkelhock (Nürburgring) and Christian Fittipaldi (Monza) come to mind, as do Stefan Bellof (Nürburgring) and Yannick Dalmas (Road Atlanta). But Le Mans 1999 was different, because it was the same type of car that flipped. Three times.

During Thursday qualifying, Mark Webber's

CLR (the '99 racing version of the GTR) took off as he was about to break through the slipstream of the Audi R8 in front of him. Contributing factors were transverse ridges in the road and a poorly adjusted front ride height. During Saturday's race warmup, it happened to Webber again. This time, the slipstream of a Dodge Viper and a brow on the straightaway were to blame. During the race, Peter Dumbreck's guardian angel worked overtime. The Scotsman had just lost one of his CLR's front winglets after a brief contact with a Porsche when he started reeling in the Toyota in front of him. Aware of the critical aerodynamics, he pulled out early—and hit the curb. That, the axle lift enhanced by the following crest, and the turbulence created by the Toyota made his car perform one of the most spectacular somersaults in motor racing history.

After Webber's two flips, the Mercedes and HWA race engineers had been cautiously optimistic. They had, once more, carefully fine-tuned the front suspension and added four small

downforce-inducing winglets to the outer edges of the front fenders. And they had added wheel-load sensors to ensure that there was enough downforce. But they did not have enough time to check the CLR in a wind tunnel. When HWA refined the '98 CLK-GTR into this year's CLR, they produced an ultrawide machine with very long front and rear overhangs and a flat hood. Its floorpan covers a swept area of almost ten square meters, and the sculpted underfloor at the nose and tail are larger than those of the other Le Mans cars. In theory, these venturi-effect tunnels make the bottom act like a fast-moving suction cup. In reality, however, the ground effects are too easily disturbed by crests and brows, by the CLR's pronounced front-end pitching, and by turbulence. In stable aerodynamic conditions and on a mirror-smooth track, the car is said to be benign and safe. But encountering bad air on undulating blacktop, the CLR in three short days earned a damaging reputation as an uncontrolled flying object. Will this UFO pull the plug on the new-generation silver arrows? —GK

The CLK-GTR can be trimmed as the customer desires: This car apes the 1955 300SLR sports-racing car with its plaid seats. The large silver button on the center console engages reverse gear.

■ Quick Silver

and the back end threatens to break loose, an alarming tendency that's repeated when you're overexuberant on the throttle out of tight corners. (And that's despite the presence of traction control. According to CLK-GTR project leader Helmut Barth, the car would be virtually undrivable in the wet without it.) After a few laps, the tires become as soft as chewing gum and seem to stick to the ground with the same kind of tenacity. Despite having 3.9 inches of

ride height compared with the racing version's 1.5-inch maximum, the GTR rides on the hard side of firm—just about acceptable for road use, with the emphasis on the "just."

Complementing the speed is the gearshift, which is a bit clunky and agricultural, but as quick as can be. One problem with having the paddles mounted on the steering wheel becomes apparent when you need to snatch a sudden downshift on entry

into a turn—oops, the paddle just moved. Formula 1 cars overcome this obstacle by having negligible steering lock, and Ferrari overcomes it on its "F1" shifter road cars by mounting the paddles on the steering column rather than on the wheel.

I'm not sure that I would have liked driving this beast on the road. Apart from its size, its lack of rear visibility, and performance that is overwhelming enough on the track, maneuvering might be tricky. For one, you have to go into neutral on the paddle shifters before deploying the reverse lever. Then, steering lock is hardly impressive. Sometimes you have to ease the car into first gear before it wants to get away. The clutch is hard work. And despite being relatively lithe, I found getting in and out of the car a clumsy process.

Yet, this car is so nutty, it's brilliant. The idea behind GT racing was to build the best possible road car and then adapt it for racing, which is what McLaren tried to do with the F1. Then the rules changed and manufacturers simply built some road cars that were based on their racers. The CLK-GTR is the result of that kind of thinking, and it's unlikely we will again see anything this outrageous for quite some time. As for comparisons with cars like the McLaren F1, who cares? This thing is just great, even if it is irrelevant as an everyday car. ⬤